KU-143-385

Gaia Foundation
www.gaiafoundation.org
Works to revive bio-cultural diversity, regenerate ecosystems, build resilience to climate change and challenge corporate dominance.

Greenpeace
www.greenpeace.org
Greenpeace exists because this fragile earth deserves a voice. It needs solutions. It needs change. It needs action.

Humanade
www.humanade.org.uk
Campaigns on human rights issues and abuses and supports a number of environmental causes.

Inga Foundation
www.ingafoundation.org
Helps rainforest people and farmers implement Inga Alley Cropping – the sustainable alternative to slash and burn.

PETA
www.peta.org.uk
People for the Ethical Treatment of Animals (PETA) and its affiliates are dedicated to the protection of animals worldwide.

Reprieve
www.reprieve.org.uk
Provides free legal support to vulnerable people facing execution, and those victimised by states' abusive counter-terror policies.

Sea Shepherd
www.seashepherd.org
Campaigns to end the destruction of habitat and wildlife in the world's oceans in order to conserve and protect ecosystems.

EDINBURGH LIBRARIES	
C0047265167	
Bertrams	21/10/2016
	£16.99
SB	TT505

GET A LIFE!

The Diaries of Vivienne Westwood

2010–2016

WWW.CLIMATEREVOLUTION.CO.UK

WWW.VIVIENNEWESTWOOD.COM

First published in Great Britain in 2016 by
SERPENT'S TAIL:
3 Holford Yard, Bevin Way
London WC1X 9HD
www.serpentstail.com

Copyright © 2016 Vivienne Westwood.

1 3 5 7 9 10 8 6 4 2

Typeset in Sabon and Golden Plains.

Printed and bound in Italy by
Lego, Viale dell'Industria 2, 36100 Vicenza.

The moral right of the author has been asserted.

All rights reserved. Without limiting the rights under copyright
reserved above, no part of this publication may be reproduced, stored or
introduced into a retrieval system, or transmitted, in any form or by any
means (electronic, mechanical, photocopying, recording or otherwise),
without the prior written permission of both the copyright owner and
the publisher of this book.

A CIP catalogue record for this book is available
from the British Library.

ISBN 978-1781254981
eISBN 978-1782831822

FSC
www.fsc.org
MIX
Paper from
responsible sources
FSC® C023419

CONTENTS

ACTIVISM AND FASHION: THE BEGINNING

AUTUMN 1970

Let it Rock 430, King's Rd. Our first shop – I was together with Malcolm McLaren. I began fashion as a rebel expressing myself through clothes. We chose the '50s for our inspiration because that seemed a time when youth rebelled against age: See you later, daddy, you're too square! The hippies politicised my generation and I hated a world of torture and death organised by the western world. Sow the whirlwind, reap the whirlwind. The older generation was responsible. We were against age – because age had abdicated its responsibility to us – and the political system.

Every time we did a new collection we changed the name of the shop: *Too Fast To Live, Too Young To Die; Sex.* Then *Seditionaries* – that was when we did punk. I did the Anarchy sign. Punk was a culmination of previous collections. We were trying to form a band of rebels who would topple the system. Johnny Rotten really meant it when he sang 'I want to be Anarchy / I want to destroy the passer by/ Your future dream is a shopping scheme'. But of course it couldn't sustain; we had no plan beyond 'Don't Vote'.

How to change the system! But back then we didn't realise how ultimately important it was. Then I was thinking, punk is over, we need ideas. We changed the name of the shop to *World's End*. I still have this shop and I still use fashion as a vehicle for activism.

MARCH 1981

Pirates, my first catwalk show. This collection was designed for *World's End*. Malcolm and I were splitting up and he wanted me to put my name to the collection. Though he gave good ideas to this collection he concentrated on his music. The idea for *Pirates* was culture. Let's get off this island and explore history and the third world / Exchange black for gold. Subversion lies in ideas.

It was at this time that I met my friend, Gary Ness. He was thirteen years older than me and he died a few years ago. He was a painter and reader. He opened up the world for me, directed my reading: Aldous Huxley, Bertrand Russell and the French in the last quarter of the nineteenth century and up until the First World War; music; we went to the ballet, *Petrushka* (that's where I got the idea of the mini crini); painting – we went to see seventeenth-century Dutch painting, and he turned me on to Chinese art. He did my perfume, *Boudoir*.

From Gary I realised that there is no progress in art: great art is perfect and timeless, original and alive.

I continued to research history for my fashion ideas; I copied the garments and tried to make them like the originals, yet taking into account that they have to be machine made. No designer did/does that. I tried to prove by example that the past is alive to us, that ideas come from traditional skills and copying.

This was my rebellion, my activism against twentieth-century dogma: 'The past is over, do your thing! You are wonderful and everything comes from you?' No! Ideas have to come from somewhere. Where else can they come from but the past. No roots, no art / no laboratory, no science. Culture is necessary for human beings to evolve into better creatures. I read.

Fan Kuan: Travellers by Streams and Mountains (hanging scroll, ink on silk, c.1000. 206.3 x 103.3cm; National Palace Museum, Taipei). I have seen this in Taipei and I bought a replica for home, half measurements – they didn't have it full size.

Thus the mini crini, the eighteenth-century corset I named the 'Stature of Liberty' (SoL), slashed denim taken from the slashed clothing of soldiers at the Renaissance; the *Portrait Collection* which attempted to represent the gamut of rich fabrics and qualities in portrait painting throughout history, including furniture, china, landscape and architecture (seen through the window), and finally the paintings themselves (photographic printing of the Wallace Collection's *Shepherd Watching a Sleeping Shepherdess* by Boucher, printed on the front of the SoL). I wanted the 'woman' to look as if she had stepped out of the painting and I gave her a pedestal – the high platform shoes.

MARCH 1990

Andreas came to work with me. I love working with him. Men do put women on a pedestal.

Andreas … pedestal. By studying clothes and how they were made, since he was a child, Andreas came to understand couture. He was able to take the construction and manufacture of clothes to the top, beginning with the secret of the SoL – you can attach much fabric to it and it will hold it comfortably to the body. So we had grand dresses with trains half the length of the catwalk. Andreas says clothes should feel light as if they were made by angels.

MARCH 1995

Vive La Cocotte. Working together, yet I would never have gone so far, Andreas creates a new silhouette, extreme female, for the supermodels.

MARCH 2005 PROPAGANDA

Caring about the alienation of young people from politics and culture, I asked myself: what would I tell them today? Huxley said, 'The world has three evils: nationalist idolatry (NI) which has taken the place of religion, non-stop distraction (NSD), and organised lying (OL). The greatest of these evils is non-stop distraction.'

Gary suggested the acronym, NINSDOL – have you had your daily pill? I thought these three evils were the constituents of propaganda. I designed graphics for six T-shirts and put them also on other clothes and bags in the collection, which was called *Propaganda*.

OCT 2005 ACTIVE RESISTANCE

Having analysed that culture is the antidote to propaganda I named this collection AR = Active Resistance (to Propaganda). The only real hero on kids' T-shirts seems to be Che Guevara so I put Rembrandt – wearing his beret – as a hero of culture.

Active Resistance is founded on the idea that the Art Lover is a freedom fighter for a better world because he thinks, and his exploration of the past gives him a perspective from which to form his own opinions and to act.

ACTIVE RESISTANCE TO PROPAGANDA
Culture versus Dogma

AUTUMN 2007

We set up our Active Resistance website. I had been writing an AR Manifesto in the form of a handy pocket pamphlet. It is a journey to find art with a cast of twenty different characters – among them Alice (in Wonderland), Pinocchio, Aristotle and Leonard Peltier. And we perform it as a reading – it takes about forty minutes – the first being with our colleagues in our studio. We launched it officially with our next reading at the Wallace Collection. Young Georgia May Jagger read Alice.

Its aim is to encourage people to become art lovers. 'You get out what you put in.' We had eighteen readings travelling all over the country. Some in universities. People made costumes.

The Royal Shakespeare Company did it with me at Wilton's Music Hall.

MARCH 2008

I read an article in *The Guardian* by the famous scientist James Lovelock. He guessed that by the end of the twenty-first century there would only be one billion people left due to climate change. I did not know we had run out of time. We must tell everyone! What can we do? We must get people talking!

My brother Gordon and my friend Cynthia did a pilot with me for a TV chat show, with Tony Juniper as our climate guest. It didn't work because I also tried to include discussion on culture which didn't fit a chat show formula.

Anyway, there wasn't time. We had to start now working through the social media. But, the first thing we have to do is save the rainforest. During our research for the show we met many important people from NGOs and charities. We were particularly impressed with the working model to save the rainforest by Cool Earth. I think they're amazing and I am full of gratitude to them – working with the indigenous people. What is so incredible is that they need only £100 million to save the equatorial forest in Brazil, Congo and

Papua New Guinea. We support them as much as we can; most importantly I gave them some money to boost them along. NGOs are our hope. Governments are doing nothing – and at the same time they support the wrecking of the earth by the fossil fuel industry and by austerity. For ten years the World Bank has been sitting on $1.6 billion specially donated to save the rainforest. They have spent some of this money on administration and meetings but have not yet saved one tree.

I began my Diary for our AR (later Climate Revolution) website. I had just rewritten my manifesto. I wrote the Diary to try to influence people because without public opinion we are lost. I want to warn people of the danger we're in from climate change; and I talk about fashion to alleviate the hard focus which nevertheless we must apply to save the world. Fashion, too, is my life and I want to let people know it's not easy and it has to be built on tradition, and inspiration comes from genius – from all the artists who lived before us. It gives me the credibility to open my mouth and say, 'I can't tell you the inspiration for my fashion, I have to talk about climate change.'

The only way out of this is a green economy.

"WHAT'S GOOD FOR THE PLANET IS GOOD FOR THE ECONOMY"
"WHAT'S BAD FOR THE PLANET IS BAD FOR THE ECONOMY"

What's good for people is good for the planet.

NOVEMBER 2010

WEDS 3 NOV LETTER TO A PRISONER

I've been a supporter of Leonard Peltier for many years now. He has been in prison in the United States for thirty-five years, more than half his life, as a result of a trial based on a flawed and dishonest case full of false evidence given by the FBI.

Leonard is a Native American activist, considered by Amnesty International and many others to be a prisoner of conscience. I've got to know Leonard through a long exchange of letters and books. Here are the first of our letters, which Leonard has now agreed to share with you. *[The idea was that Leonard should write a diary from prison, send it to me, and we would put it on our website, then called AR – Active Resistance. Leonard never did it.]*

Dear Miss Vivienne!
As always it is great hearing from you. Hey I was just being honest; it is exciting to receive your letters, being as I find you a brilliant unique lady! Before I forget, 'Yes' I did receive the books you sent, quite some time ago it seems, I just did not know who sent them, they are very expensive books I might

add, especially the Rembrandt book!! Thank you. Although they are great books I must admit I did read them before; we studied Rembrandt in College. I took Prison Course (5) when I was at LVN (Leavenworth USP), but now I have my own copies for my Private Collection ... Again, thank you very much as I did enjoy them again.

I do understand the Humanist theory, and more and more all the time as I age ... And I also believe very strongly we earth people are not alone in the many vast universe(s). I also understand life comes in many different forms, as science is proving I might add! Some life is completely invisible to the naked eye! But to answer your question, Yes I'd love to work with you, on one condition! That you will guide me and help me to write things!! Or correct me and edit me, I meant! And you're welcome to quote me!

One of my first cousins is coming to visit this weekend. I have not seen him in over forty years that I can remember. This is going to be cool I am sure. The two days we are allowed will be filled with question after question! Our mothers were sisters, both deceased now. I am awaiting approval for one of my grandsons to visit. He will bring one of my great grandsons – I have eleven great grandchildren so far. The sad part is that I have not seen any of them. I'm too far from home!

O:k in your next letter – Send me some of your ideas etc, And I will try to respond to them, Hopefully this will work out to be something good?! I better put this in the Mail, you take Care tell Everyone Hello for me!. In the Spirit of Crazy Horse DOKSHA. Leonard!...

Dear Leonard

It is more than two months since I wrote to you. I spent all my spare time in August re-writing my Manifesto. August is the one quiet time in the fashion business and I was waiting for a block of time to write. So I kept my head down and did just that. I think my Manifesto is now clearer and more profound.

It is still not finished – you know it is only 20 little pages – but I have nailed it and I know how to finish it. I need about three more days to do it. Anyway I really am pleased with it. But it was surreal it took so long – I really think it took between 600 and 700 hours – you know when you count the days and writing eight or ten hours a day. One interesting thing is that you form the ideas by the actual writing; you think you know what you want to say and then you realise there is more to it and by re-thinking the idea starts to 'come' because you are trying to find a way to communicate. (I say 'come' because the idea seems to have a life of its own.)

The Manifesto is about the fact that we are dangerously without culture and how to *GET* culture – through art, of course – and the way it connects with *STOP* Climate Change. We are an endangered species. How do you 'Get a Life' for future generations (instead of mass deaths) and what about your life now? How do you 'Get a Life' now? (ans. Culture). Leonard, it sounds boring when I just try to sum it up but it really is exciting. I will let you know all about it and send you the finished Manifesto. The name of the TV programme I want to do would be called 'Get a Life'.

Dear Leonard, for days, at least for the last three weeks I have thought of you because I wanted so much to write to you. Just shows you how busy (but not always) I am. (We did a super fashion show and collection – I will send you pictures.) There is no excuse except that you need a bit of mental space before you sit down to write a letter and when I get home at night even then it doesn't seem possible after I've cooked and eaten – together with my husband. *Very* important.

Thank you so much for your letter. I'm re-launching my website now. And I will put in the space we keep for you all the lovely things you say about your life, e.g. people will be so interested about your cousin coming. It is all these ordinary things we all experience but people will imagine themselves in your shoes and get a real idea of the importance of your life and what is important to you.

Leonard, did you receive *1984* and *Brave New World*? I want to tell you why I think they're so important. Did I tell you that I consider them to be the most important books in English in the twentieth century? *1984* is about Power for the sake of Power, *Brave New World* is about Organisation for the sake of Organisation. We could put your comments on the website 'Get a Life'. Let me know as urgently as possible. And let me know about your cousin's visit and good luck seeing your grandson.

♡ *Always, Vivienne. Please write to me soon*
i promise never to be so long again with my reply.

Please do write or send cards to:
Leonard Peltier, #89637-132, USP, Coleman I,
P.O. Box 1033, Coleman, FL 33521, USA.

THURS 4 NOV AT THE NATIONAL GALLERY

We made a five-minute film, at the National Gallery, for a pilot TV programme we wanted to do on great art. This is my script:

I believe that the art lover is a freedom fighter for a better life for himself and the world. Great art is a series of windows on the past, it gives us an understanding of where we are and who we are. We question our priorities and the world we live in and through this we're always discovering something new, something we didn't know before. We can change society and my next story is an example of how this happened in the past. Around seven hundred years ago there was a seismic shift in people's outlook right across Europe. We can see this change through looking at paintings, so I went to the National Gallery in London. You can just pop into the National Gallery or spend all day, if you have the time, looking at the greatest paintings in the world – it's free.

Left column, from top: Duccio, Masaccio, Giovanni Bellini, Peter Paul Rubens; right column, from top: Hieronymus Bosch, Jan van Eyck, Rembrandt van Rijn.

We're going to look at three Italian paintings with the same subject matter – a mother's love for her child – Mary holding the baby Jesus as they contemplate his future death on the cross. The first is from medieval times and it's by Duccio from around 1300. It's outside of time and space. And it has the authentic stamp of the Church because the truth is witnessed by saints, prophets and angels. Their size is not realistic; rather it's in proportion to their importance in the spiritual hierarchy. It's a direct appeal to Faith – no doubt, no questions; a background of shining gold – no contact with the outside world. The message is spiritual: we are nothing. Yet we can become one with God. The earth was flat, heaven was above and hell below.

Masaccio, our next painter, comes a century later. This is the time of the Renaissance. Renaissance means rebirth, when people rediscovered the art and ideas of ancient Greece and Rome. Masaccio's work was more naturalistic and was inspired by ancient Greek sculpture. The rules of perspective had just been rediscovered. He uses this and rational lighting to place the stone throne and figures in real space. The child tastes the grapes which are a symbol of the blood he is prepared to shed for us.

It's now 1500 and the high Renaissance. Our next painting is *The Madonna of the Meadow* by Bellini. It's the same familiar subject but now the world has been let in. Mary sits in a field. The baby is allowed to sleep like a real child. We can feel Mary breathing as she watches over him. *Christ Mocked (The Crowning of Thorns)* by the Flemish painter Hieronymus Bosch is from exactly the same time as Bellini. It is still a religious subject but it's crowded with horrible characters – it is set in the drama of life and shows what humans are really like when they're about to torture Christ.

Worldly subject matter entered painting through portraits. The *Arnolfini Portrait* (1434) – a double portrait of Arnolfini and his wife by Jan van Eyck – documents the rise of a rich middle class who took advantage of the new techniques in oil painting to record themselves in their finery and among their expensive possessions. The world is becoming more materialistic.

Wealthy merchants, bankers and princes decorated their palaces with scenes from ancient Greek and Roman mythology, like the painting of the *Judgement of Paris* (1632–35) by Rubens. They were showing off their new, modern and worldly outlook, which included the pleasures of the flesh. Many important events coincided to cause this radical change in outlook of Renaissance thinkers and artists. But the most important factor was the rediscovery of the Greek mind where freedom of thought triumphed over medieval dogma.

In Rembrandt's *Self Portrait at Age Sixty-Three* (1669) we enter right into the private life of the painter. God has been replaced by man as a source of ideals. Freedom from the Church's authority led to experimentation and science, and the cult of the individual.

Change happened in the past and we need to change our outlook again – radically – to get the world we want.

SAT 20 NOV REWRITING THE MANIFESTO

I am re-writing my Manifesto. Now that I've lived with it, I feel I can penetrate more deeply into the ideas – what I want to say – and strengthen the links with climate change. It's taking me ages – at least 600–700 hours so far – because I'm actually working out the theory as I go along. When I have three clear days I think I can finish it – but I'm not sure when that will be because I'm so busy at the moment. I've decided to post it online as far as it's done. I'm still working through it and will add more as it's completed.

My Manifesto is about feelings – these feelings are our primary and direct contact with reality. They are primitive, earlier than language. What art struggles to do is to communicate these feelings directly. It is through art we touch reality.

My aim in life is to understand the world I live in. I think that to become an art lover is to become a freedom fighter for a better world. Being an art lover is an activity – you're active, not passive. You're investing everything you've got when you really look at a painting. The motto of this Manifesto is 'You get out what you put in'. It's the opposite of being a consumer. You're not just passively sucking things up. This applies to all the arts but, for the moment, we're just thinking of what can one person do. Right now you can start going to art galleries if you live in or visit a city.

When I was teaching in Berlin, I sent the students to the galleries and said to them, 'Before you move from one room to the next, think which painting you would save. And, if you keep going, in six months time you won't choose that painting – you would choose something else because you're developing your powers of judgement and discrimination. Being an art lover is the best education you can get.'

In my studio I send the students who come for work experience to the Wallace Collection – it's great because it also has furniture and other applied arts, especially Sèvres porcelain. Remember when you go to an art gallery that, as far as I know, there's nobody in the world who can do anything like that now – not even paint one little flower on a teacup. How fulfiling it is once you realise how relevant art is to your life. It helps you understand the world. Why don't you dress up and go with a friend? You get out what you put in – Get a Life!

DECEMBER 2010

SUN 12 DEC ONCE UPON A TIME ...

The Adventures of Pinocchio and *Alice in Wonderland* should be at the top of any reading list. They are key characters – as 'The Travellers' – in my Manifesto. It would seem that *Pinocchio* is the most popular book that has ever been written – it's been translated into more languages than the Bible. I think it's so brilliant!

> *Once upon a time there was ... 'A king!' my little readers*
> *will say straight away. No, children, you are mistaken.*
> *Once upon a time there was a piece of wood.*

It's just great. And remember that the person who wrote it, Carlo Collodi, was a theatre critic. *Pinocchio* is so dramatic as a story that for anyone wishing to be a writer it's an absolute model of literature.

Now then, the circumstances under which this was written: Carlo Collodi was the eldest of ten children, only five of whom lived past infancy. His mother did washing for the local duke. The duke noticed this boy and how clever he was and he educated him.

Collodi became a member of the Risorgimento, the movement in Italy that was trying to unify all the little

petty kingdoms and principalities and to have a national identity and a country. This all happened in the mid-nineteenth century (1815–71). The challenge was that most of the people at the time were peasants – they couldn't read and write. The Risorgimento was going to create a republic: putting the people in power – that was their idea. In fact, they put the king in power; but the people needed educating. They launched a children's newspaper to educate children and *Pinocchio* was serialised in 1881 as the first story for kids. It was so popular that it became a book in 1883.

The Adventures of Pinocchio is a guide for living. It's a philosophy for life – a way to live. It's a terribly exciting book. Pinocchio is the most wonderful character you'll ever meet. He's so naughty but he's got a heart of gold and that's what saves him.

Pinocchio is very useful as one of the travellers in the Manifesto because we've got him after the book's action – what once was a wooden puppet has now become a real boy. He's now more clever than he used to be – he's learning and, of course, he wants to learn. He's decided he wants to be a freedom fighter, like his creator, Carlo Collodi. Next time, I'll talk about our other traveller, Alice.

MON 20 DEC CURIOUSER AND CURIOUSER!

I have now finished revising my Manifesto. One of the reasons I decided to re-write it is that in my first attempts I felt I was climbing on a soapbox and telling everyone what to do. And I don't like sounding bossy even though I've got strong opinions. I thought it would be ever so much more acceptable to people if a little girl could do this – someone about the age of Alice. She was a precocious child and I think she is a much more charming way to present my opinions.

Alice's Adventures in Wonderland was written in 1865 by the English author, mathematician, logician, Anglican deacon and photographer Charles Lutwidge Dodgson – better known as Lewis Carroll. It was originally written as a gift for Alice, the daughter of fellow deacon Henry Liddell. How old is Alice Liddell in this picture, dressed as a beautiful beggar child? I think she's about nine or ten. As Carroll was a photographer – and there weren't many around in those days – mothers were pleased to have him take photos of their little girls. They obviously thought of photography as art. When people discuss Lewis Carroll today, they sometimes have a problem with his interest in young girls but that certainly wasn't the case in his time.

I would like to say that, even as a woman, I think little children of Alice's age, especially girls, have something special about them – they're so open to ideas and so curious about things. They're the most delightful people to talk to and get involved with. It's happened to me more than once but I do find, like Carroll did, that when children reach a certain age – eleven, twelve, definitely thirteen – they start to get a bit boring. They're really just interested in their friends, not in the world around them. They want to look grown-up and get involved in all the things that make teenagers feel that they've got an advantage over everyone else. They're not looking at the world or trying to be unconventional or willing to stick their necks out in any way. The hope is that they'll come out of this way of thinking when they're older.

Why do I like this story? Remember, Carroll was a mathematician. And, fifty years before Einstein, he was very much aware of the idea of relativity because *Alice's Adventures in Wonderland* are seen from this point of view. Everything is relative to everything else. A

Alice Liddell, photographed by Charles Dodgson and transformed by Tenniel.

wonderful example is when Alice is playing croquet and hits the ball, which happens to be a hedgehog, with a mallet, which happens to be a flamingo. I remember reading once, when I was trying to understand relativity, Bertrand Russell's explanation that it was just as useful to measure something with a metre rule as it was with a live snake. That's exactly how Lewis Carroll saw the world – everything is relative. Another example is in *Through the Looking Glass*, when the Red Queen is running full speed with Alice holding her hand. They are going so fast that Alice's hair is pulled almost off her head. And then you find that they haven't moved at all and in this world you have to run fast just to stay on one spot. Of course, this is what's happening to us in our world today.

Perhaps my favourite idea is revealed at the Mad Hatter's Tea Party. It shows that 'Time' is a man-made invention. 'Time' and the Mad Hatter have quarrelled and now that 'Time' won't cooperate anymore, the time stays at six o'clock – and that is why they have to stay at the tea table.

The importance of *Alice's Adventures in Wonderland* is that things are never what they seem. They can have their own strange logic which has nothing to do with any kind of conventional logic but yes, yes it is just as real. I think this is a very good attitude or lesson for a child to have – so they're not always so complacent about getting near the truth by applying conventional logic to things. Of course it's also terribly, terribly amusing – the logic of Wonderland compared to our conventional logic. The Mad Hatter's Tea Party is the gem of the story. I love the bit when the Dormouse tells the story of three little sisters who lived in treacle well. Alice wants to know what they ate and the Dormouse answers, 'Treacle'. Alice says they couldn't live on treacle because they'd be terribly ill. And the Dormouse replies, 'Oh they were – *very* ill'. Hilarious!

The *Alice* books make you believe you could be in a parallel world – or that the world we think we know reflects the way we are programmed to see it. Maybe it's not like that at all!

JANUARY 2011

SUN 16 JAN LIBERTY

Shami Chakrabarti, the Director of Liberty, is a great friend of mine. I've been a supporter of her work for a long time and I stopped by to visit her recently. Anyone who listened to the discussion last week on BBC Radio 4 *Any Questions?* will have heard my thoughts about the controversial scheme of control orders which gives the UK government the right to hold anyone suspected of terrorist activities under indefinite house arrest. At present, control orders allow suspects to be indefinitely tagged, confined to their homes and prohibited from communicating with others – all without a police interview, trial or charges made against them. It's up to all of us to put pressure on the government to scrap this system and replace house arrest with surveillance to gather evidence for prosecution. We don't all get to take part in radio discussions but you can still have an effect by contacting Liberty (*www.liberty-human-rights. org.uk*) to make your voice heard.

TUES 18 JAN A PERFECT BALLET

Fernando Montano, a young First Artist with the Royal Ballet, surprised us with tickets to the Royal Opera House to see their performance of *Giselle*. Of all Romantic ballets *Giselle* is the one to

Woodcut of *Giselle* from Arnold Haskell's *Pelican Guide to Ballet.*

see and know. It's a real drama – a story of betrayal, nights filled with supernatural spirits and love that transcends even death. *Giselle* is not merely an excuse for dancing, but lives because of the drama it expresses. It's not just a regular favourite of ballet lovers but also a wonderful work through which anyone can discover the enduring appeal of classical ballet. The brilliant British dance critic Arnold Haskell wrote of *Giselle*: 'The scene of madness cannot be naturalistic or it would be altogether out of the picture. It must be lyricial and fit perfectly within the classical convention. The latitude allowed the actress is minute, every gesture is circumscribed. To succeed in Giselle means a triumph of personality, a unique example of true personality that is technically disciplined.'

FEBRUARY 2011

FRI 11 FEB ONE MAN'S ADVANTAGE IS ANOTHER'S SUFFERING

The financial crisis is an exact match of the ecological crisis. More than 90 per cent of the world's natural resources are owned by private interests, business and government – and they are exploited to the hilt. There is nothing left to exploit cheaply! That is why we have a financial crisis.

The pundits keep these complementary facts apart and suggest money spent on climate change would make us suffer, whereas the only people who would suffer are shareholders. When they talk about growth they are lying. It is very clear today that one man's advantage is another's suffering. Or as John Maynard Keynes put it: 'Capitalism is the astounding belief that the most wickedest of men will do the most wickedest of things for the greatest good of everyone.'

At the end of the Second World War, the Allies got together to consider implementing the economic system which Keynes had worked out. Everyone was excited because they thought his system would be an end to war. Keynes's idea was to have a world bank which would balance the world economy and create the same opportunities for all. The nations with a surplus would be obliged to balance their accounts within a year – or have the surplus confiscated. The surplus (and help) would be given to countries who had a trade deficit. (The present World Bank creates more harm than good.)

America rejected this plan. All the other countries were in debt to her, so they had to obey. America stated: The world is finite with diminishing resources. The American standard of living is sacred and the level of wealth must be maintained. Therefore, from now on, America must have a greater share of the cake. (These are not the exact words but this is what America said at the time. I am shocked that they dared to be so blatant.)

The consequences of this decision for the poorest countries have been ruinous to their development. Today, we can see the global impact this has had financially – matched by the catastrophic environmental consequences for us all.

To read more, see the article on Keynes by George Monbiot ('Clearing up this mess', available in his online archive). The details are fascinating!

MARCH 2011

TUES 15 MARCH **CREATING WORLD WIDE WOMAN**

I was so carried away by my last Gold Label show that I have decided to describe in some detail how a collection is formed.

Sometimes I know the idea for a collection but this time I started really late with no idea except for a fragment of precious ribbon I had seen pictured in an old sales catalogue I discovered among my books. I wanted to get a copy woven, a ribbon I could cut up into same-size pieces and sew on to T-shirts instead of graphics. I thought I'd love to wear a bit of old fabric instead of a slogan for a change. The original was medieval and the design had such a feeling of that time, formalised eagles in silk and gold threads circumscribed within an undulating chain motif.

Our prototypes are done in our Battersea studio but our production is in Italy, so I asked our studio there to find a ribbon factory. Then I had to choose fabrics which they had pre-selected from the fabric fair. The less fabric the better, I think; too many and the possible permutations become endless as the ideas gather, and I like to 'cook' with basic ingredients. I kept to basic fabrics; with some, I let in the natural colour of the fibre as it comes from the loom. For other plain fabrics I stuck to black, grey, indigo, brown, flesh, cream, white. Set against the fabrics we took gold, a lamé looking like metal – gold sequins.

I love our toiles, our prototypes which we make in the natural calico before we decide the final fabric; it's as if the garment epitomises the first idea of itself. I took a very conservative man's tailoring fabric (I love conservative fabrics – they have so many ideas to play with), a fresco in grey chalk stripe, and made a suit comprising a jacket from two years back and a favourite skirt – the 'alien' skirt – *World's End* customers will know this skirt. We didn't sell the jacket at the time because it has a lot of volume around the shoulder (masculine? But cross-dressing is as old as the hills) and over the breast – but I adore it because it makes a woman look important and there is nothing more sexy than that. I shall wear this suit. Next autumn it should go into our archive but it will come home with me instead. One thing I knew about the collection – I wanted the woman to look important.

Plain fabrics show off the cut of clothes. I like to mix garments from different times and places: historical, ethnic, twentieth-century couture – I copied a coat from Balenciaga and a dress from Chanel.

The suit I want, and it's coming home with me.

I sometimes copy from myself, re-doing clothes from way back in my archive. I like new things as well as things repeated and developed from last season. Most of all, I like 'do it yourself', as if the wearer has spontaneously put her own creation together in an afternoon. I introduced colour by printing. Until recently printing was done only on screens or rollers but now we also have digital printing. The cost of full colour is less because it is all done in one go. There is no setting-up cost so you might as well have every print different. That's what I did and found every print in my small booklet of fabrics from the Museum of Fine Arts, Boston.

Then I chose three yarns for knitwear which we had used for MAN – ordering a greater quantity keeps the price down and because the men's collection is in progress I have the advantage of already having worked with these yarns. We always choose fabric and yarn before the concept of the collection materialises – but this choosing helps the decisions. Andreas was very keen on this finest wool yarn, especially in a butter colour; perfect would be a classic cardigan, undone at the throat, fitting close over the body. This we did, except my clothes cannot be straightforwardly classic. People expect that dynamic power of drape in the cut.

Sweater with brocade sewn on pocket.

One of the first things I usually do is to try out new cutting principles on a miniature dummy. Our friend Iris, once our full-time pattern cutter who now manages to come two or three times a season, arrives to work on new cuts and ideas that Andreas and I have each thought of separately. Last year, she brought her own idea – a dress made out of a cushion cover. She and Andreas worked on this idea lots. We have fittings which involve toiles begun by our in-house pattern cutters (it can take weeks for one dress) and with Iris's help we get to a point, even sometimes as far as working out which fabric we will use and the sewing method. (A design is a result of hundreds of decisions through trial and error.) Even Iris who, until now has always triumphed, tells me that she is never sure she's going to make it. For me, she is so clever she walks on air, she has a unique talent that is properly trained. It is wonderful to be able to trust someone completely.

It's now time to find out why there is still no sign of the brocade eagles ribbon. The original hand-woven sample – using real gold thread – measured ten inches and there are no ribbon machines wide enough. It is interesting to note that antiques cost more in their day than they would do now. It could happen that someone could take a lifetime to make a cupboard with moulding, lacquer and inlay, or months to weave a yard of Venetian velvet which then cost the price of two cows.

The answer to my eagle brocade would be to use a full-size loom with several repeats across the whole width – then cut them through into ribbons. However, I don't need all these repeats. So I take advantage of this fact by including an image of Dionysus in the weaving programme, keeping the gold thread on the surface of the fabric. Meanwhile, Andreas, whose heroine as a woman and as a fashion icon is Marlene Dietrich, has produced dresses inspired by her. Brigitte, our head of couture, organised the embroidery on versions of Marlene's nude-effect gowns. Andreas worked with tulle with Marlene in mind.

Hats are important. They bring gravitas to a show. We suggested helmets, which always look heroic. Prudence, our milliner, chose the American GI helmet as absolutely generic. When we were deciding how to decorate them she produced a square of gold leaf which she

Inspired by Marlene.

could press into the felt and so cover entirely in gold. I asked her how much this five-inch square would cost: £5. Incredible that you can beat gold so thin.

Andreas had also designed gloves and jewellery, but when the sample shoes arrived they were not nicely made. Therefore, he got them done in the gold sequin fabric and asked for a gold catwalk. Nobody will see them because of the reflection. When they arrived they were nicely made anyway and coincidentally Andreas's friend Tony, who does the look and lighting of the show, had prepared ideas for a gold catwalk.

The people we work with are crucial, though there are things only I can do or Andreas can do. But our design assistant, Luca, must not forget a thing and keep things moving.

Our fitting model was Jenny. Because she has a perfect body proportion, the collection, when it is produced, will miraculously fit everyone else. The last thing I did before leaving for Paris – Andreas was already there working on casting and logistics – was to have Jenny stand quietly while I pinned and cut a spontaneous dress in Dionysus fabric. It took only a couple of hours because essentially, by using a live model instead of working on the mannequin, I could see how the whole thing fitted and worked in motion.

I called the collection World Wide Woman. A collection is more than the sum of its parts and this one entered a realm I had not envisaged. The final alchemy came from Andreas's suggestion to Val (make-up) and Jimmy (hair): make the girls look like horses.

The effect was Out of this World!

[*We do three main collections every six months: Gold Label, Red Label and MAN. We are always designing one while presenting another, which then is delivered to the shops six months later.*

We promote the shows on the main Vivienne Westwood website and sometimes I add stuff to the Diary, which belongs to the Climate Revolution website. That is why covering the fashion shows here seems a bit spasmodic, not of equal importance. We have just fused the two websites.]

APRIL 2011

In my Manifesto, the True Poet says, 'The present is always the present moment of the past. We *are* the past. Art links past, present and future.' So far, so good. But when he goes on, 'Cut off from the past there is only habit,' it's important to grasp the connection. Cut off from the past there is only the day-to-day continuum – no comparisons – therefore no ideas and no foresight. For what is it we really compare when we look at the past? How the world could be different, more wonderful; where we went wrong; how people see things.

Jared Diamond's book, *Collapse – How Societies Choose to Fail or Succeed*, tells some of the stories of societies who thrived, flourished, then died through habit. The most horribly fascinating story was that of the Greenland Vikings, Norwegians who colonised Greenland from AD 984 to the 1400s. They built churches and a cathedral, wrote in Latin and Old Norse, wielded iron tools, herded farm animals, followed the latest European fashions in clothes – and finally vanished in one winter. There were five thousand of them and they lasted almost five hundred years – which is longer than the English-speaking society of North America has so far survived.

They were contemptuous of the native Inuit – who were adapted to the environment and did survive – and learnt nothing from them. The Vikings even had a taboo against eating fish. They were culturally hampered in making the drastic changes that would have helped them to preserve their habitat. By default they chose death to change. There is a connection between culture – the way we see the world – and climate change. Let us not die from habit.

What we're doing on the website revolves around the AR (Active Resistance) Manifesto and I've realised that what we're building here

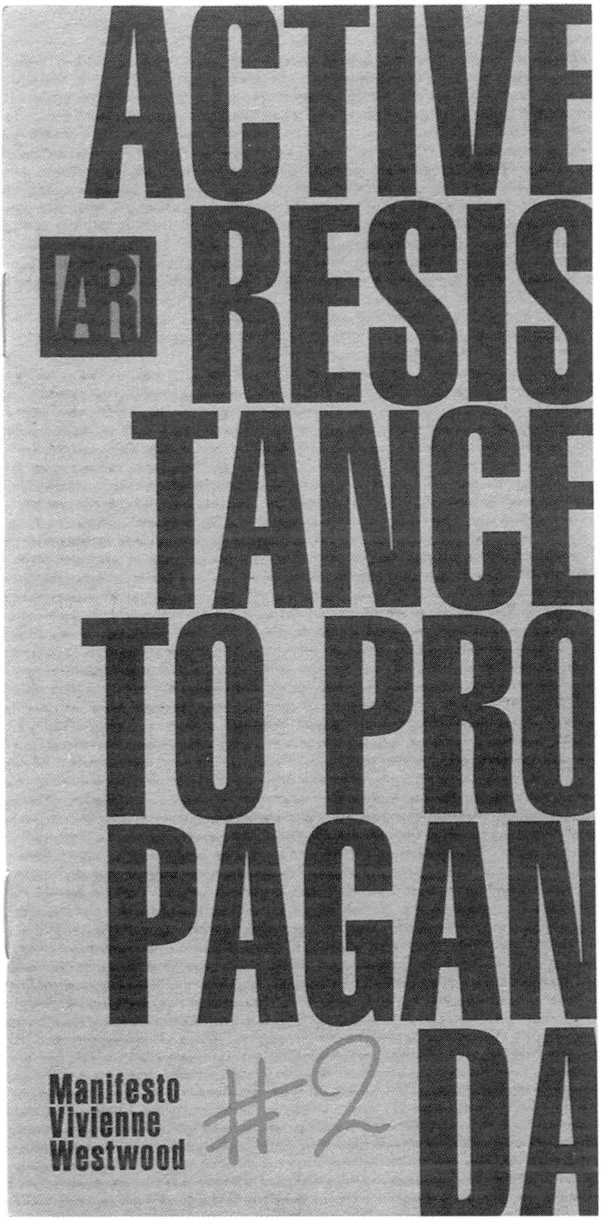

ACTIVE
[ÆR] RESIS
TANCE
TO PRO
PAGAN
DA

Manifesto
Vivienne
Westwood

#2

This slim pamphlet is of a size to fit the pocket, and the text is of a width that the eye does not need to travel across as you read – as in a newspaper.

can be transformed and published as a book with the Manifesto as its heart. I think the book should be called 'The Art Lover and the Lost Generations' – or even 'Get a Life', because that's what it means.

AR's (Active Resistance's) speech in the Manifesto is particularly relevant to 'The Art Lover and the Lost Generations'. The idea is 'culture for beginners':

> 20th century progress was a bad idea. Smash the past and the future will take care of itself. Follow the trend, keep up with the times. Artists and intellectuals jumped on the bandwagon. Progress and future were automatically linked. March on! Don't stop to think. You have nothing to lose but your chains.

What I mean is this: in the twentieth century we were not engaged in the world. We took everything for granted – and also the future – so today we're an endangered species. Culture comes from our engagement with the world of a shared experience. We have allowed ourselves to become alienated from deep contact with each other and manipulated by politicians.

We launched the new Manifesto #2 yesterday evening, taking advantage of the first glorious day of spring to do the reading on the roof of our office in London. It was a real social event, with wine and snacks for the performers and audience. The speakers were in prime form – everyone was completely engrossed in their roles – and I felt very encouraged. The Manifesto is very clear to everyone. It just requires concentration on the part of the reader because it is heretical to received opinion. It would be great next time to combine the reading with a workshop.

Of course we had a lot of students here and they really enjoyed the acting – they were all cheering, right from the beginning – especially when Luca (our design assistant) jumped in as Pinocchio. Chiara, from our purchasing department, played the True Poet, and Brigitte, the head of the studio, played the Art Lover; Theo, who deals with the Japanese market, played Whistler – his long speech with its American accent was spellbinding. We were delighted that

Lily Cole (model, actress, studying History of Art at Cambridge) arrived from Paris to play the role of Alice. Although she hadn't seen the part before she did a wonderful job.

I was particularly happy to welcome our guest, Matthew Owen, Director of Cool Earth. I'm going to be working closely with this charity in the coming months. Matthew made the point that the best way to get anything done is do it yourself, referring to the work Cool Earth is doing to save the rainforests. Cool Earth uses a bottom-up method, working with the indigenous people who live in the rainforest to help them protect the land they own. This is already having a dramatic effect – over 150,000 acres have been saved in the last eighteen months, protecting an additional million acres by their strategic location. I've decided to get involved with people who take the Do it Yourself approach to things.

MAY 2011

WEDS 25 MAY THE PROCESS OF DISCOVERY

Brian Sewell recently criticised the Tracey Emin retrospective at the Hayward Gallery, London. This is how I see the problem:

The academic dogma today is that tradition belongs to the past, and we must forget the past otherwise we can't be original. It goes on – you don't need to draw, that's old-fashioned. You don't need to be able to represent anything. Just take the actual objects of real life and, if necessary, rework them, which you can do by sending your concept to an engineer or factory workshop. Art schools teach you how to do this through 'presentation skills' and this is what is now called conceptual art.

Well, you do need real skills to express yourself. You learn skill by studying tradition, trying to copy the techniques of great artists; only by doing this have you the means to express what you want to say. Art has to be representative. A representation is an epitome of a point of view, an overview. I believe that an idea is formed, and it is in the very process of applying one's particular skill – all those extraordinary decisions, the decisions of a lifetime – that the artist discovers their idea; the simplification must be spontaneous, a matter of the artist's spirit transmitted to the work. By illusion, creating an illusion through representation, the true artist achieves a totality – a world which the art lover can enter. The conceptual artist makes an arbitrary selection from the real world. He discovers

nothing, nor can the art lover. His work is sterile.

In answer to Tracey Emin's question, 'What's it all about?' Brian Sewell ends his review by answering, 'You, dear Miss Emin, you – but you have never been enough.' No artist was ever enough in themselves, not Titian, not anyone. It was what they did – the skill that gave them the means to discover their vision – that was enough.

THURS 26 MAY OUR FIRST TRIP TO AFRICA

Travel less, stay longer. I think it's gross to rush off just for business, then straight back. I always try to do more than one thing on every trip to discover something about the history of the country. Andreas and I, with members of our team, were away for ten days working and travelling from Nairobi to Segera, in the very centre of Kenya. We've been working with the United Nations Ethical Fashion Initiative to produce bags and accessories in Kenya. The idea of this programme is to lift communities out of poverty using environmentally sustainable materials and processes. Charity = dependence; Work = control over your own life.

Simone Cipriani, who runs the project, had the idea of bringing our designs to local craftspeople so they can produce attractive fashion items for international markets. Now, after working with them for two seasons, we have 250 locals directly involved in Vivienne Westwood manufacturing. We were really pleased to see what a difference the project has made to their communities. Andreas and I spent time at the workshops to work with the craftspeople to add more designs to our range. Eventually, we aim to employ five hundred people.

In the Nairobi slums, we met a man called Stephen who has a team making the brass fittings for our bags. He's become quite an entrepreneur – known locally as 'Stephen Brass'. And we were amazed to see how people take bones directly from an abattoir and make them into buttons and jewellery. Simone's team deals with every challenge and tries to turn it into something positive. A lot of dust is produced when the bones are cut – it was allowed to blow away and was inhaled by the workers who didn't wear masks to protect themselves. Simone decided that the dust could have value and now plans to use it in rose fertiliser and then, possibly more ambitious, for bone china. These plans have made the dust precious to the men who now conserve it and wear masks to protect themselves. Everything at the rubbish dump is recycled – and some of it is used for our production. It's an important source of income for slum dwellers. Waste food and rubbish from airlines is collared by slum hierarchies.

I was surprised to find that rents for small concrete houses are not cheap. There's a whole social structure and economy in the slums – the houses double as shops and workshops. People are healthy, though I'm told the life expectancy is below average. They were happy and friendly to us, especially the children who always greet you with a 'How are you?' Second-hand clothes are a very important business here – given free by charities but then often sold on.

I believe the UN programme is making a really positive impact on the people's lives. Another small business they started is the production of fuel from paper found at the rubbish dump – like a kind of papier-mâché briquette. Andreas and I went to a school in Nairobi to meet students who had previously been working on the rubbish dump – some of them as young as four years old, abandoned

Juergen Teller's image of Ajuma modelling our clothes in a Nairobi shanty town.

by their parents. They were rescued by the UN and are now being taught about farming so that they can return to the land and lead healthier lives.

Our photographer, Juergen Teller (who we always work with on our fashion campaigns) also travelled with us to Kenya to visit the communities involved in the Ethical Fashion Initiative. He shot a reportage of the visit which will be displayed as an installation in the Pitti Palace, Florence, in June. The video highlights issues such as education, access to water, recycling and the ways in which the Ethical Fashion Progamme is helping to improve the quality of life in these communities, though damage to the environment is not addressed.

As Juergen was to be with us in Kenya for the UN video, we decided to shoot our next fashion campaign there. It's a lot of work doing a fashion shoot – it takes two or three days to prepare and, as the clothes only arrived the night before, we had been busy.

It's always hard work (but I enjoy it) because Andreas and I model in our own publicity – so we are dressing models and ourselves in a van and then coping with doing the shoot outdoors – right amongst people's lives. People were curious and one lady told me that she admired me for doing such a thing at my age. We brought so many accessories with us to Africa that Juergen suggested we pretend we had a shop and were selling things like everybody else.

After Nairobi, Juergen went home but we went on to Segera Ranch on the Laikipia Plateau – 50,000 acres, only twenty miles north of the equator. It was started in 2008 by Jochen Zeitz (owner of Puma) as an 'ecosphere retreat' – it is carbon neutral and is one of several of the Zeitz Foundation's tourist-driven enterprises supporting community development and cultural stewardship, sustainable development, ecosystem management and conservation. I think it's an amazing achievement in so short a time. Our plan is to provide more work for the people there, using their skills to make accessories.

There's a new scheme in Segera that we were very impressed with. The idea is to provide people's homes with solar panels. It's obvious that the bush has really deteriorated and the plan to re-establish it depends on the people not chopping firewood. This saves them a lot of time – and, importantly, using solar for cooking instead of burning firewood prevents the serious respiratory illnesses which are endemic in the area. The solar panels also provide lighting – this is a real advantage because the children are able to do their homework in the evenings.

Segera provides schools for the children. All Kenyans have both English and African names given to them at birth. Their lessons are taught in English and all the signs you see are in English as well. Andreas and I were welcomed by one of the teachers, Millicent, who lives at the school, as do the other staff, because of the remote location and the difficulty of travelling. There are as many as sixty children in a class but they do their best. We were shocked that they don't have reading books – so I shall send them some when we return to London.

JUNE 2011

THURS 9 JUNE SEMELE WALK

Zeus was the king of the gods. His jealous queen, Hera, tricked Semele, telling her to ask Zeus to come to her, not in human form but in his full splendour. Zeus granted this favour and Semele was consumed by his lightning fire and from her pregnant womb their son Dionysus (Bacchus) was born. The story of Semele was made into an opera by Handel, which premiered in London in 1744.

I love Handel; he is a great composer whose operas are wonderfully human, ironic and sexy – and great music is timeless. To open the Herrenhausen Festival, near Hanover, Handel's work was magically transformed into Semele Walk, a musical-theatrical performance staged in the perfectly restored Baroque gallery where ancestors of Britain's George I once held banquets – a wonderful setting for the catwalk that forms the stage.

The theme of the festival is 'Worlds Unleashed', which focuses on the danger we face from runaway climate change (once it hits +2 degrees). The key speaker at the opening was Lord Giddens, who is passionately convinced of the urgency needed to stop climate change. I agree with him and believe that the weight of public opinion must be brought to bear on business and government.

Semele Walk incorporated fashions from my spring/summer 2011 Gold Label collection, Get a Life, which is all about climate change and saving our planet, Gaia. We also specially designed key outfits for the performers and musicians which added to the Baroque grandeur of the story and reflected the famous gallery. Baroque is the tension between restraint and grand gesture. My clothes echo this – they have a dynamic rapport with the body which is body conscious and keeps you centred and moves with every breath.

MON 27 JUNE WE SEE THROUGH THE EYES OF THE ARTIST

We went to Florence for the exhibition of our African bags before going on to the menswear show in Milan. Andreas managed to squeeze in a visit to the Uffizi in Florence. When he returned, he talked of Titian and his painting the *Venus of Urbino*.

ANDREAS: This is the painting of all time; it says everything. There is nothing before it and nothing after it. The idea is that there is no idea – just this woman – it doesn't mean anything. For the first time in painting, she's not Diana, she's not Eve, she's not Judith; she's not Venus (the title 'Venus' has been given to her later): she's an image of life. This image of life, it had to be a woman – the woman gives birth; no, it couldn't have been a man, a man can't just cover his cock with his hand. We all know it; it's mesmerising. Manet's *Olympia* is very similar. Manet is more direct; Titian is more stylised. Its sfumato is the finest sfumato ever. It's not lit, not diffused; not clear, not blurred; not real, not fake: it's in perfect equilibrium. It's a world you think you know, yet it's invented ...

VIVIENNE: Andreas, you said that the impact of Renaissance painting is full of colour but when you came to the room with the Titian, it was all one colour.

ANDREAS: I can never understand the colour: there is hardly any; it's the way it's put together, the weight of it. It's not the real world, yet it seems to reflect it more than anything.

VIVIENNE: I think we all search for perfection and truth, as well as outlook on life. Sorry, I know generalisations don't interest you.

ANDREAS: Well, Titian is known as 'the painter of the poesie'.

VIVIENNE: What do you think of the dog?

ANDREAS: The important thing is that there *is* a dog! It's the woman's companion – a King Charles spaniel, a pet. It's part of the subject matter. It would be a horrible painting without it. And the hairstyle! The way it comes down on her, into her neck. There is nothing like it. And she's holding the violets. And the two servants, getting her clothes from the chest? The painting is talking. What will happen next, what is she up to?

Titian's *Venus of Urbino* in the Uffizi – what do you think of the dog?

That's what we mean by 'the painter of the poesie'. Poetry tells a story – reduced to its essentials; you get the idea in one go. The detail helps – the universal in the particular. But of course it's the way it's done that makes it – that's the mystery. Andreas is a visual person: he understands everything from what he sees. He has obviously entered the world that Titian has created and can look into it and also out of it. This illustrates my point in the AR Manifesto that each work of art is a window on the world, an artist's view, throughout time, which we can concentrate into our own experience.

Let's carry on talking about Titian and his Venus. What else do I get? Let's try to pin down further the comparisons art gives us and which help us understand our world.

Most important: There once lived on this earth a man, Titian, who developed his gigantic talent to an extreme which still seems to go beyond the limits of human potential. Even so, such an event cannot just happen: the man must take advantage of the situation. Others must prepare the way. It has to be a development of skills made available by previous artists. This was the time of the Renaissance and men were inspired by the Greek genius to push themselves to the limit. And so much was opening up: the world itself. Innovation teems. The painting not only mirrors the world, it creates it.

I love what Andreas says: 'The painting says everything – nothing before, nothing after.' I think this applies to each real painting. There is no progress in art.

JULY 2011

THURS 14 JULY A WEEKEND IN PARIS

I am busy every day with something different. But the most special thing I just did was to travel to Paris with Andreas for a party held at the Grand Trianon. It was for the opening of an exhibition – *The Eighteenth Century Back in Fashion* – and to mark the end of Couture Fashion Week. The Trianon is a 'small' royal residence

– one storey high – in the grounds of Versailles. On display were fifty designer dresses inspired by Versailles' fashion of the eighteenth century; this has always been such an inspiration to us and quite a lot of our dresses were on display. I was thrilled by the poster which superimposed a dress – originally worn by Nadia Auermann – on to a portrait of Marie Antoinette. We all know Marie Antoinette loved fashion – though she went to the scaffold in a long cotton shift, she was permitted to wear a favourite pair of purple silk embroidered shoes under it: shoes of the Queen of France. Andreas was telling Tizer, our assistant, about the event and I surreptitiously took notes. The brackets = what I'm thinking or what I think Andreas is thinking.

There is Versailles and the sun going down – and had we been quarter of an hour earlier or later we wouldn't have got the sun – the backlight of the last beams and the gold and Louis XIV on his horse, an enormous statue in front, and the dazzle on the blue slate roofs and the gilded metal and the windows shining gold. You realise that this was planned for exactly this time in summer, when they had all the important guests and parties? Le Roi Soleil: The Sun King (*Propaganda*); Louis in splendour rises and sets with the sun.

And then at the party, five or six hundred people – all the women in evening dress, everyone different – everyone went to such trouble *(crazy)*. And an incredible mood. When the French are in a good mood! The champagne, so good! *(Like it never happened before)*. And at 11am – standing on the terrace and sitting on the parterre overlooking the gardens where the King sat – the Fireworks! Not kilometres high *(Rococo)* but like a theatre show high in front of you. Gold and silver against a blue, what do you call such a blue? *(Diffused but still bright)*

Our dress worn by Nadja Auermann.

Midnight blue? And the Fireworks sizzling high or crossing each other from all directions. And the moon. And the end an absolute golden mess and a drizzle of golden rain.

And now the disco tent! The sweets, one thing after another. And in every corner a different ice cream.

And the Trianon is pink, a bungalow *(pink and yellow marble)*. French: so light – so big – and therefore so small, so arrogant, so cool! Once the most powerful man, the most powerful nation, in the world *(Andreas was thinking of Louis XIV. But I imagine more Louis XV having his summer residence there)*. After this, everybody wants to be in this way: Showmanship!

Then, I visited the Musée d'Orsay to see the exhibition, *Manet, the Man Who Invented Modernity*. Manet is one of the greatest of the great painters. Nobody paints like him. Everything I say in AR about great art pays homage to Manet. I am going to look harder at Velázquez to try to see how Manet used his methods. Andreas says the French wouldn't be French without Manet. They are so proud of him. Take him away and our idea of France wouldn't be so complete.

Something else I had to do (secret) involved spending time with my friend Lawrence. He has just got a very important job in communications and, while we were talking, it occurred to me that the biggest problem in today's world is the *isolation of intellectuals*. That's where we need communication if we are ever going to make the world a better place. That is what AR is about. I am trying to engender communication between people who are intellectually inclined like myself.

AUGUST 2011

WEDS 24 AUG IMAGINARY FEARS

James Lovelock, the originator of the Gaia theory and inventor of the electron capture detector (which made possible the detection of

Talking about Gaia and climate change with James Lovelock.

CFCs and other atmospheric nano-pollutants) has always been a strong and outspoken supporter of nuclear energy – and a person whose ideas I have the deepest respect for. In the aftermath of the earthquake and tsunami in Japan and the consequent damage to some of the Japanese nuclear plants, I asked James if he had reconsidered his stance on nuclear – if his opinions had changed.

In reply, he sent me an email outlining his reaction to the tragedy and, in particular, the reaction of the world's press and the actions taken by many governments. In James's own words:

'The reactions of the media and of Green lobbies to the Japanese earthquake and tsunami are in my opinion obscene ... Had Fukushima been a chemical plant and the accident allowed the escape of a small quantity of toxic gas, and if no one was hurt or killed, we would probably not have heard about it. But such is the fear of nuclear radiation and a fear endlessly stoked by the media, Green lobbies and ignorant politicians, that a local event such as Fukushima became a global scare. What

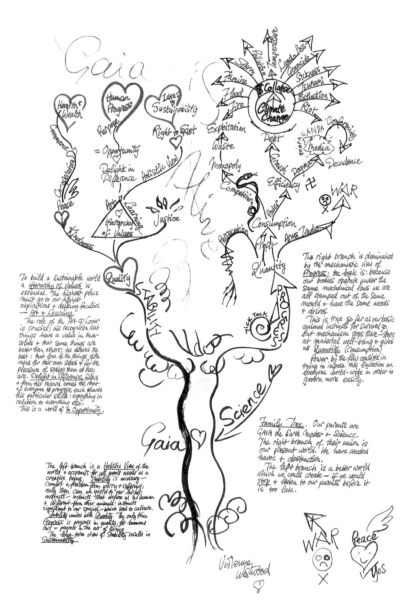

Active Resistance has a mission to promote the green economy. To promote this I drew a family tree as a poster. It looks like Daphne with her two arms/limbs of a tree thrown up. First GAIA married SCIENCE. The limb on one side branches into a loving relationship, on the other side a destructive one. PROGRESS marries QUANTITY. He should have married QUALITY.

is inexcusable about this tiny event in the Japanese tragedy is the way that the media have used it to sell their stories and the politicians cravenly used public fear to justify closing their perfectly safe power stations. This act immediately increases the flow of carbon dioxide to the air. Carbon dioxide is a substance that, unlike the minute quantities of radioactivity, will, if we do not see sense, kill most of us.'

We can't have nuclear: (1) it's too late, (2) emotion against it is too strong and based on anecdotal testimony, and (3) we should promote green energy.

OCT 2011

TUES 4 OCT KYLE NASH-BAKER IN PARIS

We featured the composer and pianist Kyle Nash-Baker at our Gold Label Spring/Summer 2012 fashion show last week – and the feedback has been wonderful. He wrote a comment on our website in May and sent me a piece of his music to listen to – we were so impressed that we asked him to perform his work in Paris.

Kyle is just sixteen and originally taught himself by watching YouTube videos of pianists' fingers (really!). He has a condition called synaesthesia, which means that he sees colours when he plays or listens to music. The music he played at the show consists of selected excerpts from a range of his own compositions – music that has been either totally or partially inspired by the visual aspect of his condition. It was Kyle's desire to combine the audio and visual experiences of his music that first drew him to the Active Resistance Manifesto – particularly its ideas on the relationship between the artist and the world around him. These ideas inspired Kyle to write and develop much of the music he played in Paris.

THURS 13 OCT ABOUT OUR LIVES

After the Gold Label show in Paris I went to Sicily. Although this diary is about my ideas – mostly outside of fashion – I think it's good to include every now and again bits of my private life to give a more rounded picture of what I'm doing. So here is an idea of my trip to Sicily in a postcard to Leonard Peltier. Our friends are what our lives are about and news of a friend's death touched one of us whilst we were there.

Dear Leonard,
As you know I am always thinking of you. I just took a short holiday with Andreas and Ben. The towns are all untouched Baroque architecture and ruins going back to before the birth of ancient Greece and a large Greek amphitheatre (Syracuse was a Greek colony but larger than Athens) and a modern cathedral – a kind of enormous star-shaped cone built because of a ceramic plaque of a Madonna who cried real tears for three weeks in 1948.

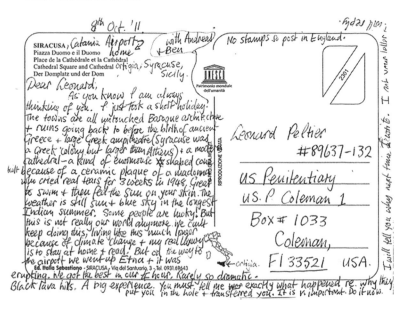

Great to swim and then feel the sun on your skin. The weather is still sun and blue sky in the longest Indian summer. Some people are lucky! But this is not really our world anymore. We can't keep doing this, living like this much longer because of climate change and my real luxury is to stay at home and read. But on the way to the airport we went up Etna and it was erupting. We got the best in our ¼ hour. Rarely so dramatic. Black lava hills. A big experience.

You must tell me exactly what happened re why they put you in the hole and then transferred you. It is very important. Do it now. I will tell you why next time I write. I got your letter and will reply.

DECEMBER 2011

WEDS 21 DEC IT'S THE WEEK BEFORE CHRISTMAS …

We've been very busy in these last days before the Christmas break: putting together the Gold Label collection and moving ahead with Cool Earth fundraising work. The campaign has really been gathering momentum since its launch at the end of November. As well as raising money, raising public awareness of the urgent need to save the rainforest is really important if we want to achieve our goals. Our friend, Daniel Lismore, hosted a party at Whisky Mist in London – I think we were all amazed at how much money was raised and how many people wrote us letters of support.

This morning I did a photo shoot and interview on climate change for the March issue of *Harper's Bazaar* with models from the Storm agency – we are so grateful for all the help and on-going support Storm are giving us with our project. I was also really pleased to spend time with the models: Lily Donaldson, Poppy Delevingne, Jacquetta Wheeler, Sadie Frost, Paul Sculfor and Max Rogers. I

Our 'No Fun Being Extinct' spread in *Harper's Bazaar* with models from the Storm agency.

knew Jacquetta and Sadie already; they all looked wonderful but I was impressed by how interested they are in our work and how willing they all are to help us.

On Thursday, we're off to a meeting at the prime minister's office to talk about the rainforest and climate change.

JANUARY 2012

What would I like to do in 2012 – apart from fashion? The first thing is we need to see everything from the main problem of climate change to find the right solutions to all we want to do.

CLIMATE CHANGE We have helped the Cool Earth campaign to gain momentum and plan to keep raising public awareness and fundraise. The faster we fundraise, the faster the plan to save the rainforest operates. People can see the practical results and then the more they will want to help. The big idea is that our demonstration of people power will encourage governments to join in with financial help. We want to save not only the rainforest but the planet.

Harper's Bazaar and Storm Model Agency are planning a big fundraising event for February, to follow my interview and photos. We have also been approached about a possible TV documentary – for this it would be good to visit Peru and see for ourselves the impact our investments have had – and to find out how the people there earn their living and what is important to them culturally.

HUMAN RIGHTS We should never forget the plight of Leonard Peltier, still languishing in jail after thirty-six years. Protecting human rights is now more important than ever, considering the danger of climate change chaos, the growing numbers of climate refugees (there are already 38 million) and the breakdown of society as we know it. I'm encouraging Leonard to write more about his life in prison but, in the meantime, this is a quote from his book, *Prison Writings*, which gives some insight into his thinking:

> We need each other. Each of us is responsible for what happens on this earth. We are each absolutely essential, each totally

Leonard Peltier took up painting in prison. This is a portrait that he sent to me.

irreplaceable. Each of us is the swing vote in the bitter election battle now being waged between our best and our worst possibilities. How are you going to cast your all important ballot? Humanity awaits your decision ... One good man or one good woman can change the world ... and their work can be a beacon for millions, for billions. Are you that man or woman? If so, may the Great Spirit bless you.

If not, why not?

FINANCIAL TURNING POINT I went twice to speak at Occupy, outside St Paul's Cathedral. The way out is the Green Economy. They should nail these demands on the church door, like Luther.

ART AND LEARNING I don't know if I can manage it this year but I would work with a museum to curate an exhibition which answers the question 'What is Art?' I want to challenge received opinion that art can be anything; everyone's opinion is as good as anyone else's, therefore anyone can be an artist. My own opinion involves a hierarchy of values (see my Family Tree).

One day I would like to have access to a theatre to produce important works which could be vehicles to understanding the world we live in today. I would start with Peter Brook's dramatic adaptation of the twelfth-century Persian verse poem 'The Conference of the Birds' – visually so exciting. The underlying reason would be to promote the fact that Arabs have an amazing culture. The format of Brook's adaptation inspired that of the journey to find art in my AR Manifesto.

Then I would go on to dramatise great books I have read. I am mulling over the idea of Faust who sold his soul to the Devil in exchange for knowledge – knowledge for the sake of power. Well, in today's situation, we seem to have sold our souls for the knowledge that brings power and destruction. That seems like an important message – it could be the idea for a new ballet. And the ballet is one of the great achievements of the human race.

So, how much can we do in 2012? Let's start now and see ...

WEDS 11 JAN *THE IRON LADY* FILM

Years ago when she was in power, I impersonated Margaret Thatcher ... the suit I wore had been ordered by Margaret Thatcher from Aquascutum, but she had then cancelled it.

Margaret Thatcher was a hypocrite. That's what I put in my head. I thought: there's the child in the hospital bed and there's the TV camera. I'm going to show the world how much I care. The photographer Michael Roberts was going mad with delight, 'and it needs one more thing, you need to put a little doubt in your head, do they believe me?' That's how we got her. This cover for *Tatler* was blown up on billboards during London Fashion Week – even I had to look twice to believe it was me. One week later *Tatler*'s editor Emma Soames got the sack. I've never asked Emma if there was any connection.

The Iron Lady is now a film. I don't think it is going to show the real damage that she caused in the world. She helped to release financial madness and now the pyramid scheme has crashed. She's definitely a woman of her time and our time. When will we wake up and take the long-term view? Financial crisis is a symptom and the herald of climate change – coming soon, apocalypse in 2020. When are we going to listen to the scientists?

Thatcher got the North Sea oil bonanza and used the money to help business. If I had really been Thatcher I would have used this wealth to reduce the size of classes in school. Education is the thing that could really enrich our country and surely all those extra teachers would help the circulation of money and wealth. You need heart and head to have vision and that's why I call her a hypocrite: she did not care and used her status as a woman to pretend she did.

TUES 17 JAN: FROZEN PLANET – GREENUP!

We've just returned from our MAN Autumn/Winter 2012/13 Show in Milan. Our collection is in support of David Attenborough's documentary series *The Frozen Planet*, which will go to America

April fool

£2

this woman was once a PUNK

SEE PAGE 104

9 770263 716000

Double take. Michael Robert's notorious photo of me as Mrs Thatcher on the cover of *Tatler*, published in April 1989.

but, unfortunately, without the final episode where he explains that we humans are responsible for the ice melt. So we took the polar explorers as our heroes, and we love polar bears.

Barack Obama never mentions the words climate change. If our leaders would admit the fact of climate change and conduct their politics from that perspective then we might have a chance – we have ten years at the most to stop it. How impossible it is for us to imagine ourselves victims of disaster. We suffer for the poor people who were thrown into the sea from their cruise ship off the coast of Tuscany, some losing their lives. Imagine a world of accelerating natural disasters, one after the other so that nobody can help anyone else. Public opinion is the only thing that will save us.

I was approached by the UN Environmental Programme to design a T-shirt for their GreenUp! campaign – when you start doing things you find people come to you. They're starting with a terrific idea, which is to plant corridors of trees to link Europe's forests. This new initiative is about triggering new habits for a greener Europe and for greener economies. It's a really practical idea and it raises public awareness – it's great for the environment, great for people, great for animals.

Milan, backstage at our Frozen Planet show, with *GreenUp!* 'tree-shirts'.

I have created a design for UNEP in support of the project. It has been printed on a T-shirt provided by sustainable manufacturers, Anvil. The 'Tree-shirts' will be sold through YOOX.com and in our Milan shop during menswear Fashion Week, with all proceeds to be donated to the GreenUp! fund, helping to re-plant trees in Europe's worst-affected regions.

FRI 20 JAN SEVEN WONDERS

A few months ago I did an interview for *L'Officiel* magazine in France. They asked what seven things I consider most important for our time – this is the English version as I wrote it.

(1) THE GAIA THEORY OF JAMES LOVELOCK This is as revolutionary as the theories of Einstein or Darwin; indeed it is a more complete theory of evolution. It has changed our perception of the world – and this will change our behaviour. Gaia is the name the Greeks gave to the earth goddess and Lovelock chose it because of his insight that the earth is alive; Gaia and her life-forms have evolved together in a self-regulating system, and together they create the atmosphere which keeps her cool. If this harmony is broken then Gaia can no longer sustain or tolerate those same life forms; she, herself, will find a new equilibrium by moving to a hot state.

(2) IMAGINATION Should we disappear from the face of the earth, Gaia would never again have the opportunity to create creatures as wondrous. No other species has our powers of understanding and expression: our imagination is a model which mirrors the world. All our sensations and experience are represented by coded imitations of reality which are stored in our imagination like a kind of blueprint. We decode these imitations by the power of insight, which we also call intuition. This is how we get our ideas – by connecting these flashes and impulses which our imagination feeds back to us; then we strive to convert them to real form, expressed externally. We can cross-reference the codes in our blueprint. No

Four Wonders, Hatto and Aamon playing diabolo; Titian at the National Gallery; my friend Nina Ananiashvilli of the Bolshoi ballet; and the Amazon rainforest.

other animal can imitate an object or an idea by drawing on paper, or can dance to music.

(3) THE HUMAN RACE: OUR SURVIVAL We are an endangered species. Our survival depends on becoming more human; for that we each need to engage with the world – not consume but live in harmony. I suggest: a) when possible prepare your own food ('Do it Yourself'). My own diet is without meat or grains. I am one of the world's privileged people and can choose what I eat. Fruit and vegetables is my preferred food, delicious and aspirational. It is convenient to prepare and the most efficient for your body to use, supplying all the goodness and energy you need; b) engage with the past through culture in order to understand the present. This will give you an anchor in life and a sense of personal progress; c) inform yourself about climate change, listen to the scientists; your outlook and behaviour will change ('Get a Life').

(4) NATIONAL GALLERY, LONDON Twentieth-century doctrine aimed to smash the past, break the mould of tradition. They managed to do this in the visual arts but by breaking tradition they also

rejected skill: nowadays, anybody can be an 'artist'. No point, therefore, in running around to catch the latest thing. Go to the National Gallery. Without judges there is no art. We need art lovers because we are dangerously short of culture, which means we are short-sighted, blinkered in our thinking. Great art aims at perfection and is timeless; there is no progress in art. Each of us, at different stages of our lives has had different points of views on the world. A painting is a mirror of the world, an outlook on life, and we find ourselves discriminating and comparing one world with another and with our own; criticism of our present world brings understanding. We are living in the present moment of the past, we are the past: art is true.

(5) THE RAINFOREST: COOL EARTH With the exception of Norway, governments seem to be doing very little to stop climate change. They talk only of growth and in the same breath they talk of the collapse of the economy: the financial crisis is a match of the ecological crisis because the world has nothing cheap left to exploit. Hope lies with the thousands of NGOs, charities and individuals doing practical things. I have joined Cool Earth in their plan to save the rainforest. They aim to save the three great forests of the equator, efficient factories of our atmosphere – because the plan is simple and cheap

and because they are working with the people who live and work in the rainforest. This is a bottom-up approach and the big idea is to link this with government – to get governments to support great ideas which are already working.

(6) RICHARD BRANSON: CARBON WAR ROOM   Branson is a businessman who cares. He is tackling the problems of climate change by use of business methods and by means of the Carbon War Room. He created the Carbon War Room to put forward the idea that over fifty per cent of the climate change challenge can be addressed today, profitably, by existing technologies, in ways that achieve billion-ton-scale carbon reductions. Since the first summit two years ago, the Carbon War Room has specifically targeted shipping, resulting in a rating system for ships that allows customers to choose the most efficient, least polluting ships for their businesses. Large multinationals need to use them. Can you believe it? Fifty per cent of ice melt can be traced to pollution from shipping! And the world has not bothered to try to regulate it. Good luck to Branson and his business methods. Clean shipping is also cheaper.

(7) THE ORCHESTRA In London you can experience a live orchestra at the Barbican or Festival Hall for as little as £7. To someone who has not experienced this it's like nothing else you'll ever see or hear – when you have all these instruments playing together as one and in universal synchronisation of movement. So much depends on the conductor and every time they play it's different. The music completely enters into your body – it's a total experience. The sound of the orchestra and its instruments has been built up over centuries. There are no wires, no amplification – only the acoustics of the building and the very shape and dynamic structure of the instruments which have evolved from simple pipes and sound boxes. The Greeks thought music was the most pure expression of imitation. While you listen to the orchestra it does mirror the world: it is a completed whole, not one note too many.

FEBRUARY 2012

WEDS 29 FEB NO FUN BEING EXTINCT

We have had three fashion shows to present over six weeks. The final show is in Paris this Saturday – we are calling it 'London' and we want to link it to saving the planet by asking, why do all the empty buildings in London have their lights switched on all night? {*We talked to Boris Johnson for weeks – he was very keen, but nothing happened.*}

Stella Tennant modelling London Blackout.

Besides the fashion shows there have, of course, been many other things happening. At the end of November we launched the 'No Fun Being Extinct' campaign to raise £7 million to kickstart the rescue of three of the world's most endangered rainforests. The *Times*, *Guardian* and *Telegraph* interviewed me and covered the Cool Earth story, which went viral in the national media. As a result, the World Bank contacted us and Cool Earth have just met with them in Washington DC.

Storm Model Agency has backed the project enthusiastically. Stephen Fry tweeted to Save an Acre – and within an hour the Cool Earth site received nearly 2,000 hits. The funds raised have enabled them to extend their work: a new Green Teen Philanthropy project was started to teach students how to use their skills to protect rainforest. Ovo Energy is protecting an acre of rainforest for each of their customers with Cool Earth. This number is now 70,000.

Cool Earth's Matthew Owen (left) and anthropologist Dilwyn Jenkins (centre) signing an agreement with César Bustamante (right) of the Ashaninka tribe in Peru.

Matthew Owen, Director of Cool Earth, visited the Aguaruna communities in Northern Peru to scale up the conservation project and include more communities fighting against logging. Several of the Ashaninka communities in the Amazon received a clean water supply: a joyous moment for families who have had to cope with polluted water and walking several hours over arduous terrain to collect fresh supplies. Each village also received a medical outpost. Now there is medicine to deal with venomous bites and malaria.

I donated the original artwork for my Family Tree (see p.46), inspired by the Gaia theory, to help save James Lovelock's archives for posterity. It was auctioned at the Science Museum's fundraising dinner last week. Together with other funds raised, it will make it possible for the museum to become the perfect permanent home for these invaluable records of a lifetime's work and discovery.

I went to a book launch and signing for *Dispatches from the Dark Side* by Gareth Peirce, the famous human rights lawyer. The book is on 'torture and the death of justice' and the political misuse of the law in England and America that has accompanied the war on terror. Torture today is easier to read about because most of it is of a kind that doesn't leave physical marks – when it does, the victims are killed. Today, the agony of torture is prolonged; it destroys people over an indefinite length of time.

MARCH 2012

SAT 3 MARCH 38 MILLION CLIMATE REFUGEES

Experts estimate that there were more than 38 million people displaced by sudden-onset, climate-related natural hazards in 2010. Climate refugees now outnumber refugees fleeing persecution and violence by more than three to one. What we're talking about regarding climate change refugees is total chaos, where natural disasters are more intense and more frequent. I have been working

No Place Like Home, our new T-shirts in support of the Environmental Justice Foundation, modelled by Naomi Campbell.

with the Environmental Justice Foundation's (EJF) 'No Place Like Home' projects and recently recorded a video interview in support.

Every year climate change contributes to the deaths of over 300,000 people, seriously affects a further 325 million people, and causes economic losses of US$125 billion. Four billion people are vulnerable to the effects of climate change and 500–600 million people – around ten percent of the planet's human population – are at extreme risk. Climate change has been recognised as a fundamental threat to human rights and developing countries stand to bear almost all of the burden: 98 per cent of seriously affected people, 99 per cent of deaths from weather-related disasters, and 90 per cent of economic losses. Recent disasters show the potential scale of the problems: 1.5 million homes were destroyed in Bangladesh by Cyclone Sidr in 2007; floods in Pakistan displaced around 1.8 million people, and damaged or destroyed up to 1.6 million homes and 6.8 million acres of crops in 2010; more than 950,000 Somali refugees were displaced to neighbouring countries between January 2011 and January 2012 as a result of the complex East Africa crisis.

Unlike refugees recognised under the UN Convention Relating to the Status of Refugees, climate refugees have no legal status. There is no legislation, agency or institution specifically mandated for their protection and assistance. No existing framework or institutions in the domain of migration, displacement or climate change specifically address the issue of climate refugees, and no international institution has a clear mandate to serve these people who so need human rights protection and humanitarian assistance. EJF's No Place Like Home campaign is working to get the voices of those most vulnerable to climate change heard internationally, with the goal of securing a legally binding instrument for the recognition, assistance and protection of people who often have nowhere to go and no means to survive.

I have designed T-shirts to support EJF's campaign. They have a 90 per cent smaller carbon footprint than an average cotton T-shirt; they are organic, ethically made and manufactured by renewable green energy.

APRIL 2012

TUES 10 APRIL THE PRADO AND VELÁZQUEZ

The weekend before Easter, Andreas and I went to Madrid for three days and, apart from one morning when we visited the superb Thyssen Collection, we spent each day in the Prado.

We had promised ourselves for so long to visit Velázquez. His *Las Meninas* or *The Ladies in Waiting* is the most famous painting

Velázquez's masterpiece, *Las Meninas*, or 'The Ladies in Waiting'.

in the gallery. Nothing, no reproduction, could ever prepare you for the shock and power of the painting – you are confronted by another world, a parallel universe, the fourth dimensions of space and time. The surface becomes a room and the focus is on this little thing, this child who still hasn't a clue of why she is so important: the Infanta. She's blonde – everyone else is dark – and in a silvery white dress; the hair is important; it suffuses down over her shoulders, infiltrated by the rosy haze of the air which fills the room; the dress is silk and her skin has the liquid softness of a child who is still a baby. The way it is painted! The lady in waiting bending over the Infanta from our right has a knot of silver ribbons in her hair, but when you open up your eyes you see her head is just a twizzled daub of black and thick white which grabs you and pulls you into the picture. Eyes looking at you can be smudges and a hand can be lost. I'm always thrilled how much brush strokes and paint applied on a flat surface can emphasise – or not – and therefore represent – the movement of real life around us, where we never focus on everything at once but only according to our interest. The composition is highly original: so much going on, caught in a moment of time; Velázquez himself in the act of painting, and the images in the mirror of the King and Queen, as if they were really standing next to you looking into the picture.

The Prado is one of the world's great galleries. It has loads of the best landmarks of innovation. The museum has just been re-done and they've done it so well; the paintings are grouped and hung in such an exciting way – they seem to have all the Velázquez paintings in the world. And all the Goyas – so many and all so different. Goya had such skill he seems to have been able to paint in any way he wanted. Manet came to absorb himself in the collection and learn, and described Velázquez's *The Buffoon* to be the most wonderful thing the world had ever produced. The man really stands in a space of his own – no background. The sense of reality is overwhelming when you are in front of it.

Coming back to London, the plane was delayed by six hours, most of it spent on the tarmac. Two weeks before, coming back from France on the Eurostar, we had a nine-hour delay because of a pylon on the tracks. It was all very friendly but uncomfortable and some people were moaning because the delay was caused by French strikes. We are so used to the facilities of our consumer society. In a shrinking world economy and with more problems from climate change we are going to have more of this. For me it is the 'Beginning of the End'. Normally, I try to fly less. We got to bed at 4 a.m.

THURS 26 APRIL SHELL MUST CLEAN UP THE NIGER DELTA

Shell has been extracting oil in the Niger Delta area of Nigeria for over fifty years. They are the major operator there and have made billions and billions of dollars out of the country. And what have the people of the Niger Delta received in return? The vast majority have been subjected to grinding poverty, little access to clean water, a polluted environment and ongoing violence and conflict.

Amnesty International believes that leaks and spills from Shell's pipelines have devastated the livelihoods of millions of people in the region. Amnesty research has revealed that the fish they catch, the water they drink and the air they breathe have all been ruined by oil pollution. I support their campaign to end the needless suffering of the people of the Niger Delta. Shell makes billions of pounds of profit each year. It is a profit that is being subsidised by the poverty and ill-health of the people of the Niger Delta.

For decades Shell has ignored repeated calls to clean-up the mess they have left behind: a mess that they are responsible for; a mess that has blighted the livelihoods and health of thousands upon thousands of people. Shell needs to get around the table and put a proper cost next to the liabilities they are responsible for and to fund new structures to ensure that the life and health of the people of the Niger Delta are protected once and for all.

The Niger Delta is one of the most polluted areas on the face of the earth. Decades of oil pollution has seeped into the water, the soil and the burning of oil waste pollutes the air. Where once the people could fish and farm in order to support themselves, their families and their communities, now they are reduced to begging. Their government has abandoned them to the oil companies.

But they are fighting back. Communities in the Niger Delta have taken Shell to court in the US, UK and Netherlands. Shell is starting to be held to account for its devastation in Nigeria. You can add your voice too. No more excuses, enough is enough: Shell needs to clean up its act.

STELLA TENNANT

Came home after a glorious day with Juergen Teller shooting Stella Tennant for our publicity campaign. We had worked exhaustively over days to prepare it and it went well. We shot clothes from both the January MAN show and the February woman's show on Stella, and created an atmosphere of seventeenth-century interiors. We

A glorious day with Juergen Teller, shooting Stella Tennant for our campaign.

wanted to present the clothes with the noble gravitas of Velázquez portraits and posed the shots accordingly. Stella was superb.

SAT 28 APRIL THE STORY OF THE STONE

Yoga. Decided every Saturday will be my day of rest and glory! Reading for pleasure in bed. I have a queue of books waiting, most of them non-fiction, but my current one is *The Story of the Stone* – it is fascinating, profound, exhilarating. It really is a book of life – a Chinese eighteenth-century classic in five volumes. Read until I slept.

MON 30 APRIL TOILES

First fittings for Gold Label – designing fashion is continuous. Our fitting model tried on the toiles. A toile is a draft – a work in progress of a design, executed in calico, which we develop and fit until finally we make the finished garment in the correct fabric. Iris really enjoyed working on some of the clothes inspired by beetles. A kind person had sent me a little book on beetles thinking it could inspire jewellery designs.

MAY 2012

TUES 1 MAY WE ARE THE MAJORITY

Yoga. Then long talk with Julian Assange: WikiLeaks and their problems raising funds to ensure their survival. They've been fighting an unlawful economic blockade by giant US finance companies for over a year. This has destroyed 95 per cent of their revenue from the public. Our politicians are in default on every level – climate change created by squeezing everyone with a crazy financial system and decreasing regard for human rights. It causes people to think only of themselves. Yet it's all connected. When I read the newspapers (I expect TV is the same) they make you think the public agrees with all this. But I don't think we do. We know they are exploiting us. I am not alone. You are not alone. We are the majority.

WEDS 2 – THURS 3 MAY IRIS AND FABRIC CUTTING

Worked on collection. It's hard. On average, if you can make one decision a day – that is speed. With Iris here we can work more quickly; Iris develops the new ideas for a cut. She is so light and so quick because she is technically trained; she brings more than one idea to a point each day; she helps us and our other pattern cutters. We can pin our ideas down at the fittings and I can check with her the use of fabrics for the designs. Andreas thinks the most important thing is to catch the accident, keep it, use it. Right use of fabrics is the hardest part, matching the idea – the toiles – with the fabric. This continues throughout the building of the collection and includes how to sew and make up the garment.

You have to let the fabric do what it wants to do. At the moment we only have small samples of fabric – some are only 2-inch square, the rest 12-inch. Nothing has arrived, yet I need to work it out in the air because: a) I need to get a potential overview for the collection, e.g. what blouse goes with what skirt/jacket (through such practical solutions you develop the collection and the feeling); and b) this will show me what other fabrics I am going to need so I can still order before it is too late. Some fabrics – I think, why on earth have we ordered this; what am I going to do with it? Print it? Cut it full of holes? Then I might get an interesting idea. When the fabrics do start to come then it often happens that the idea and the fabric just don't work together; then you have to design something else for the fabric and something else for the idea which is still at the toile stage. Anyway, this is the hardest thing. Luckily, Andreas is genius at all this and only when the fabrics arrive will he start to commit himself.

Knitwear is much easier to design. One day I'll explain why.

WEDS 2 – THURS 3 MAY KEN FOR MAYOR

I voted for Ken Livingstone for London mayor. He's done great for London throughout his career. He made you feel we were all in it together, that London was our town. I liked Siobhan Benita – an independent – she was very specific and practical. Boris adopted the bike idea from Ken and, apart from that, he's shown no imagination – just hard-line Conservative policy. Yet people like him, like him because he's disruptive. I remember some years ago I attended a discussion at the British Museum, run by the Telegraph, 'Do we live in a free society'. Boris was on the panel and sabotaged the whole thing by showing off and saying silly things.

FRI 4 MAY WILL.I.AM

Met Will.i.am. He popped in to see me about an idea he has for fashion. We talked a lot. He had helped Obama get in with his hit song, 'Yes We Can', but he is quite politically aware. Because Obama is a fan of drones and because Will believes in technology, I talked about drones. We now live in a world worse than *1984* for surveillance, and drones can be targeted at anybody the Ruling System decides to kill. Do we really believe they're killing only terrorists and that they know who these terrorists are? (To me a terrorist is often just someone who is in the wrong place at the wrong time.) Will thinks that social media and the internet provides a transparency so that no-one can lie.

I say: for two centuries Western people have agreed with the belief system which masqueraded as democracy, especially in the US. Movies, bombs, War is Peace – we believed the myth. Even in the face of the lie, we believe; the more blatant the lie the more we believe. We do not see our own face in the mirror. We can only hope that as the lies become more blatant, more of us will admit to the reality. It will be great if the internet increases our disbelief. Will works hard and donates a lot of money for education. He connects education with being able to use technology in a creative way. He took my point that education doesn't start from you and what you can do. You have to know the past in order to understand the present and to launch into the future. He laughs that I don't have a mobile phone, etc. but acknowledged what I also said – whatever the marvels of technology, the internet can't read a book for me.

He is a very good, sweet, clever man. Apart from his other charities, he's interested to help with Cool Earth and I told him about Leonard. There is no better way to know things than from the motive: how can I make the world a better place?

Re the collection: another milestone attained! I had not found a tailoring fabric I liked. Now we've decided on three and I have some idea of 'how it's gonna be'.

Will.i.am wearing our Spring collection.

SAT 5 – MON 7 MAY **READING**

Spent all three days reading. Newspapers: I don't usually read them except when I travel – and I don't travel much. Then I read them from cover to cover. I prefer surveys in book form, e.g. environment: Lovelock, Mark Lynas, Jared Diamond; politics/human rights: John Pilger, Gareth Pierce, Jung Chang – and for real solidity and overview: Bertrand Russell. I've been reading him for years and always recommend his books *Freedom and Organization 1815–1914* and *The Problem of China*.

I read *The Week* (which is a survey of the week's news) but not always, and the *New Statesman* for Pilger. Cynthia King, who works on our political campaigns, finds and prints articles for me, too. So, I was reading articles, dipping into my books, making notes and thinking. I must read novels again, soon.

WEDS 9 MAY CONCERT AT THE BARBICAN

I am usually awake at 6.30 a.m. but thinking for at least thirty minutes. Wrote a letter to James Lovelock. 11 a.m. called in to see a neighbour. The council want to evict him and others from their homes so I will write a letter against this. At work: spent rest of the day with Andreas designing a label. Labels are the important thing. We will see samples and then we may have to rework it.

Concert at the Barbican: piano and violin. Andreas loves music and gets tickets. He is usually totally absorbed and carried away but, for the first and only time I can remember, he was distracted by stress. He takes responsibility for the way everything on the creative side of our company is done; he carries it with him and anticipates everything that can go wrong – he's the boss and I'm the assistant, though he depends on me doing lots of design without him as well as designing together. He really lives for fashion, whereas I have all these other things.

I used to be, 'When I finish this pair of trousers I can read my book', plus human rights. But now I have a general worry: climate change is the overriding worry. How to get through to enough people to promote urgent action? Noam Chomsky has been trying to get through on politics all his life. Now he thinks the Occupy Movement may be that catalyst. I enjoyed the concert (Mendelsohn, Greig, Frank).

All day Thursday with Andreas styling our Red Carpet Collection for a photo shoot. On Friday, a person-to-camera video campaign for Liberty and interview for *GQ China* with Robert Johnston. He asked me, 'Are you political?' I answered, 'Well, a political person tries to influence people and that is what I try to do.' The difference (between me and politicians) is that I know the problem we absolutely must solve and they ignore it. Robert asked me, 'Is fashion intellectual?' I answered, 'It has to have a story.'

Concert at the Barbican: Stravinsky, conductor Valery Gergiev. Andreas and I had a lovely time: snack and cup of tea, wine in the interval. There's nothing more modern, therefore universal, great and exciting than Stravinsky (no progress in art). His fame came from the Ballet Russes; by age twenty-seven the world was at his feet. He looked an intellectual but he caught people's imagination.

Valery Gergiev conducting the London Symphony Orchestra.

He was a romantic hero. The age of the Ballet Russes had an amazing impact, and Diaghilev, its creator, was one of the great artists of the twentieth century, along with Matisse and Picasso. Tickets for the Barbican concerts start from £10 and it's the greatest music in the Western world.

SAT 12 – SUN 13 MAY SUDOKU

Yoga. Reading – articles and dipping (take it for granted that I read in bed). I must mention cooking and talk about it in full one time. Also, I often spend an hour doing Sudoku – I enjoy it too much to consider it a waste of time. On Sunday I read only my book, *Story of the Stone*. Pleasure from morning till night.

TUES 15 MAY *WORLD'S END* AND *OEDIPUS REX*

Yoga class, then to work. By the time I'd had lunch and Tizer (our PA) had gone through stuff – you know, invitations, appointments, etc. – it was 3.30 p.m. But I was able to work at last – I'd been promising myself for months – on my favourite shop, *World's End* (opened in 1970). Going through, making sure everything is happening and building ideas for more to happen.

In the evening, Andreas and I went again to the Barbican (I told you he books tickets at the beginning of the season – but it's so large you can always get tickets on the night). Stravinsky's *Rite of Spring*, perhaps the most famous musical event ever staged (it's a ballet but tonight it was the music alone) due to the furore which erupted in the audience on the opening night. People had never heard or seen anything like it before – it's a great driving cacophony of strange rhythms and beats and overwhelmingly beautiful strains. The tribes surge around the Chosen Maiden who must dance herself to death; they lead the pounding rhythms along with their heads leaning to one side on their shoulders. Amidst the row somebody calls out, 'A doctor!' someone else, 'A dentist!'

During the interval I met Mary Greenwell, a very fabulous make-up artist, a friend whom I've often worked with. She was raving! She talked of how an orchestra is at a pinnacle of evolution in music, a highly complex unity. I said I thought that's what Plato had meant when he said, 'Man is a political animal', political referring to *polis* or city – that he moves towards more complex social structures which culminate in the city and that the hierarchy of different functions provides the means for humans to express and develop more and more the human genius, to evolve into more perfect humans. Mary thought that African music was not so evolved as our orchestra. I said that it might seem so to us but let us be aware that man has forgotten more than he knows.

The second half was music from Stravinsky's opera *Oedipus Rex*. You know, it's one of the great stories which obviously has its source in primitive ritual: Thebes is afflicted with plague because the king, Oedipus, had unwittingly killed his father and married his mother. Gergiev was great. He had once told me that the most important thing for a conductor was to listen to the audience; a member of the orchestra had told me that it's different every time they play, they never know what to expect. At the end, Andreas said, 'I love the mess! Wasn't that so Oedipus Rex? So meaningless, so tragic, so great!'

WEDS 16 MAY CRAIG AND VANESSA

Did my roots with henna. Worked on *World's End*. Afternoon: photos of me by Craig McDean and stylist Vanessa Reid for *Interview* magazine. Amazing how clothes can help and give you such a feeling of adventure – powerful, important, funny, heroic. The photos seemed very nice on the monitor (Juergen doesn't seem to use one; he says it's important to look at the subject and, I guess, look for the subject). Craig gave quite a deal of direction to me and to his lighting assistants – the light was on wheels. I enjoyed myself.

I do publicity and interviews so I can talk about climate change. I'll be doing the interview later.

One of Craig McDean's shots for *Interview* magazine.

THURS 17 MAY JOYCE DIDONATO

Morning: interview with Francine Lacqua on the London Eye for Bloomberg TV's *Eye2Eye* series. I was so concentrated on what I wanted to say that I didn't look at the view and though we were back on the ground in the blink of an eye, she was very nice and I made some good points. Worked two hours on *World's End*.

Late afternoon: interview – i.e. filmed conversation – with opera star Joyce DiDonato for the Arte TV network (French/German). I met Joyce because she noticed me in the audience at one of her concerts and sent me a CD. Since then, we have designed for her stage wardrobe. I had never really talked to her before and I didn't know what to expect. She has a beautiful warmth and sincerity of manner. She grew up in a small town in Kansas but her voice and intellectual curiosity have taken her far from home. She is proud of her home town and brought me some chocolates which are a local speciality. She has thought a lot and is intellectual and artistic. Joyce is so kind and we had a really inspiring talk. I am looking forward to seeing her in a dramatic red gown we are preparing.

FRI 18 MAY JUERGEN TELLER

Juergen came to help decide which photos from the shoot to use for our publicity. Stella Tennant has such total class. Andreas enthused, 'She is just the most perfect representative of the human race; she is everything: young or old, child, woman, man! The mouth alone! Beauty incarnate.'

I had told Craig McDean that Juergen thinks there are only a few good photographers and Craig replied, 'I think he thinks there's really only one.' I told Juergen and he grinned and put his hand to his forehead, acknowledging the point that he has strong opinions. Juergen admires the work of William Eggleston – not a fashion photographer. Because Eggleston inherited a private income he photographed according to his own lights and never compromised himself for commercial success.

SAT 19 MAY MORE SUDOKU – I DON'T RECOMMEND IT

Morning yoga class. At home with Andreas. Instead of reading I spent all day doing one killer Sudoku. Of course I will probably be quicker next time but it's a terrible investment of time and I only want to do the extra-hard ones. So many hypothetical factors to mark and hold in mind before you can advance one square. I shall really have to limit this. I won't do any more this month. However, it really is stimulating. I didn't even feel hungry; I only had breakfast – two bananas and a pear. Please, no comments about Sudoku. I don't recommend it because I think it's addictive – but it is an exercise in pure reason.

MON 21 MAY GOOGLE ZEITGEIST CONFERENCE

Weather glorious. Left home at 8 a.m. with Cynthia for Google's Zeitgeist conference at the Grove Hotel in Herefordshire; due to talk in the early afternoon. We went early to get an idea of what the conference was about. The audience was mainly Google advertisers and employees – people with a lot of money and influence.

The first panel discussion on the current political situation – Greece and the euro – bludgeoned me into incredulity. Worthless discussion about upturns, downturns, cycles and growth and not including the factor of climate change: like preparing the Sunday roast and not turning on the heat because the house is burning down. Why am I here? I can read this stuff in the papers. Anyway, I'm a vegetarian.

We first met our friend, Marc Koska, at a previous conference. These things are networking opportunities to raise support for our causes. And Marc has a wonderful cause: he invented a disposable syringe – only one-time use is possible – that has saved millions of lives. Massive spread of disease in poor countries is due to using the same syringe and needle on a string of patients. After twenty years of finding ways to combat the practice of drug companies, his safe syringe will become the only model used, supported by the World Health Organization. Great news!

Lily Cole and Jimmy Wales (the founder of Wikipedia) were interviewed by CNN anchor Becky Anderson. Jimmy is endorsing Lily and her project, giving her the technical help she needs to inaugurate her 'gifting' website, ImPossible. I was next. Nobody had yet mentioned climate change and I was bored by the audience and didn't care what I would say. But I was angry and it all came out anyway – my mantra: climate change is caused by the bad financial system; talk of human values instead of abstract sums about money. When Becky tried to ask me questions I told her, 'You're trying to interrupt me', and carried on in full spate until I was finished. Then! The members of the audience were delighted and clapped and hooted. I was surprised and of course really pleased.

Then! The lightning struck! Annie Lennox and a presentation on HIV/AIDS and its impact on women and children in Sub-Saharan Africa. 'Did you know?' she asked us. 'One in three women and children die from AIDS in Africa.' I did not put my hand up; one or two did. She told us that there is treatment to prevent transmission from mother to child at birth. I have never heard anything like this speech. The power of this woman is a phenomenon! Passion and oratory on a grand scale. I told her later and she rang with laughter, 'Nobody would have listened to Hitler if you'd been around.'

TUES 22 MAY DINNER WITH JOE

Yoga class. Shopping (food) and letters. 4 p.m. at work. A photographer called Joanna Brown took an impression of my finger to cast for a charity exhibition (Freedom from Torture). Andreas and I set off on our bikes to a Condé Nast Traveller event where I accepted an award for sustainability on behalf of Cool Earth. Then, as we were in the West End, we made it an evening and met my son, Joe, for dinner. We have lots to talk about but I won't tell because Joe is not really part of this diary, but he does 'stuff'. He has a human rights charity called Humanade. He supports Leonard Peltier and also the Inga Foundation, which is an agricultural project which replaces the slash and burn agriculture of the rainforest. On the way home, I looked

in at the windows in *Selfridges* promoting the *World's End* shop and showing my graphics, e.g. the Family Tree, which has drawn a lot of attention.

I loved being out with Andreas. We are so lucky in life and, who knows, this might be the last age of great material wealth. Before I went up to bed I stayed in the kitchen adoring the flowers in the middle of the table. Andreas had bought them. It's always lovely to choose the flowers yourself rather than letting the florist do it. These are still in their glory but tomorrow it will be over. Thank you, flowers.

WEDS 23 MAY LILY COLE AND THE RA JUBILEE PARTY

This evening the Royal Academy hosted a Jubilee party for the arts. The Queen will give the awards.

I usually borrow something but almost all the Summer collection was in Hong Kong. I spent all day messing about at home but I couldn't find the right thing in my own wardrobe. I had been asked to go with my muse, and that was Lily Cole, who I was supposed to meet at work. These things can take ages. (One reason for wearing the same things over and again. Chanel had all her clothes organised as outfits with numbers for each.) If it weren't for Lily, I think I might have just not gone – there were at least 1,000 people there and I wouldn't have been missed. When I got to work, Andreas had managed to collect a rail of outfits for me and for Lily to choose. So it was all sorted. Andreas did it.

We arrived, I thought early (it was still only six), but in fact we were late. The organiser kept saying, 'Please come, I have to get you

Lily Cole, my Royal Academy muse.

in.' But I, true to my own bossy character, delayed in order to talk to the BBC because I'm a great fan of the Queen. The result was I missed being in the group picture of British dames, but never mind.

I was able to talk to Lily. She said that the next day at the Zeitgeist conference, former president Clinton gave a good speech and that he did mention climate change. She also told me about a group called World Land Trust (*www.worldlandtrust.org*), who sound like people we should be working with. I did some networking: Annie (again), Bono and Paul Smith. I hope to involve them in our big event in July – celebrities to lead the way – saving the planet from climate change. It must have been about 8.30 p.m. when I left. Piccadilly was thronging plus total traffic block. I headed for Green Park tube and headed home. I quite enjoyed being so dressed up on the tube even though the trains were packed.

THURS 24 MAY PRINCE'S DRAWING SCHOOL

 Dentist. Worked on *World's End*. Evening: Andreas and I went to the Prince's Drawing School for a private view of their club's annual exhibition. For my speech I had planned to talk of the imagination: insight and the fact that we are cross-wired; that the appreciation of art is direct knowledge and that the foundation of visual art is skill in drawing; the importance of art in creating true culture. The place was packed, half of the audience young children. I hadn't expected this so I had to adapt my speech and I really enjoyed the task of explaining these intellectual ideas so that young people could understand something of it.

Prince Charles has identified a well-felt need in establishing this school and its regional drawing clubs. Our stale academies of visual art (e.g. Goldsmith's) teach only dogma, not skill. Andreas and I were blown away! This school is so great. The facilities are a dream. Kids attend from age ten; with parents' consent they can do nude life drawing from age twelve (they are taught by artists); students can take an MA arts degree here. There is also a department of Islamic crafts with an incredibly high standard resulting in beautiful

At the Prince's Drawing School. The Family Tree is printed on my dress.

objects. The atmosphere vibrates with potential. Andreas and I were really inspired. He can't wait to receive a drawing of a horse and rider he was allowed to choose.

FRI 25 MAY THANK GOD FOR GREENPEACE

Thank God for Greenpeace. They're the ones who got us the Antarctic. It's international. No one can disturb it. Now they must do this for the Arctic. We must put an end to the obscene quarrels for ownership between the US, Canada, Russia, Norway and Denmark or agree to our own suicide. Greenpeace will do it. The plan is simple genius. More of this another time. John Sauven, Executive Director, Greenpeace UK, and his colleague Sophie came to see me at work. I guess when you plan such a smooth operation as is required you need all the help and support you can get and talking adds to and fixes the idea. Andreas listened, too. He is so visual and auditory (I am more literary). He was so taken by John, by his presence, tranquillity and grace, clarity and determination (these are my words). Small things, bits and pieces for the rest of the day.

MON 28 MAY SEEDS OF FREEDOM

Stayed at home until 5 p.m. getting this diary up to date. I can't seem to find the time to do it day by day. At the moment the pressure for designing the Gold Label collection is off because technical work has been delegated (it's going to hit again soon). And I like writing this diary. It marks the time so the days don't all merge into one.

At 6.00 p.m., I joined Cynthia for a screening of *Seeds of Freedom*. The film exposes how GM seeds give monopoly of supply to a few giant companies, e.g. Monsanto. GM foods are promoted as providing future food security for the world's vast population. There is no evidence for this and all the facts are against it. There is more food security in tradition: seeds which have developed thousands of years of resilience to changing conditions and crops which adapt to the environment and diversity of crops. Farmers who changed to GM seeds are locked in a spiral of dependence, increasing poverty and often ruin. Aphid-repellent wheat sounds like a good idea but it's not; it results in superbugs, monoculture with the risk of entire crop failure and having to buy your seeds for planting each year.

TUES 29 MAY GEORGE MONBIOT

Yoga. Shopping. Then meeting with George Monbiot. I am a fan of his writing but I had not met him before, and he very kindly came to see me and Cynthia. My idea is to talk to a few influential people, starting with George, so that we all frame our opinions in the context of climate change.

Given the state we're being dragged into, George would have expected thousands – millions – to be out on the street. My son, Joe, says that after the massive demonstration of two million to try to stop the war on Iraq was ignored by the Labour government, people have become too pissed off to bother. (Ignore the public and they'll go away.) I also think that the twentieth century trained us up to be consumers – we suck up and expect somebody else/the system to provide the solution.

When I told George about my neighbours facing eviction, he was really touched and shook his head despairingly at the short-term thinking of councillors and bureaucrats. Perhaps we should go out on the streets as the whole thing ties in with being anti the austerity measures. George has just finished his latest book – how by doing right in respect to Gaia she will repair the damage in a very short time, e.g. re-introducing a few wolves into Yellowstone Park has in eight years changed the behaviour of other animals, and the vast park is back to what it was a long time ago.

WEDS 30 MAY PAMELA AND COOL EARTH AT THE LORDS

Worked on *World's End*. Then to a House of Lords event to mark the fifth anniversary of Cool Earth, to thank everyone for their donations and do a bit more fundraising. Matthew Owen told us what Cool Earth had accomplished so far – and what the plans are for the future – both short and long term.

When we arrived, the person getting out of the car in front of us was Pamela Anderson, a vision in one of our lace dresses. I was so confused – it was surreal; I wondered where I was. She had come to help us. Darling girl – I couldn't get over it. We all gave speeches and had many photos taken; friends I hadn't seen for ages were there. Pamela talked to everybody and had a tour of the House of Lords. Several people came to tell me what lovely people were there. I met Eliza Doolittle and we are going to visit the art galleries together. She was dressed to perfection, sexy and chic.

Johan Eliasch, the founder (along with Frank Field) of Cool Earth, invited some of us to dinner. Pamela is magic for me, she wrote in

At the Lords with Pamela Anderson and Cool Earth founder Frank Field MP.

an email: 'How I cherish the two of you (Andreas, too). And I really am impassioned about saving the world, spreading the word... I was up at 3 a.m. ... thinking about our dinner. Half afraid, half hopeful.' She is such a serious person who tries to learn everything she can. Her beloved grandfather was a Finn. She wrote, 'He taught me about fairy tales, symbolism, alchemy and woods. He was a logger in Canada. The trees spoke to him.' He used to dance on the small circle cut off at the tops of trees a hundred feet in the air.

JUNE 2012

SAT 2 – TUES 5 JUNE TO JOE'S PLACE IN CORNWALL

On the train with Andreas to my son Joe's place in Cornwall; we'll be there with my son Ben and Joe's girlfriend Faye and friends. One trip to the beach – a bit cold to go in the water. You have to do it straight away. Joe went in. Spent most of my time reading in bed. Too much time spent on Sudoku: you get so you only want to do the really hard ones. I've stopped.

WEDS 6 JUNE I AM NOT A TERRORIST ...

Transition time between holiday and going back to work. At work at 11a.m. and talked strategy to Cynthia, who works with me on everything to do with climate change and manages our political work. After lunch, Cynthia went to a discussion about Julian Assange's TV interview series, *The World Tomorrow*. I had to get on with Gold Label which I've have been dangerously neglecting.

What are we doing to help Julian in his hour of need? He is now appealing the UK court decision to extradite him to Sweden, and the Pentagon is determined to get him one way or the other; his sources of public funding have been effectively cut off by the

Cindy Palmano's photo of me with her son, John. We are wearing my 'I am not a Terrorist, Please don't arrest me' T-shirts, designed originally for Liberty.

Bank of America and US-based credit cards. My T-shirt, 'I am not a Terrorist, Please don't arrest me' has even greater significance today than when I designed it for Liberty. We need to fight these emergency laws which our governments are using to trap people – not terrorists, not anyone who has done anything illegal but simply anyone they don't like – like Julian, who is a public hero for exposing their hidden secrets. Of course, Bradley Manning – whose trial has now been delayed until late November – is an even greater hero.

If Julian's last-chance appeal doesn't work, he faces years in jail for sticking his neck out and telling the truth. Put yourself in his shoes; I would be terrified. Orwell's *1984* is happening in our world now.

THURS 7 JUNE A DURIAN

Awake at 5 a.m. thinking about *The Story of the Stone*. The characters in the book are so alive to me. I just have the feeling that every person who ever lived, who took part in the vast timeless circle of time, is important, every little life counts and some of those lives are so beautiful even if they don't manage to survive beyond youth's golden spring. Early to the dentist. Long session but painless. Popped into Chinatown and treated myself to a durian.

Work, after lunch: answered questions for a journalist friend's book. (Fashion is so much about public face, interviews, etc.). Now it was 5 p.m. Did one thing for Gold Label. OK!

FRI 8 JUNE RAIN, AUSTERITY AND *LE MONDE*

Rain, rain, rain! In my lifetime never have we had such rain continuing through spring into summer. I consider it part of the chaos point of climate change. Afternoon interview with *Le Monde*. It is really a fashion profile, which I try not to do unless it brings in climate change, which the journalist, Veronique, was interested in. I tried to make the point: Everything is connected. If governments would only see everything from the point of climate change, we might be able to solve the problem and the financial problem.

We all know that money is debt. Governments pretend that this debt will be paid by the future taxpayer. Even if the future were secure there is no way the debt will ever be paid. The debt will increase because that is what our financial system is based on. Every baby in Britain today owes £20,000 from the minute it is born. Anyway, the status quo right now is that governments must be seen to manage the debts so that the rate of increase can be controlled.

Hollande is doing the right thing in France by relaxing the austerity and perhaps borrowing money. By this he acknowledges the money is debt and the debt will never be paid. I believe it also acknowledges the need for human values. Nevertheless, he should stop talking about growth. Stability is what we need. I believe in Europe as a political federation because that's about co-operation – and we need the European Court of Human Rights. I hope it stays together financially because in that way – if everybody helps everybody else – we will find a better financial system.

Tried to do a bit more knitwear.

SAT 9 JUNE JACQUETTA'S WEDDING

Yoga. Then to my friend Jacquetta's wedding. She's a model and also works for the human rights charity, Reprieve. We went by train to Canterbury and then on to her parents' home.

I had never been to Canterbury before and we went inside the cathedral for a half hour. Those stones erected in the service of a principle and a way of life is beyond the depth of my understanding. Where are the books I should have read that would give me an insight into this world? It's like I said: knowledge is insight. One day I may discover something which will make the connection – illuminate the life that this immense time capsule holds in suspension and without some other piece of information my imagination is powerless. I am primed for this flash of inspiration because now this stone phenomenon is part of my life. I would need to come again, stay longer, read Chaucer.

Chilham is a little, perfectly pretty, really old village with an early Gothic church. The sun was out, the church was decorated full of flowers – lots of blue delphiniums and white daisies. I loved the service though I have to substitute my own metaphors for the idea of God. I enjoyed especially the singing – we do miss something these days; my childhood was full of singing. The bride was brimming with happiness in a lovely dress by Alice Temperley. After the service we walked over to Jacquetta's family home, which is a Tudor mansion: Chilham Castle. The view looking down from here was unbelievable, a sea of blown-green grass and blue sky filled with ranks of fluffy clouds, framed at the back with the ridge of the North Downs and not a soul or a house in sight.

Quite a few of the male guests were connected by their careers in hedge fund activity. Jacquetta's husband works in this field but part of his work is directed towards philanthropy. Jacquetta is active in human rights. These are influential people; among the journalists, the editor of *The Economist* asked me what I thought about drones. These people are not the same as me or a campaigning journalist like George Monbiot. George and I try to form an overview of what would make a better world, whereas these people are more establishment, more content with the status quo and how it will pan out for the best. I really need to talk to one or two of them – good to talk to people who don't agree with you to find out if either can influence the other: we need to find agreement to work towards a better world. These people are movers and shakers of the establishment.

We missed the last train home. There we were, Andreas and I in the middle of nowhere in an empty station and the train didn't come. We moved off and found a taxi. The driver, who was the other side of thirty, had never been to London. Andreas couldn't imagine how he could avoid the urge of driving on to the motorway from Canterbury up to London. The driver had the time of his life – Tower Bridge, the Tower, Elephant and Castle! Wow!

SUN 10 JUNE **LA MER**

Reading – news articles, sleeping, eating. Evening: to Royal Festival Hall. Orchestra of the Age of Enlightenment, conductor Simon Rattle. Fauré, Ravel, Debussy. Last piece, *La Mer*. This is what is called 'Impressionist' music. It began with a series of notes drawn with the bow across the double basses. The sea was at once before us, grey in the first light and with each stroke the waves moved towards us, expanding until the sun caught them up. Divine when sometimes we represent one thing with another.

MON 11 – TUES 12 JUNE KEEP YOUR TEETH

On each day, I spent half a day going to the dentist. Advice on how to clean your teeth: keep your gums healthy by aiming your brush under the gum and use those little twizzly brushes to clean between the teeth and up into the gum. Try to visit a hygienist for cleaning twice a year – ask your dentist. This way you will keep your teeth.

Wrote up the diary. Made three decisions re Gold Label.

WEDS 13 – THURS 14 JUNE CHELTENHAM SCIENCE FESTIVAL

I travelled with Cynthia to the Times Cheltenham Science Festival at the invitation of Jonathon Porritt and it was out of respect for his work that I accepted. Over the course of two days – there and in Bristol – I gave the same talk five times: twice for local BBC Radio stations, twice with live audiences, and lastly on the train in an interview for the *Independent on Sunday*. The theme of my talks was Get a Life: (1) for the next generation by preventing mass extinction due to climate change and (2) what about your life right now?

I do get through to people: I focus on them and what they can do. The main point is that the twentieth century was an age of consuming, sucking things up – including opinions; the dogma was that we would all be better off if we left everything to technology and Big Business. The way out of this is culture not consumption: consumption you just suck up, whereas you have to invest in culture, engage in the world, past and present. My motto is, **You get out what you put in.** Through reading we understand the past and this knowledge is what gives a purpose in life and creates the individual. Also this individual strength will help you in any fight for the environment. The most important thing I want people to take away is my mantra: the main cause of climate change is our financial system; the way out of it is by concentrating on human values and the long term instead of the financial abstract quick fix.

I think it is important to talk to people face to face. It's the best chance to influence people and hope they act. Also live radio and TV is direct communication. But being interviewed for a newspaper is not direct; it's up to the journalist and they may misrepresent you. I was tired during my interview and chatted to the young journalist who, at age twenty-five, had a very important job – she was going to Uganda on Sunday to research a story on family planning, ahead of a major London summit with the aim of getting quality family planning to 215 million women worldwide who want contraception but can't get it. She told me that the highest cause of death in Africa for girls of 14–19 years is pregnancy because they are often immature and don't have access to health care.

However, though she had listened to my talk in Bristol as well as doing the interview, she missed my message and just came up with a standard profile. I had said to her, 'Here's a tip. Tell your editors: Give people a choice – sell just the Sunday newspaper without all that bumpf, all that sport and culture chit-chat (people don't know what culture is any more: non-stop distraction). I would buy it!' She said, 'Oh no! That's where they get the advertising revenue from.'

THURS 14 JUNE **THINKING OF AN AFRICAN GIRL**

On Thursday night, we went from the train to our studio in Battersea to pick up Andreas and thence to a reception at St James's Palace to meet Prince Charles and to celebrate 'English Menswear'. Then on to the Festival Hall. András Schiff, one of the world's greatest pianists, conducted the Philharmonic as well as playing the piano in Mozart's famous piano concerto no. 21, and then conducted the Jupiter Symphony, Andreas's favourite: it is total, it is the 'all' of music; nothing goes beyond it. It is galactic. András Schiff – this music is flesh and blood to him. A small man, every fibre was electrified. He was a conduit for the genius of little Mozart, who died aged thirty-five. The piece is pure bliss and joy but I was sad; for some reason I was thinking of an African girl, about seventeen, who died during a reality TV thing where an English nurse spent time in an African hospital. The pregnant girl had been advised by people at home to put certain leaves inside herself but, instead of aborting, she had killed the foetus and it was rotting inside her. She lay on a mattress in the hot hospital; she was a beautiful slender creature, short unkempt hair, wild-eyed and out of her mind, never speaking. The hospital had no drugs and no means of operating. After three days, they announced that she had given up her fight for life.

SAT 16 – SUN 17 JUNE CORA'S BIRTHDAY TEA

At home, thinking about Gold Label, reading, writing. Saturday evening: intimate dinner hosted by *ID* magazine. I very much like Terry Jones (editor-in-chief) and Trish, his wife. On Sunday, an invitation to my granddaughter Cora's Fifteenth Birthday Tea. One of the things that Cora enjoys at school are discussions on philosophical, ethical and cultural questions. You have a choice to save either one great thinker or two people who don't think; or discuss artists like Damien Hirst – he's an artist because he says so. If you called yourself an artist would that make you one? No, because I'm not Damien Hirst.

 ### MON 18 JUNE IDEAS FOR GOLD LABEL

This week I pinned down the ideas for the Gold Label, knitting, sitting with my assistant, Luca, so that he could draw the diagrams properly and send instructions to Italy. I will be able to get an idea of how well they will work out when I go to Italy on Friday for the menswear show because the finished men's samples include the same yarns. While working on this, I took a square-foot sample of

Finale at our Milan menswear show.

knitted stitches I liked which had a corner cut off it and placed it on top of a similar sample. I decided to make a dress from the first sample with cut-out holes patched with the other sample. I thought I might copy the placing of coloured patches on some of the beetles. (At this point, beetles are one of the inspirations for the collection.) I told this later to Andreas and he said we could apply this idea to these dresses – this will mean that these dresses will be all pulled around and ragged. I was really excited because this is a real key to the collection – it helps pull other ideas together in my mind.

TUES 19 JUNE *THE STORY OF THE STONE*

Reading before going into work, I finished my book, *The Story of the Stone* by Cao Xueqin. An eighteenth-century Chinese classic, in five volumes, it has been my most important reading experience. It is as if I have lived two lives – my own and the life of the people in the book.

The story is about Bao Yu and twelve Beautiful Girls, companions of his youth, and the love between him and Dai Yu, who is surely the most romantic heroine in fiction. It is a fictional tale of real people and real events but begins with a myth: when the goddess repaired the sky, one vast stone was left, unused and rejected. The stone had magical properties and the story of its life was written upon it. It shrank itself down to the size of a fan pendant and Bao Yu, our hero, was born with this magic jade in his mouth. He is the stone incarnate; his name means 'Precious Jade'. As a pubescent youth, he visits the Land of Illusion in a dream where he is allowed to read the official registers – riddles which tell the fate of the Girls. On the archway leading to the Land of Illusion, Bao Yu reads: 'Truth becomes fiction when the fiction's true; real becomes not-real when the unreal's real.'

It is astonishing to understand the enormous wealth of this family whose ancestors were legendary for the service they performed for the Emperor; and to follow the circulation of this wealth as it is distributed to so many retainers, along with their families and friends in mutual support. The family purpose is to keep up and

The Emperor Hui Zong's painting, *Auspicious Cranes*, from the year 1112.

enjoy a grand protocol. And this protocol – their ceremonies and daily duties – is an outward show of family integrity, which is an unfailing testament to the importance of the Emperor in his role of maintaining stability and the perpetuation of heaven and earth. Each girl's character is forced to shine so strongly under the pressure of her prescribed role in the scheme of things.

Bao Yu and his girlfriend relations live in the pavilions of the Imperial garden with their personal servants. The garden is wonderfully described; it is a place of poetry and refuge. It was built for the visit home for one night of Bao Yu's elder sister, the Imperial Concubine. The things they say to each other; who they are! The structure of events is rooted in kharma; the rhythm, the voice which tells the story, recreates a world of people who are immediately intimately present to you. The things that happen are so unexpected, so real, so original – because the characters are alive.

Collapse of the fortune looms and when it comes so soon it is seen to have been dependent on the events caused by human behaviour.

WEDS 20 JUNE THE GAIA FOUNDATION AND GM SEEDS

Liz and Edward, founders of the Gaia Foundation, invited Cynthia and me to dinner. We met at their film showing of *Seeds of Freedom*, and they realised that we needed to know more about their work and about seeds. The Gaia Foundation (*www.gaiafoundation.org*) works internationally to regenerate cultural and biological diversity and aims to restore a respectful relationship with the earth. They work with indigenous people to secure land, seed, water, food security and sovereignty so that they can better cope with climate change.

They explained to us that GM seeds have been modified to be resistant to pesticide, their growth boosted by fertiliser. The seeds from these crops are not good for replanting because they have been force-fed; the farmer must always buy new seeds. That's the first problem. Another is that the pesticides which coat the GM seeds destroy all other life and poison streams and groundwater. Superbugs come along. You lose biodiversity – crops that have developed resistance to changing conditions and are tough through experience. We learnt, too, that it is a myth that GM drought-resistant seeds could be developed, especially as this is not in the interest of the food corporations (like Monsanto). In fact, GM seeds have a negative effect on soil fertility and also the nutritional value of foods – the GM plants are not able to absorb the minerals we need to be healthy.

Talking, we lost all track of time, until we realised it was 1 a.m.

FRI 22 – MON 25 JUNE MILAN SHOW

Andreas and I travelled to Milan. It was hot! Andreas was working on the show and I didn't need to join him until late afternoon on the Saturday. They were still doing the casting and the fittings at the showroom. I chatted to the models and helped with styling some outfits and the running order and wrote the press release. Andreas was able to leave with me at 3 a.m., leaving our team to finish the organising and, as the show was not until 3 p.m. on the Sunday, we had a good sleep.

The show was lovely. In the evening our friend Gian Mauro, who is a lawyer, gave us and our friends a big party in his apartment on the roof. On Monday we worked in the Milan showroom. It is crowded with our other lines and our staff from all over the world and we present and sell.

We flew home by 7 p.m. but we were too shattered to go to see Pamela, who was in London. She was attending the thirtieth birthday party of Prince Azim of Brunei – and she gave him a present of thirty acres of rainforest from Cool Earth. Wouldn't it be great if he gave us some more money?

TUES 26 JUNE BUY LESS, CHOOSE WELL

Iris (brilliant guest pattern maker) is staying at our house and Andreas is working with her. I do two big interviews which take all day – one for Bloomberg TV's *Eye2Eye*, another for *Kulturmontag* on Austrian TV. People want to interview me because I'm a fashion designer (Bloomberg needed footage of me and our couture in Davies Street), though of course by now they are also interested in the mix: fashion designer/activist. In answer to the question, 'Buy less, choose well, make it last, how does that reconcile?' I tell them, 'A healthy business is supposed to expand; I wish to grow in quality, not quantity – yet keeping prices down; my customers help me by choosing well. It would be nice if the Queen would set an example by wearing the same thing over and over again.'

FRI 29 JUNE SELFRIDGES SUPPORT THE EJF

Finally managed to join in with the work on Gold Label with Iris and Andreas – fittings and discussion of fabrics. It is really starting to happen, really exciting. Worked on a print.

Evening: *Selfridge's*. Talked on their roof garden to some of their customers; following on from *Selfridges* having featured window displays to sell our T-shirts for the Environmental Justice Foundation (EJF). The talk was on my usual subject of the connections between climate change and finance and politics and the need for true culture (my mantra). The focus was on the Family Tree (a blow-up of which had taken up all of one window) and the question 'what can one person do?' Start with informing yourself and become an Art Lover (get off the consumer treadmill).

I was really delighted to see young celebrities there – and particularly young models. I want to keep in touch with them all through what I'm trying to do. I asked people to buy the Family Tree poster for £10 and if they could not afford that to give £5. We also included a Cool Earth brochure; all proceeds to go to Cool Earth. I think it's a real token of commitment, a formal pledge to donate even £5, so I was really pleased. It signified to me that I had got through to people in my speech. And I don't just give away the poster indiscriminately.

SAT 30 JUNE JEMIMA KHAN'S PARTY

Yoga. Then Andreas went to work with Iris (she stays in our house when she is in London). But because I was tired he told me to go and do my thing. I read in bed, had a sleep and joined him at work at 4 p.m.; they had done really good new things.

At 5.30 p.m., we boarded a coach near Sloane Square to travel with other guests to Jemima Khan's house-warming party in the countryside. I took the opportunity to ask one of my fellow travellers, Neil, a social media journalist working for the *Wall Street Journal* – owned by Murdoch – what was happening with Julian Assange's reputation in social media. This man has no clue what is happening in the world. He told me Julian faced no danger from America; as to Obama's regular Tuesday drone killings he replied, 'What else can Obama do?' and went on to enthuse about the schoolgirl who had photographed her school dinner and was all over the papers. That's where it's at. Neil makes me sick!

At this point, I'd had enough. I went to the back of the bus to talk to my friends, Noreena Hertz, economist and author of books on global capitalism, and David Fenton, an American PR activist. David says, and I agree, that Rupert Murdoch has done only harm in the present world. He owns Fox News, which is the same lies repeated over and over. 'Everybody in the UK should be made to watch Fox News for a week', David says, to wake up to how ridiculously unbelievable it is.

Now we are arriving. The house is an eighteenth-century architectural gem. The setting! A perfect landscape between lush hills and woods. Inside, I never saw such flower arrangements, such wanton gorgeousness of colour and blooming magnitude – thrown into the vases. It's a great party. Trudie Styler's long legs as she descends the staircase feeling so hot in her hot pants. Drinks. Andreas points to the Grayson Perry tapestry. Jemima: 'Do you like it? I saw the programme he did on TV and he is such a sincere and highly intelligent person with such an interesting view. That's what made me decide to buy it.' Andreas had told me the same and that he has such original observations to make on the working class. I would like to listen to this. We don't talk much about the different classes any more. We talk about the haves and have-nots.

Jeanne Marine takes us up to her and Bob Geldof's bedroom to look at the view. Over the bed is an artwork in neon writing by my dear friend, Tracey Emin, 'Those who suffer love.' I go, 'Oh, dear!' Andreas says, 'It takes two.' (She who did it and she who bought it.) Without judges there is no art. We look down on the terrace – at one side is a pool – overlooking the French rose garden with lavender and set in geometric box hedges and leading down to a stream then up again to grassy hills.

I try to speak with Joseph, Assange's assistant. We go into the kitchen with Bella Freud to be on our own and Joseph says that Julian never told anyone, not him, not anyone, that he was going to seek asylum in the Ecuadorian Embassy; he also said that people would not lose their bail bonds because asylum takes precedence over other bail conditions. Then we were joined by a boring man holding forth on a stream of borrowed opinions and Bella and I walked off, leaving poor Joseph who was too polite.

Then a lady, Helen Lewis, introduced herself to me, a writer from the *New Statesman*. I suddenly realised who she was and said, 'Oh, you're the one who wrote your bad opinions about Julian Assange.' She said, 'I would have been very pleased if he had defended himself in the Swedish Court.' And went on about justice.

Julian is unlawfully detained. [*The UN have now called for his release.*] Julian has not been charged because there is no evidence against him. I said, 'And who are you to be very pleased? You're a journalist, get the facts.'

I was delighted to meet Tracey Worcester whose film *Pig Business* you can watch on the internet (*www.farmsnotfactories.org*). It's about the harm done to pigs and the whole world by corporate factory farming. This woman is so strong and beautiful. What she

Tracey Worcester – campaigner against factory farming.

does comes from the most refined human motivation. Please see it and act for change: for hundreds of years animals have had no rights and are seen as there for our use. All rights are identified exclusively with humans; we have become disoriented, alienated from the planet – we have lost touch with reality. Let's get real and stop the devastation. Start with cruel bacon sandwiches.

At night I stood on the terrace by a brazier with Andreas and Rifat Ozbek who was telling us how he enjoys the London club scene. Once he did fashion but now, after three year's work, he has just finished decorating Robin Birley's new London club, *Rupert's*. There were hundreds of glamorous guests and Jemima was the centre of it all, running around in her lamé mini-dress, talking to anyone and everyone. She's witty and sarcastic and full of fun, radiating energy. Andreas says she's a sphinx, 'I can't make her out, perhaps it's all that hair.' (She said to her sister-in-law who was wearing jeans and a sweater, 'Oh, I see you made an effort!' 'But I didn't know there was a dress code!' 'Nevertheless!').

JULY 2012

SUN 1 JULY AN EGYPTIAN AMULET

I go with Andreas to an antiques fair, 'Masterpiece'. There are really precious wonderful things that you can have an intimate relation with and here I am, trying on the best pair of diamond earrings, Georgian ones that suit me perfectly; holding in my hand a glazed pottery amulet of Thoth, twelve centimetres high, from Egypt, fourth century BC. After having lived a little *The Story of the Stone*, I very much fancy living in my imagination, close to whoever wore the amulet.

Embroidery was once such an important part of the lives of privileged women, who would sit talking while they sewed or one of them would read aloud. I know that even after Henry VIII

Guardi's tiny Venetian masterpieces.

divorced his first wife, Catherine of Aragon, she continued to make his embroidered shirts. I learnt so many interesting details talking to the vendors of embroideries. I hadn't realised, for example, that education was widely available to children in the sixteenth century where girls were taught embroidery.

If I could choose one thing, it would be a set of three miniature paintings by Guardi. In reproduction you cannot see the air. You have to look at Guardi's paintings themselves to see a never-ending horizon in each of these tiny masterpieces. In his views of Venice, he worked exclusively on depicting reality such as the eye saw it. His new approach to painting and the manner of painting influenced the Impressionists and modern painting. Even so, he was a master of the tradition of oil painting – the indirect method – which gives unlimited possibility of expression, and he pushed the technique into his own original method. 'He was prolific and 'churned them out' for the tourists of Venice though he was not so popular as the more traditional Canaletto,' Andreas told me. 'I love small,' he said. Small when it's great is any size at all.

MON 2 JULY Q V Q AND GOLD LABEL

Our pattern cutters are working on the patterns and sample toiles created last week by Iris and Andreas and bringing them a stage closer to finish, so Andreas and I carry on with Q v Q (*Quality v Quantity*). Then on Friday afternoon Andreas and I work together trying to put outfits together for Gold Label – of course this brings us nearer to deciding which fabrics to use. We do this again at work on Sunday. And the next week, too, is occupied by Gold Label fittings.

TUES 3 JULY TRACEY EMIN'S BIRTHDAY PARTY

Cynthia and I had a very exciting lunch with Michael Stein and Jon Snow, who is a friend of his. Michael has a solid strategy underway to mobilise business in the fight against climate change. He has a new baby; he's very concerned and clear about the danger we face. We really believe in the power of his conviction. His plan is so sound, he's got it all worked out. It's about crowdfunding for green energy projects.

In the evening Andreas and I go to Tracey Emin's birthday party at Annabel's. Tracey is one of the sweetest, most kind, loyal and reliable people I know. She is so generous to her friends and she always celebrates her birthday with a big party for them and we all love her (she writes us letters and postcards).

I first met Tracey at a photo shoot and I talked to her because I found her attractive to look at, with her super-feminine figure and legs. I think she could make more of an effort with her art but she is happy with it and with success. She likes me, so she ignores the fact that I criticise her. She knows I dismiss all these modern artists, e.g. Andy Warhol, as artistically irrelevant. Tracey said to me, 'Aren't we lucky to be friends!'

10–17 JULY **PRATO AND LUCCA**

Andreas and I are off to Italy for a week to work with our people there. Rosita and Paola have a company in Prato, an old town near Florence. They produce our Gold Label. The company is a studio which does more than manufacture and dispatch but helps from the start of the collection, helping us source and develop fabrics and yarns, and we work step by step with them changing, building and, through our assistants, sending emails and patterns and samples to be copied. It is obviously efficient for Andreas and me to go there personally for a few days. We get so much done face to face. We have worked with these two women for around twenty years and they have become dear friends.

We arranged to work either side of the weekend and to visit Lucca together on the weekend. By the time we left on Tuesday evening we had made so many of the small decisions that pin down a collection; I now feel that I have grasped its identity.

Paola comes from Lucca and though it is only a half-hour drive from Prato I had never visited. We all stayed in an apartment in

With Andreas in Lucca.

Palazzo Pfanner belonging to a friend of Paola's brother, Alfredo, who still lives in Lucca.

Medieval Lucca was an independent republic for almost five hundred years, rivalling Florence, and the old town is preserved intact as it is enclosed and protected by a wall. It sits in the middle of a flat area (once marsh), surrounded by the Tuscan hills. It really is beautiful. Paola guided us through the narrow streets, against the old walls of the houses. She showed us her old school and house. The church interiors do not beautify themselves with added pomp and splendour; it is the church buildings which are important, the experience of entering the church itself – the sparse clarity. Andreas, who has loved churches since he was a tiny boy, had never seen the like before; he described them as 'shockingly elegant'.

WEDS 18 JULY **THE HOTTEST YEARS ON RECORD**

When we left Prato the temperature was 36 degrees centigrade. When we got home the weeks of rain still continued and we had to put on the central heating. In America, this year has been the hottest since records began, and in the last twelve years, ten have been the hottest on record worldwide. The Met Office says that climate change may be the cause of the extreme weather conditions. If climate change *may* be the cause, why aren't we doing something about it? If we don't, then the catastrophe we face will be unprecedented.

Back home I write a piece for the *New Statesman*. They are doing an issue on 'My London', so I talk about the importance of art, how I have engaged with it since I came to London when I was seventeen. London is the greatest city in the world for high culture.

FRI 20 JULY **THE SAMPLE COLLECTION**

Worked on Gold Label – we have already sent some of the final samples to Rosita. She needs to copy them, and also in other fabrics, to prepare the sample collection and to do as much as possible before the August holiday in Italy. At this stage we make charts of all the permutations, so that we arrive at a scheme of all the collection. Our job now is choosing those final fabrics and how they are to be manipulated – we take the toile and rework it so that it becomes one with the fabric. I have only just begun on the dresses and each one has a life of its own; we make it come alive.

I spend about four hours on this and then have to go to the Wallace Collection which is being used by Chinese *Harper's Bazaar* as a location to shoot some of our designs and they want me in the pictures. The cover will be my Family Tree.

SAT 21 JULY ANTIGONE AT THE NATIONAL THEATRE

Yoga. Reading. Can't remember if I had a little sleep – I usually do on a Saturday. Evening: went to meet my friend Peter Olive at the National Theatre. I met Peter a few years ago when I gave a talk at Oxford University where he was studying Classics. I was really excited to meet such an interested, interesting person. He's a musician and he teaches Latin and Greek. We saw *Antigone* at the National Theatre. The staging was a cabinet war room, with a chorus of Creon's staff, chipping in with commentary across their desks. Soon after the play began – I hadn't looked at the programme – Peter and I had been talking too much, catching up – I whispered to him, 'Is this play by Sophocles?' I couldn't believe it hadn't been written today, now! The ringing economy of the language, efficient instrument of the unfolding drama, transfixed me with its power and beauty. There was no interval, thank God. I was held in a state of such intensity that I think it would have harmed me to be interrupted.

MON 23 – FRI 27 JULY THERAPEUTIC KNITWEAR

Gold Label work all week. Worked on two more knitwear pieces, mostly to do with sequences of coloured stripes: therapeutic – absorbing but easy.

Spent most of Wednesday with my PA, Tizer, who had a backlog of so many requests to do things or to attend events, so many charities these days who need patrons and help, so many things to ask me. I can only do one or two.

AUGUST 2012

SUN 29 JULY – SAT 4 AUG CHALET IN THE TYROL

Andreas and I go to see his family in the Tyrol for a week. We stay in a chalet, high on the mountain, belonging to his brother, who is a farmer. The chalet is three hundred years old and is self-sufficient with no mod cons. Electricity is solar. We will walk and read.

We walked every day and did yoga outdoors. The views were exhilarating and always different depending on the weather – especially when the sun goes down, which was the same time as the moon was rising. The thunderstorms this year came at the end of the day. I love them – being so high you're in the middle of the clouds with the lightening and thunder all around you, and once we had buckets full of hail the size of peas bouncing back up as high as a metre.

The people there are so sweet. Apart from Andreas's family, one day we met a man from the neighbouring farm – just a chalet and a barn for his cows. His name was Thomas and he was in his eighties. He invited us in for a schnapps and we noticed the toys of his grandchildren. He was so pleased. He and Andreas at the table in his rustic home and in his check shirt. I noticed he had a proper handkerchief to blow his nose – a check one like my father used to have years ago. I was so happy sitting there listening to them talk and laugh, though not understanding. The scene was like something Van Gogh would paint.

Before I left, Theo gave me a copy of an article called 'The Reckoning' by Bill McKibben which was published in *Rolling Stone*. Cynthia tells me it is all over the internet. It is the best political thing

Bright sunshine and lederhosen in the Tyrol. Behind me is the little chalet.

I've read since an interview with James Lovelock first shocked me into understanding the scale of the danger we face from climate change, about five years ago. Every word hits the target. I shall tear out the pages and frame this article as an important document. (John Milton framed his copy of the death certificate of Charles I. I felt sorry for Charles – he acted according to his beliefs.)

McKibben nails the madness of the fossil fuel industry, whose assets are the proven coal, oil and gas reserves (and don't forget tar sands and shale gas). If these are all burnt, as they are planning, the amount of carbon this would release into the air is 2,795 gigatons – five times higher than the figure of 565 gigatons which scientists say is the point of runaway climate change. (In reality, the figure is much lower – McKibben explains.) So, once everything is out of control and we have runaway extinction of the whole earth community, including humans, the industry will still be drilling away, will they? (*Drill Baby, Drill!*) No wonder we have a financial crisis when the corporate industries are running the world.

SUN 5 – MON 6 AUG STAYING WITH IRIS

On Sunday we left the chalet and said goodbye to the family on the way as we drove down to the station. We took a two-hour train journey in order to spend two or three days with Iris, who lives on the edge of Lake Constance. The train followed the River Inn for much of the way. Its bed lies in a narrow strip of land left by a glacier cut between great walls of the Alps. The soil is so rich, the land so cultivated and the total view so mind-blowingly spectacular. There used to be silver mines in the mountains. Iris and her boys, Aamon, nine, and Hatto, seven, met us – all in bare feet. This whole area is green hills, rising up to the mountains and it is like a garden. Andreas said you probably would not find anywhere equal to it in the world – not in Italy – for such rich land.

Three years ago, without warning, an avalanche on Mont Blanc swept Iris's husband, a doctor and a climber, to his death. She is glad she had two boys; they helped each other and are close friends.

They are a sporty family. From the house you just walk thirty yards down the road in your bare feet and onto a patch of grass beside Lake Constance – it's like having your own private lake. There is a sailing boat, surfboards, skateboards, skis, a trampoline. Aamon is a wonderful gymnast and Hatto is strong and trying to copy him. Each summer evening they jump and dive off the pier into the lake. Iris says they're on the move all day. They are also creative, like her. They go to a school in the woods and are allowed freedom

Hatto (the younger one) and Aamon – Iris's boys.

with responsibility. They have ceremonies to honour the natural world and the world of the spirit at important times of year.

I had a lovely time at Iris's house. One day I stayed reading while the others went out. Otherwise we talked, ate and drank (one night her friend Roland came and prepared us a meal fit for gods), swam in the warm lake, played games and watched the Olympics on telly. I felt like we all had a party.

TUES 7 AUG ANNA PIAGGI

Came home to hear that Anna Piaggi has died. Dear Anna. What a lovely person! Had she been ill? We missed her at the last show because she always came. She was one of the first important fashion people to come in my shop, then called *Let it Rock* in the *World's End* in 1970. She worked at Italian *Vogue* but she loved London and some of her best friends lived here, like Gene Krell from the shop *Granny Takes a Trip*. He came from New York and his personal style influenced the whole look of the 'Swinging Sixties', especially the Rolling Stones. He told me that, meeting Anna in London, she came out of the taxi with seven suitcases of clothes for the weekend. She liked to try things on and experiment, every time she went out she had a different ensemble. Gene is now fashion editor of *Vogue Nippon* and *Korean Vogue*. Another of Anna's friends, Vern Lambert, had a very influential shop in Chelsea Antique Market; he bought up a load of bell bottoms from the navy and they became the whole style right through the 70s (when we were selling drainpipes). Vern went to live with Anna and her husband in Italy. Anna did five or six terrific ad campaigns with us. She was really, really talented and her personality and work helped to give the fashion world its identity for us. Andreas and I will miss her.

THURS 9 AUG NAOMI'S OLYMPICS PARTY

Evening. Naomi Campbell hosted a party at *Cipriani's* in Mayfair to mark the Olympics. Naomi's in great shape. Tall and slim in black, with black, fine, straight hair falling over her shoulders and down to her waist. She is happy and we liked her man – he seems a serious person. Yes, lots of our friends were there, Kate especially and Sarah Ferguson. She is doing work in the Congo – Sarah's very capable, always doing charity work. We must see if her activities there tie in with Cool Earth. At the party, we watched Usain Bolt win the 200m. I had seen him win the 100m at Iris's. Cool! I also watched some of the opening ceremony at home where Andreas has his TV at the top of the house. What I really liked about Danny Boyle was his inclusiveness – we're all ordinary people, including the Queen, and we all share what it means to be British. Thanks, Danny, for the comfort. We'd better wake up to reality, get rid of our complacency and confront climate change – or die.

FRI 10 AUG STEPHEN EMMOTT'S 28 BILLION

Andreas got up early to go to Vienna as we're opening a shop there. Then he will join the men of his family in Turkey to go sailing around the Greek islands on his uncle's boat.

I went with Peter Olive to the Royal Court to see Stephen Emmott present *Ten Billion*. He began by saying that the forecast figure of ten billion people at some point in this century was really twenty-eight billion if we reproduce at the present rate. Stephen Emmott is Professor of Computational Science at Cambridge. I have never been in the presence of a more attractive human – warm, intelligent, intense, kind (the word 'kind' comes from the same root as 'kin' and it means to care for someone as much as you do for your family).

He said that the stage decor was a replica of his office; of course, he wasn't an actor. On two screens various graphics appeared to back up his points. Two maps of the world showed dotted lines moving thick as a blizzard over the whole surface constantly, 24 hours, representing aeroplanes (I didn't know it was so bad; it's increasing

Stephen Emmott presenting *10 Billion*.

all the time), and the same thing with streaks representing shipping and cars. We are constantly moving stuff (my business does).

Two things he mentioned were important to me because they pointed to immediate action: the absolute necessity of preserving the rainforest and that the only possible energy solution right now is nuclear. (Although, whatever your opinon on nuclear, it seems late to introduce it – and solar may turn out to be a quicker solution).

Governments are doing nothing (we know they're just helping corporations to wreck the planet and don't help people at all). Emmott drew the parallel between now and 65 million years ago when the dinosaurs vanished. He talked of a time when the earth would be mostly uninhabitable, how the habitable parts would have to defend themselves from climate migrants. He mentioned that recently, when he attends top meetings about climate change, he notices that the military are always present. He asked a younger colleague if there was one thing he could do what would it be. 'Teach my son to use a gun.'

SAT 11 AUG CRAZY WORLD – CRAZY ENVIRONMENT

Wrote up Friday's diary. Yoga. Sleep. By bicycle to a friend's party, a secret space near London Bridge where we had a fire and a barbecque (I ate vegetarian barbecque – delicious). She is leaving to live in Brazil so that her family can help look after her two children. Yet she and her husband will be travelling here often because they both work here. Crazy world – crazy environment!

SUN 12 AUG THE WORLD'S PROBLEMS ARE MY PROBLEMS

Did nothing except some desultory reading. So downhearted apropos the overwhelming extent of the wrecking of Gaia as set out by the unflinching assessment at Friday's theatre. Stephen Emmott didn't mention the NGOs who really are doing things, but we have to find out ways for the public to know and to face the problem when the whole plutocracy/bureaucracy conspires to deceive us. I worry what I can do in my company. I've begun to do it re *Q v. Q*. At 5 p.m. I made a good salad and cooked some corn on the cob and decided I don't need depression to help me with the world's problems. But I've always thought the world's problems are my problems. We might have a chance if only more people knew. I still think 'Climate Revolution' is the way forward. Identify the enemy: the two big ones – the fossil fuel industry and agribusiness.

MON 13 AUG THE COURTAULD AND CLASSIC LITERATURE

I wrote up the diary at home. Reading stuff to inform myself and writing it up takes a lot of time but it is all part of my campaign to Stop Climate Change and it's very useful to collect my ideas together so that I know what I'm talking about when I get the opportunity in interviews. Culture is connected so I write about that, too, and include bits of my daily life to show when I'm busy or relaxing. Fashion is a big part of my life. But the real reason for the diary is to get my ideas across so that more people will join the 'Climate Revolution'.

At 1.30 p.m. I rode my bike to the Courtauld Gallery to see an exhibition of some of the drawings from the great masters that they hold in their collection. (Before 2 p.m. on Mondays it is free.) At 5 p.m. I met my friend, Giselle, and our mutual friend, Peter Olive, in a café in Westbourne Grove. We ate a horrible salad. (People usually make horrible salads – they should be simple – I'll tell you how to do it one day.) Then we went to Giselle's house, nearby. If I had more time, I would see more of Giselle. I'd go round and talk to her improving my French; she's French, very interesting, and she loves fashion. We talked and drank. She had just read Dostoevsky's *The Idiot*. These classics in literature. You get a lot out of them when you re-read them when you're older (more experience, therefore more to think about). Books are always focused in their time – windows on the world seen from different points in time. Virginia Woolf said the success of a masterwork is the 'immense persuasion of a mind that has completely mastered its perspective'.

TUES 14 AUG TOUCHED BY HUMAN HANDS

Had to answer some questions for Suzie Menkes. She's interested in the bags we design which are made in Africa from recycled materials under the auspices of the UN's scheme, *Work not Charity*. She does ask good questions. She asked me, 'Do you think that objects that have been touchßed by human hands are elements of luxury today?'. I thought of a pre-industrial time when everything was made by hand. And going back as far as the classical Greeks or the tribes which moved across Asia when only skilled craftsmen made beautiful things. It's not true that everyone made their own things; even in the earliest times, stone hand axes were made by specialists and traded.

WEDS 15 AUG ANDREAS AT SEA

My Andreas phones me and tells me that the four boys and Skipper Nedge have so much wind and they are sailing at a great speed – all working the boat and not many boats out there. They're

Alex, Teddy, Andreas and Robert at sea, wearing the crew T-shirts we designed.

OK because the boat, the *Vesta*, is big. Our friend, Alex, is at the helm as much as possible, getting soaked in the thrill of the boat ploughing the waves. At anchor in the Greek islands, Andreas stops and cooks and is constantly over the side swimming. I went on the *Vesta* four years ago in the Turkish islands. I was unlucky; we had no wind. But I love the idea of sailing between the islands like the ancient Greeks.

THURS 16 – SUN 19 AUG LUCY'S WEDDING, STAYING AT JOE'S

The reason I didn't go with Andreas on the boat was because on Saturday my niece, Lucy, is getting married in Devon, where her mother (my sister) lives. So we are staying with my son, Joe, who has a farm near the sea in Cornwall. He loves to be in the country and his girlfriend, Faye, is getting really involved with the garden. I travelled down with Ben, Peter Olive and our friend Krishna.

Lots of rain on Friday, so I stayed in bed reading *Sinbad the Sailor* and *Ma'aruf the Cobbler* from *The Arabian Nights*. These fairy tales are imaginative derivatives of myths which originated in primitive ritual. Joe's house is full of books and I like just to browse through whatever takes my fancy, books I don't have. I also read half of the myth of Gilgamesh; this is Sumerian (present-day Iraq), an epic more than a fairy tale, and has a different exotic identity to the Arab tales.

We went for a walk round the wood when the rain cleared. At home, Joe cooked – quick, very good. He's so capable, looks after you: drinks, music, films, discussion, affection, fun. Starting from when he was a little boy of three, he looked after me as if he were my husband, went shopping, fixed the telephone, bought a mixer, lent me money. Kate Moss says he's an alpha male. It could have something to do with his father telling him the milkman was his dad, then disappearing for days when he felt like it – so little Joe assumed the responsibility.

My brother, Gordon, joined us ... but this is all becoming enough chat for one week so I'll be quick: wedding, reception at my sister's

With my sons Ben (left) and Joe in Cornwall.

house, lots of children and an electric-blue giant dragonfly flying over the garden pond. I gave Lucy a red dress with silver and gold lurex. She looked stunning. Her friend said, 'When will you wear it?' But she will wear it, I know her, she's very dazzling and outgoing. Gordon gave everyone in the family a video he had made of our mother a year before she died. She told us the story we had heard most often – how she met my father.

Cynthia phoned on Saturday night to prepare a message of support for Julian Assange for her to deliver in London on my behalf. I wrote: 'Through WikiLeaks, Julian Assange continues to expose the lies and distortions of the authorities. His fight is our fight. It is a fight for freedom – freedom of information. We are Julian Assange, I am Julian Assange.'

TUES 21 AUG DANTE'S INFERNO AND GORE VIDAL

At home reading. While I was at Joe's, I began to read Dante's *Inferno*. I got as far as the Entrance to Hell – a dark room where hundreds of people run constantly round and round stung by wasps and horrid insects. These were people who in life had never committed themselves to anything, not to God nor to the Devil; they had never engaged with the world or learnt or changed. Therefore neither Heaven nor Hell wanted them. Do you think such people are also the gossips? They live off other people, do nothing, just get their buzz from causing trouble and confusion. They never have an opinion but just choose the worst opinions of other people. Why don't they want to be honest and do some good? The thing is, it makes them feel important. Half the journalists are like this and the other half are good – what I call 'serious people'. Would you send the stirrers to Hell – or leave them in the foyer?

An event I want to say something about is the death of Gore Vidal, the author, at the end of July. He was a hero of mine and I met him a long time ago. A German magazine had asked me if they could record an interview between me and a person of my choice. We first met at a photo shoot during which he told me (out of the corner

We are Responsible!

MANIACS = PLUTOCRATS
↑   ↑
CRIMINALS = POLITICIANS
_____
RABBLE = Democracy

of his mouth, as we sat side by side) all the London socialites he knew and, as I knew none of them, he had no interest in me. Then we met for lunch and the recorded conversation. I wanted to talk about politics. Vidal was related to the Kennedys and had worked as an advisor to JFK. One morning Kennedy was fuming about the military in the Pentagon being a law unto themselves. Gore Vidal said, 'But you're the President, you can tell them what to do.' JFK: 'It would take ten years to sort that lot out.' GV: 'I see, meanwhile you have to get re-elected.' JFK: grins.

However, GV began to talk about religion. He said monotheism was the greatest evil in the world. I thought it was because he was American that he said this and that it's not such a big deal for the English. He said that anybody in America could invent a religious cult and it was tax exempt, that's why these churches are so rich, e.g. Scientology. He was right, but I didn't grasp the depth of what he said so he was really bored with me. I realised when I thought about it afterwards that the idea of a sky god who is the one and only true god is a terrible dogma that forms the whole ethic of our society – it is why the US is always right and why they need an enemy to be their devil. It is the most horrible, disgusting ethic in the world. (By contrast, polytheism is about biodiversity. Each god represents different qualities.)

Came to work to check with Cynthia where we are in our campaign. We went out and talked over coffee. I went home quite early (still on holiday) and plucked some nettles in the park which I put in a soup with some beans and tomatoes we grow on our balcony at work. Now I've started to read a book on finance, *The New Depression* by Richard Duncan, my brother Gordon lent me. Economics is childishly simple.

At around one in the morning Andreas came home.

THURS 23 AUG THE ECONOMIST

The reason I was reading Richard Duncan's book is because today I am meeting John Micklethwait, editor-in-chief of *The Economist*. I went with Jacquetta Wheeler. She had seated me next to him at her wedding dinner. I hoped to be able to convince him that climate crisis and economic crisis are the cause and effect of each other; they are like serpents who eat each other's tails. The only way out of this double crisis is: What's good for the planet is good for the economy.

"WHAT'S GOOD FOR THE PLANET IS GOOD FOR THE ECONOMY"
"WHAT'S BAD FOR THE PLANET IS BAD FOR THE ECONOMY"

What's good for People is good for the planet.

I did not convince him. He said, 'How did climate change cause the US housing crunch?'

To him, like the rest, economics is a science and it's just a matter of adjusting to the equation. Tweaking. But he's right, this particular financial crisis does not seem directly linked to climate change. I went away. It will be a long answer.

It's clear that the Rotten Financial System (**Rot $**) caused the crunch; based on debt, it is designed to create poverty. Banks make money from interest, they don't want the principle back because then they make more money. They created mortgages for people who couldn't afford it and thereby created an investment bubble which burst. People lost their homes. Investors sell-on 'assets' like 'passing the parcel' – the one holding the parcel when the music stops loses. Fracking and the Alberta tar sands are investment bubbles which result in bankruptcies – and poison which is never paid for, and climate change.

Economics since industrial times has been based on fossil fuels, which are finite. We still have plenty of oil to extract cheaply and easily (easy oil) in e.g Saudi Arabia.

At this point it is necessary to explain that we can only use an estimated 20 per cent of fossil fuels. At that point we must either stop or fry; if we use more, we will have runaway climate change and temperatures will be out of control, leading to the extinction of life on earth. Yet investor portfolios include all known sources of oil, including oil which is difficult and mega-expensive to extract (e.g fracked oil and gas) and even oil we don't have the technology to extract. Their calculations are unreal. Meanwhile the extraction of difficult oil causes terrible accidents and pollution: it is driven by investors. Not needed.

This is why Saudi Arabia is selling its easy oil cheap because there isn't much time left for them to cash in – and this means that difficult oil can't compete. The British government still supports fracking by pledging taxpayers money to subsidise it.

How did climate change cause the housing crunch?

Answer: By ignoring climate change, not factoring it into the equation, we have crazy bankers and investors who perpetrate the wrecking of the planet. Also, whereas, drought, floods, migrants are more obviously seen to cause the financial crisis, so do all people made homeless and poor.

TUES 28 – FRI 31 AUG PINNING DOWN THE FABRICS

Iris has arrived and from today I will concentrate on fashion – the shows are starting to line up in front of me. Back from holiday, our pattern cutters have been finishing perfectly their samples and patterns; Iris and Andreas have been working with them. On Wednesday we had a major Gold Label fitting lasting all day and we found ways to make crucial improvements. We now have a good idea of the fabrics we will allocate to the designs in toile form and we have managed to test out some in the correct fabrics.

On Thursday, we began pinning down the fabrics so that we can send the remaining prototypes and all information to Italy. Rosita is here so that she can follow these last stages, then when she goes back to Italy on Tuesday she will have everything she needs for an efficient operation making the sample collection (each design is made in more than one fabric choice). Rosita travels between here and Italy by train. She stays at our house, as does Iris.

SEPTEMBER 2012

SAT 1 – SUN 2 SEPT WEEKEND WORK

Iris left early Saturday morning and I was reading from 7 a.m. to noon. Then I joined Andreas at work to finish the charts. Andreas is amazing; he has worked on the shoe collection and has already organised the tights and other accessories to coordinate the collection. I, meanwhile, did some graphics and the invitation for the Red Label collection – coming soon.

MON 3 SEPT INDIAN SUMMER

Yesterday was cold but today was suddenly Indian Summer, so called because this late-summer phenomenon happens in North America

– Indian Country – and while I mention Native Americans let me say 'Thank you, dear Pamela' for sending an email from her friend, Jon, about his work to provide clean water to the Americans of Pine Ridge, Leonard's reservation. Jon has an NGO supplying practical hands-on solutions for clean water crises; he also works in Haiti. One of his solutions is a bucket and plastic pipe and chemicals costing $50 which supplies clean water to 100 people for a year. I was also delighted to receive a reply to my letter from Leonard Peltier.

Back to our Indian Summer: I immediately asked myself, what date is it? It must be my son's birthday. On 3rd September, forty-nine years ago, my then husband Derek and our son Ben – one year old and already scampering around like a little rabbit – were on holiday in North Devon, walking over sand dunes to the sea, larks high in the sky in this glorious weather. Every year since, with just one exception, we have had this same glory: a refined heat in a big blue sky, held in suspense against the cold air that is waiting. It's great to have the last of the summer sun turn up on cue even amongst the present chaotic weather patterns. This is my Ben's weather. Happy Birthday, my love.

Now that the charts are sent, Rosita is waiting for me to check the knitwear samples sent from Italy. We do this together and she notes the corrections. Andreas goes to Italy to work on MAN.

TUES 4 SEPT CLIMATE REVOLUTION

I had the day off. I was tired and wasted two or three hours doing a 'very difficult' Sudoku (I don't do it much anymore). It was, nevertheless, good for me; it's mentally stimulating but relaxing, and I fell asleep. A sleep during the day is the best restorative. I had already been carrying in my mind the idea of 'Climate Revolution'. It is important to give what is happening a name. The revolution has already begun. throughout the world people are changing their way of life. Save a plastic bag is a first step. We are not alone. We must build it together. When I woke up, I sat down and immediately wrote out a plan of action for the Climate Revolution, which will be the new name for our website.

Joe de Campos, who does all our graphics and website, put the first Climate Revolution charter online. Climate Revolution is about working with and trying to link to other NGOs, and go on each other's demonstrations. This is Cynthia's full-time job and she is often at meetings until ten o'clock at night. She knows everyone. She also tells me what is going on in the world, especially on social media. Planning a demo takes months of meetings. We have designed logos, posters and T-shirts.

The other thing is to analyse, know your enemy. That is what I try to do. Pin it down to one go, get the idea across. That way you're clear in speeches and interviews, you deliver a strong message. I read, think and do a lot of writing. When I wake up in the morning I lie awake thinking, then I might do some notes to really pin down the idea. Everything connects.

WEDS 5 SEPT DAVID BAILEY

Main event – a photo of me by David Bailey. I chose my grand dress, which is really seven metres of bronze silk paper-thin duchess satin – the weave on the other side is midnight blue. The dress has a cord attached at the back of the neck. I can wear it as a cloak or put a belt round the waist and pull the fabric through to make it into a dress. Under this I wore a T-shirt, 'Get a Life'. Our photo is for *Harper's Bazaar* who want to give me an award for Cool Earth.

What is it about David Bailey that makes him so attractive? You enter another dimension, pulled to the centre of his attraction, totally happy but on the alert for something to happen. He has the face of a happy devil; his eyes burn like diamonds in amber. He loved the dress and marvelled at the fabric. His eye: 'Don't move!

Can I?' – moving my elbow slightly – 'Don't stick your tits out! Relax your shoulders!' – steps forward to make my hair fall a bit better. Serious focus and delight. He does a little hop and his hand dances in the air.

David subscribes to a magazine called *Bird* – he has a pair of rare parrots. In the 1970s he and another parrot fancier (rich) were discussing birds. The other one said, 'Let's have lunch tomorrow', so they went to Manila! A different world! Or do some rich Russians still behave like this?

THURS 6 SEPT THE DRESS THAT BECOMES A BANNER

Morning coffee with Adrian Cheng at the Wolsey. He is opening a VW shop in Shanghai. This is our first meeting and after five minutes he was my new friend. We are going to do a lot together. He is young and already has done so much. He is lucky enough to be the son of a family business in China, which began a generation ago with jewellery (now the distribution is twice Tiffany's), and includes many and various enterprises. The whole company strives to be green. Adrian paints and is interested in contemporary art. They have an enormous network of contacts through social media and as we are beginning the Climate Revolution through social media, Adrian will be a route to China.

Then I go to a rehearsal for the Paralympics. The artist Joe Rush has asked me to be Boudicca on a great flaming chariot. Joe and the Mutoid Waste Company make sculptures out of recycled scrap metal. They've been working for months making several giant ones which will be driven round the stadium for the closing ceremony. So now is my first look at these metal floats which are in the form of creatures (my favourite is the horse) and a galleon and (my) chariot. Mind-boggling, epic, so ingeniously worked.

I escaped quickly to go home so as to avoid questions as to what I was going to wear. My idea is to unfurl a banner for CLIMATE REVOLUTION. I shall take my 'dress' – seven metres of fabric – and wind myself up in it. Nobody will know that we have applied giant letters which spell *Climate Revolution* inside. There are two pockets sewn upside down at the top edge of the banner/dress, and my warriors, Andreas and my son Joe, will stick their spears into the pockets and lift high the dress as I undo it.

SUN 9 SEPT CLIMATE REVOLUTION AT THE PARALYMPICS

I was incredibly worried about the Paralympics idea right up until the final day – Sunday. My time was taken working it out, getting it right. What if we missed the moment to time the Climate Revolution banner for the TV cameras? (All they knew was that I would lift the veil off my helmet to reveal my face.) I had to deceive the show producers. I was so helped by Joe, Andreas and Letmiya (Joe Rush's girlfriend). But once I was on the chariot I was excited. **We did it! The inauguration of Climate Revolution.**

My make-up was crucial, too. I was supposed to be Boudicca, the Queen of the ancient Britons, who fought the Romans and used a blue dye called woad for warpaint. And because I am dead serious about the Climate Revolution, I wanted the face of war. I had discovered this face when I drew out the Family Tree – I just drew a face that was the opposite of a smiley face (Wipe that smile off your face!). I painted my face like that and painted arrows on my arms.

TUES 11 SEPT BELLA FREUD

Interview for *Harpers* to go with the Bailey photo. What a treat! They sent me Bella Freud. We haven't had a long conversation for years. We've known each other since we were punks and Bella was once my assistant. We were together in Italy. I was designing the Crini Collection and I stayed with her on weekends in Rome where she was living with her boyfriend. She drove a Vespa like the young Italians and now she came by scooter to our Battersea studio.

I have just released the dress – now a banner. I stand up and the words CLIMATE REVOLUTION go up on all the videos and are seen by 7 billion people worldwide.

THURS 13 SEPT GOLD LABEL

I've been continuing to work on Gold Label. The point has passed for Rosita to take on any more work and we continue to work on, especially, the evening dresses. I am still worrying about which fabric goes with which design. Andreas and I work together, and slowly we talk it out. Our fittings involve very much how to sew and how to finish the dresses according to the kind of fabric. Making clothes depends on letting the fabric do what it wants to do.

FRI 14 SEPT GEORGIA MAY

I colour my hair then at midday take the tube from Clapham to Highbury and Islington. Then by bus to a studio for a photo shoot for designs we did for Palladium jewellery. I could have had a car but I like public transport. Georgia May Jagger was our model and I had to join in the first session for *Grazia* magazine who wanted me in some reportage shots (photographer, Sean McMenomy).

Then Andreas and Juergen Teller arrived for Palladium's official campaign. I had such a happy time. I like to be with Juergen. He is quiet (concentrated) and at first Georgia May thought perhaps he didn't like her (she told me). What I had not anticipated was the pleasure I got from being with a young person. Her talk makes everybody feel good, she's so sensitive to other people. And how she loves her mum and her family! She brings 'Mom' into her talk all the time, tells us how she's lost ten pounds in one week in training for *Strictly Come Dancing*. Georgia May is sexy; she just needs to look at you, look into the camera. She's done no bad thing in her life. Every woman, young or old, would like that jewellery when they see it on her.

SAT 15 SEPT FRIENDS OF THE EARTH AND RED LABEL

Friends of the Earth rally in the afternoon, speaking along with Caroline Lucas and a wonderful lady from the Philippines, Lidy

The dress that becomes the Climate Revolution banner (at the Red Label show).

Nacpil. I told them about Climate Revolution and, of course, they all laughed that the fight now is not between the classes but between the idiots and the eco-conscious. All NGOs have to work together and the very naming of Climate Revolution gives us that focus.

Evening: to the offices at Conduit Street to work on the Red Label show with Andreas, Murray and Yasmine (friend and stylist). Still fitting the girls, styling the outfits and concentrating and clarifying the collection for the presentation. Shoes, bags and Stephen Jones hats. Stephen explained that he made the hats real i.e. as if in an age where people wore hats – and this would be their best hat. We are working with a hair stylist new to us, Mark Hampton. I don't know what Andreas and Murray told him – something about the Queen, for sure – and he arrives with these wigs; caricatures of wigs from the past, around the 1950s. More than half the girls would have their natural hair – the main inspiration here, Debbie Harry in the 1980s. And then when Val Garland does the make-up it really reminds you of cut-off heads in a wig shop. The face is made up in yellow and Val suggests other colours as well – pink and green. It's as if the person in the wig shop painted features on to his featureless head blocks – a black line of eyelashes on the skin under one eye, the other eye trying to be the same but a bit

Red Label models made up by Val Garland.

different. Val explained that she would grade the level of extremity so that some girls would look more normal.

Did I like it? I kept quiet, stayed neutral. Of course I liked it and I knew that with this look you would really see the clothes. It's just that Val is so crazy, more crazy than me. She and Mark are hyper-artistic. Then we have the nail lady, Marian Newman, who just does her thing. They're great. Biked home about 3 a.m.

SUN 16 SEPT RED LABEL SHOW

At the show. The venue was a great hall in the Foreign Office, nineteenth-century grand classical. Thank you so much to the government for inviting us. The pretty girls looked good in their make-up under the lights at the rehearsal. Interviews. Lights, music, great sound, colour. 'Rooster' Sara Stockbridge, singer of the band, with her lovely bass guitar boyfriend, Cobalt. Show starts. Finale, then I unfurled my dress into the Climate Revolution banner, helped by models/warriors Charlotte and Alice.

Then Cynthia and I went into an anteroom to talk with three of our guests: Suzy Amis Cameron, who is doing a lot especially on education, Samata Angel, Global Campaign Director for Red Carpet Green Dress, a fashion competition we will collaborate on, and Christiana Wylyan, environmental advocate and partner in Satori Capital, a firm focused on sustainable investing. We had the chance to get to know each other and talk about ways we can help each other. We're all doing Climate Revolution.

Suzy explained that when she needed a dress for the red carpet – she was a model and actress before becoming the wife of James Cameron who directed *Titanic* and *Avatar* – she had to instigate a whole research foundation in order to procure an ethical and ecologically friendly dress. She would like me to guide the winner of the next competition organised by her foundation from the concept to the actual dress and then a celebrity will wear it on the red carpet at the Academy Awards. I had an extra reason for wanting to do this which is to tap into this research for my own use.

MON 17 SEPT LADY GAGA, LAWRENCE AND BRUNO

Worked all day on Gold Label running order. I was thrilled to see Lady Gaga wearing a Climate Revolution T-shirt.

Evening: We were invited to our friend Lawrence's birthday party. I like Lawrence but I haven't really found out what he does – something to do with Bill Gates and at the moment getting mobile phones to women in Iraq to empower them, I think. He's American, finished his education in France, and as well as speaking French, he speaks Arabic, Kurdish and Persian. If he likes you, he loves you and tells you so – that's how we started.

We had told Lawrence we were tired and might not make it. I'm so glad we did. The address was near and in the evening we biked over. Lawrence's party was in the home of his friend Bruno, who introduced himself as our host and led me by the hand. He is Chinese and his family must have lived out of China for some time. I say this because he is cultured and a man does not gain such culture

Lady Gaga joins the Climate Revolution.

in one generation – and the Chinese revolution smashed culture and smashed all cultured people. I have never seen such works of art, Chinese and Japanese. The dinner, Andreas says he will never forget. I want to see Bruno again as soon as I can.

TUES 18 – FRI 28 SEPT WORKING ON THE PARIS SHOW

We just did the Red Label show in London; now we do the Gold Label in Paris. Working on the collection, we didn't know what to do for hats, but Prudence brought an unusual helmet-shaped block (wooden form which the hat is moulded on) and we worked out the materials with the idea that it would introduce something alien – like the metal slab did in 2001. We went to Paris on Wednesday and the collection was already hanging in the showroom there. The clothes looked lovely and we put them in the running order. Girls were still arriving for the casting and some evening dresses and shoes were still to come from London.

On Thursday I went to the showroom at 4 p.m. to advise on the hair and make-up. I don't usually know, but this time I had an idea. For the hair use three ideas – all tribal: one was taken from the young male Masai but instead of the locks swept to the back and hanging, leave the hair combed and greasy-looking like a gypsy or rocker, masculine and maybe with a quiff; another was frizz, like Marie-Antoinette; the third was blonde wigs with the comb left in the hair – I had seen this on men from an African tribe. Most of the girls have long hair but we left the ones with shaved heads. And, of course, we had our alien hats.

The make-up idea was white circular patches in the eye socket, not too strong but so that it looked disconcerting and strange, and a heart shaded around the face. I was worried that Val, our make-up artist, would be frustrated to repeat alien clones and sure enough on the day she developed the idea and the girls were individual in their make-up. But Val's idea was much better and it did look tribal and alien.

SAT 29 SEPT THE SHOW AT HÔTEL DE CHAROST

Luckily, the show wasn't until 4 p.m. the next day because we weren't happy yet with the run. But in the end we did our best – trying to include all the ideas, but with no more than fifty outfits. I wrote the press release, then we went home and changed and arrived at the British Embassy at 1.30 p.m. where the ambassador, Sir Peter Ricketts, and his wife welcomed us. The building, the Hôtel de Charost, was bought by the Duke of Wellington from Napoleon's sister, Pauline Borghese.

We went to say hello to everybody helping. The girls were still arriving and my favourite memory at this point was a group of these young black models talking and laughing between doing cartwheels on the grass before going to get their hair and make-up done. Andreas went to finish the preparations, allocating jewellery, trying the outfits on again. I talked with the ambassador and did interviews and we watched the run-through, checking the make-up under the lighting. The lighting was done by Toni, who comes from Andreas's village. He did a super job and the girls walked through splendid rooms.

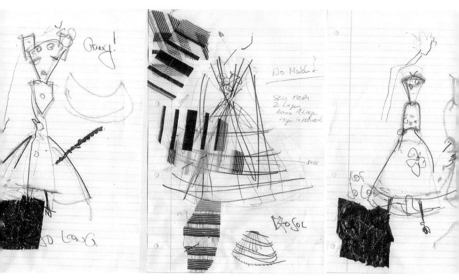

Some of Andreas's sketches for the Paris show.

At the after-show party, I talked to Trish, a kind, powerful woman who only does good things. She is the wife of Terry Jones, founder and editor-in-chief of *i-D* magazine. Some of the girls from the show came, especially one of my favourites, Marta Ortis, who's just left school and did her thesis on the rainforest. Her friend, who also did the show and lives in Paris with her boyfriend, said it's difficult to make money there: agency 20 per cent, tax 50 per cent, 30 per cent for her. Elegant, friendly party. Home before midnight.

SUN 30 SEPT LA CONFERENCE DES OISEAUX

A lovely day at home. Read *La Conference des Oiseaux*, a play by Jean-Claude Carrière adapted from a twelfth-century poem by Farid Udin Attar. It was performed in France by Peter Brook's company and must have been visually marvellous – they used bird masks from Bali. The birds have interesting characters and they meet all kinds of people on their way to discover their King (I got the idea to do my Manifesto as a journey from this play). They always talk in the most everyday expressions, though the text is poetic, and it's good for my French. I read French but I don't have much chance to speak it.

Why else do I love the play? Because it illustrates through little anecdotes and stories and indeed by the whole journey what people in medieval times thought about God and the universe. In their journey to the King – really God – they finally come into his presence, which is a mirror of themselves. It is quite alchemical. People think reading – and indeed all art – is worthwhile only if it is relevant to today. I think it's very relevant to know what people *did* think, especially when it's different. This is what gives you a perspective on your own life. And this perspective is what I consider to be culture. I don't believe in any grand plan but it is a fact of experience that we have a spiritual dimension to our make-up.

OCTOBER 2012

MON 1 OCT FONTAINEBLEAU

In Paris, we stay with my friend Andy Stutz (we use his silks in our grand dresses). His flat is across the river from the Eiffel Tower, which we can see from the balcony. But now we had to move because he was leaving that day and a friend he shares the flat with was coming. We had a room at the Crillon hotel and a driver picked us up for the move and then drove us to Fontainebleau, in the countryside outside of Paris. The style of this castle reminds you of the Three Musketeers. We really enjoyed the beautiful weather in this small French town and came back in time to go to the Saint Laurent show.

We said goodbye to our driver, Johann. I liked him so much. He had been with us all the time and once he was late so we left without him. He was so beautifully sorry, so dignified and genuinely polite that my heart went out to him.

We went to the Saint Laurent show wearing our T-shirts, me in CLIMATE REVOLUTION and Andreas with his 'I am Julian Assange' and we sat next to Kate Moss. Kate wants to meet again the next day for breakfast. She gets up early – 6 a.m.

TUES 2 OCT KATE AND JAMIE

We met Kate and Jamie Hince for lunch with some of their friends. I tell her where we're at with Climate Revolution. She's really excited and involved. Jamie has booked himself onto the Siberian Express, something he's always wanted to do. He'll work on his next songs. After, we go to the showroom and Kate tries things on. This girl really has got style. Such an intimate rapport between the clothes and her body, she really knows how to use it and she has so much energy. Talking. Never tired. It's good for Andreas and me to see how the clothes fit on a woman who really understands clothes – we

At the Saint Laurent show with Andreas.

will adjust, make one or two changes. Jamie says, 'My idea of the perfect strip show is women getting *dressed*.'

Kate and Jamie were going to the McQueen show. On the way, we stop off to see a small collection of underwear of our friend Yasmine Eslami (Yasmine helped with styling both the Red Label and Gold Label shows). Fashion people are there. Kate's so pleased to see them. All friends, throwing her arms around them. Kate tried on the underwear and bought a set. She kept the bra on and thought her vest looked better with it. She's wearing a little camouflage army jacket – a bit too small – which she won on a shooting range. Andreas says to me, 'What a lovely little thing, so kind, running around.'

They dropped us off and we went to the bar. Andreas hardly drinks but he'd had some wine and we carried on, joined by our friend Sabina, a fashion stylist, and her boyfriend, Michael, who deals in second-hand clothes and supplies them to designers to copy. He was thoughtful and seemed clever. One thing he said that I don't agree with was that now we have popular culture all the interesting things come from there, like pop music. With this he seemed to imply that we don't need to listen to 'old' music anymore.

WEDS 3 OCT BY TRAIN TO LAKE COMO

We leave Paris by train for Italy. We have an appointment in Como. The reason we stayed in Paris two extra days was because it wasn't worth travelling home; we could go on by train, which I much prefer to flying. We went down to Lyon and across the Alps (spectacular!) to Milan. At the border the police took off two young men who were illegal immigrants. Poor people.

From Milan, we drove to Como. The lake, surrounded and protected by mountains, has since the Renaissance attracted the rich, who have built their villas here. We stayed in the Villa d'Este, considered to be the best hotel in the world. I had been here once before for the silk fabric fair. Silk is important here. Why were we here? We weren't exactly sure. We had been invited by Morris, the owner of Montero, which produces the scarves we design, as a rose has been named after me. It was most important to him that we should come – therefore, we came.

THURS 4 OCT JAZZ AT THE VILLA ERBA

We took a trip on the lake and disembarked at one of the small towns where we lunched and looked around. Then at 7 p.m. we went to a jazz concert in the Villa Erba, home of the Viscontis. Luchino Visconti was one of the great, great film-makers and, as Andreas said, being born into such a family, style and luxury, no wonder he had such solidity, such standards: 'It didn't come from nowhere, did it?' The villa was immaculate in its grandeur.

It was lit up in the near distance as we approached through the green shapes of the garden. I liked the concert. I've never really got anything out of jazz but I liked this, probably because I liked the players. They were so sweet and sympathetic and dedicated and talented. But a quartet playing Mozart or Debussy is so much more profound and elevating.

FRI 5 OCT NAME OF A ROSE

Arrived at the rose 'event' at 3 p.m. Andreas explained that it was a horticultural fair – everything from potatoes to orchids to garden furniture – where people from all around Italy come to show and sell, and this year the prizewinning rose is dedicated in my honour. It is the brainchild of Morris. I really do love the rose. It has a faint but special spicy smell. Something about the way the petals curl back when the flowers open and the form changes in its different stages and also the salmon colour changes from a more yellow to a more pink hue. It grows all summer long.

Before we left Como and the Villa d'Este, Andreas told me off: 'Vivienne, you want to explain the world but you haven't understood

the magnificence of this hotel. There is nothing like it in the world. It was built in the Renaissance and has been maintained in peak condition ever since. Nothing is wasted. Look at these garden chairs – they were bought in the 1950s and every year at the end of the season they are cleaned and repaired – if necessary repainted – they just unscrew the brass knobs and paint them. Can you imagine any other hotel doing that? Through the different trends

of the 1960s, 70s and 80s – they'd just throw them out and get new ones. This is your ecology, this hotel!'

MON 8 – FRI 12 OCT A VISIT FROM TATI

The nicest thing this week was a visit from Tati, who has modelled for us in our shows and in two campaigns. She's Argentinian and came with a great bouquet of chrysanthemums. She's an art lover. She had been working with Miu Miu and told how she enjoyed it; she's fascinated by how the designers put outfits together; she loves to be part of it. Tati is creative and, like all creative people, she lives in another world as well as this one. She has been to Machu Picchu, walking with a guide – you have to chew coca leaves because of the altitude. Her guide was the wisest person she had met; if you hurt your leg they just give you something, because they understand everything in relationship, understand the planet they stand on.

Andreas has spent every waking hour of the week, even once getting up at 4 a.m. with the stress of it all, preparing for our visit to Vienna. Our friend, Gregor, is opening a Vivienne Westwood shop there and for this we are doing a fashion show. We have an invitation to present this in the Kunsthistorisches Museum, one of the six great galleries of Western painting. So the show has to be great – we will show evening wear and select from our past two collections. We are also allowed to spend all of the Monday in the gallery shooting our next ad campaign.

The problem for Andreas is the outfits have been worked on before for collections, therefore our team of colleagues could prepare all of this for the shoot and the show and it would be good; but not good enough for Andreas – it has to be super-sexy and divine and only he can do that. So he makes himself responsible for every fashion decision, logistics, budget – the lot. I got involved at points where I had to.

SAT 13 OCT MAXIMILLIAN I EXHIBITION IN VIENNA

We went to Vienna on Saturday to have time to calm down before the show. We stayed at the Sacher hotel. Andreas loved the rooms so much; he felt so at home.

We walked across the road to the Albertina, famous for its collection of drawings and prints. The exhibition was about Kaiser Maximillian I (1459–1519), who enlarged the Holy Roman Empire and established the Habsburgs as its emperors, mostly by clever marriages for himself and his children: 'Let others live by Mars: we rely on Venus'. He employed the artists of his time – famous among them, Altdorfer and the unbelievably skilled Dürer – to publish and consolidate his position for posterity through propaganda: his maxim, 'The emperor never dies'.

Maximillian made great use of printing, e.g. *The Arch of Honour*, a gigantic coloured woodcut the size of a wall which he sent around Europe in numbered sheets so that it could be re-assembled. It illustrates his accomplishments, historic scenes and a fake family tree tracing his ancestors back to Moses and Julius Caesar. The most impressive artefact was the *Triumphal Procession of the Emperor*

Maximillian by Altdorfer, a frieze of vellum sheets stuck together, half a metre high and fifty metres long (the first half is missing – it was originally 100 metres). Such skill: you can't make a mistake on vellum (as with ink on paper, you have to start again).

I would also mention the most beautiful suit of armour ever made, not least because of the proportion. It would have perfectly fitted Andreas – so Maximillian was a tall man – especially for the age – with model proportions.

SUN 14 OCT WATTEAU

I saw a painting for sale in a famous auction house. If there is any painting I would like to have it would be a small Watteau and I especially love his scenes of soldiers resting in camp. And here it was. It was the most perfect thing, though someone had once chopped away six centimetres on one side. If you bought it, you could live with it – a vision fixed in time, it would bring security into your home. We visited the new shop and then worked on preparing the clothes for the shoot.

Juergen arrived, Kate arrived from holiday with her mum, and we had supper in the really cosy hotel.

MON 15 OCT SHOOTING AT THE MUSEUM

Shooting for our advertising campaign. I know the Kunsthistorisches Museum well, the paintings are tremendous; part of my job was hurrying around choosing which paintings suited the different outfits. I had to wear a few outfits, so did Andreas, but we mostly left it up to Kate. We also shot in the rooms under the galleries where the picture restoring happens and we met my friend, Elke, working. She restored one of the world's most mysterious and precious works – a late Titian of a nymph and a shepherd. Juergen was very happy.

The show at Vienna's Kunsthistorisches museum.

TUES 16 – WEDS 17 OCT THE SHOW

Karma. Was it Andreas's angst which now produced such a beautiful show? The show was truly marvellous in this sensational setting. I sat with Andreas and watched as the girls walked their itinerary through the rooms and then saw them coming back, so there was this constant appearance and re-appearance of beauties.

Andreas left early the next morning to go to Italy to work on MAN. I went to the new shop to work on how to improve it. It just needed to be more of a mess, more tactile and attractive.

FRI 19 OCT SCHOOL OF HISTORICAL DRESS

Back in London, I attended the launch of the School of Historical Dress, founded by my friends Santina Levey and Jenny Tiramani. I am a patron and gave a speech on the importance of tradition.

Santina and Jenny each have a lifetime of experience of research in historical dress. They have been curating the work of Janet Arnold who, to my own particular benefit, made patterns of historical dress and published them in diagram so that I was able to scale them up and work from them.

I have a book on lace by Santina herself – of comprehensive magnitude – you can guess what period the examples come from, so exquisitely do they mirror the aesthetic of the time. It is a work of great scholarship. Like Janet Arnold, these curators carry the baton of tradition. Without them we would not have the key to the past. I would do anything for splendid Santina. At the moment the school is peripatetic – they are looking for a building and I think with the bright fire of Jenny's dedication they will get it.

WEDS 24 OCT WITH JULIAN ASSANGE

Together with Andreas I managed to begin work on Gold Label, starting with fabrics and yarns. At five I went to visit Julian Assange with Cynthia. We were wearing the 'I am Julian Assange' T-shirts; the face is mine, looking like a man (photo by Juergen Teller). They will be on sale soon and all profits will go to WikiLeaks. You know, they've had 90 per cent of donations blocked by Visa, MasterCard, Western Union, PayPal, Amazon and Bank of America.

I support Julian Assange because he's clever and brave and the founder of WikiLeaks – a brilliant organisation in the public interest which exposes facts concealed and misinformation published by the authorities for their own protection. Therefore the authorities wish to punish him; they're out to get him at all costs. The Swedish government is asking for Julian's extradition. This is a ploy to extradite him from there to the US. The press constantly re-iterates that Julian has been *charged* with sexual offences. He has not been charged. He is the subject of a preliminary investigation involving *allegations* of sexual misconduct.

Julian is so full of facts – a visit is like going to school to learn the world political situation. We agreed that it's not profitable to battle

Supporting Julian Assange at the Ecuadorian Embassy.

against the wilful confusion directed at him by the press. I hope that this will eventually bore people by its negativity and they will be more interested in those journalists who tell the truth. The totality of his actions has been in the public interest. I don't propose to say anything about his present living conditions – that's his business, he made the decision. If he had not made that decision, I am sure he would be in solitary confinement in the US. (My opinion of Sweden – and Britain – is, of course, at rock bottom.) I personally applaud and am grateful for Ecuador giving him political asylum and standing up to the US.

I took Julian wine but he would rather have had fruit.

FRI 26 OCT CLIMATE RUSH AND THE INGA FOUNDATION

Visit from Tamsin Omond of Climate Rush and her colleague, Juliet Chard. The idea is that activists should try to work together. It was an exhilarating meeting. We will be able to help each other a lot with the Climate Revolution. Cynthia and I have begun to meet key people who often contact us with a view to the application of our agenda for the Climate Revolution. We are saying little until we fit our plan together – but it's happening!

We talked about the documentary, *Up in Smoke,* about the incredible work being done by the Inga Foundation in Latin America. The farming system developed by its founder, Mike Hands, over twenty years of experimentation, can make the destructive slash and burn farming techniques – which contribute so heavily to rainforest destruction – a thing of the past. *Guardian Online* is running the story in three sections.

After work, biked over to Belgravia for my friend Steve's party. He sells art. Large drawing room, thirty-odd people – possible to sit – servants, buffet with exquisite food, conversation. Rich society people from different countries who contribute to charities, diplomats, property developers, people who buy art, artists. A teenage Asian boy (fashionable) was introduced to me and he was so sweet, having to cope with his outrageous father – who has tried to buy (offering many thousands) some of our amazing MAN showpieces for his personal wear.

WEDS 31 OCT I HATE AMERICA! WOMAN OF THE YEAR

Recorded a short film for Amnesty: my freedom to think and do in contrast to the terrible things that happen to people. I talked about kindness. Kindness is what makes us human and our intelligence is rooted in empathy – by putting ourselves in somebody else's shoes we start to understand. The film ended with the stark detail of what happened to Azza Suleiman for helping someone. Human rights are part of Climate Revolution because it will lead to a better world.

Not for sale! This showpiece jacket – entitled 'Slave to Love' – was embroidered by Mr Pearl. A 'cut' at the heart bleeds with dripping red beads.

After work, I called in to see Renaud Poutot, a designer of speciality bikes, who wants to give me a bike – but these were so luxurious I wouldn't know quite what to do with one and I like my own bike. I will think about it. Then on to the *Harper*'s 'Woman of the Year' awards at Claridges. Sitting next to Dinos Chapman, I mentioned in passing that I hate America. Chrissy Blake, wife of Peter Blake, the artist, berated me, 'You can't hate America. The music! You can't hate a country!' I think I can hate a country, at the same time as not hating every person in it. Myself, I am very grateful to the hippies who politicised my generation – not only in America, but worldwide. I would guess that half the NGOs in the world are American and these are people who are trying to right the wrongs of US and world policy. My heroes are 'Hanoi Jane' Fonda and Gore Vidal, who fought American injustice; as well as the American Indian Movement, Leonard Peltier, Black Equal Rights Movement, Martin Luther King.

It is the case that foreign policy in the West is determined by the US and that it dominates world policy institutions. Europe follows its economic rules and China copies it. Though most Americans have never been out of the country, they believe America owns the world. What's good for America is good for God. And for this reason, they are the most hypocritical country. As for music, black music and Elvis. Elvis was as great a talent as any opera singer. I'm not so sure about Hollywood, their horrible hamburgers and their drones. I am not patriotic about Britain.

I received an award for inspiring people. So in my speech I talked about Cool Earth (I hope we get some contributions) and the Climate Revolution. The most serious honour (for journalists) was awarded posthumously to brave Marie Colvin and the acceptance speech on her behalf, by war photographer Don McCullin, was proud and heroic: regarding the Syrian oppressor Assad, he said, 'We will continue our reports; we will get them in the end.'

There was a dazzling woman. In real life, I didn't know who she was, although I now realise I had seen her starring in a film on Edith Piaf. She was Marion Cotillard who was given the International Actor of the Year Award. Ralph Fiennes gave the encomium: he loved her for her spirit, the loving and generous life force which flowed through her. On her way to being photographed, she stopped and bent over our table, telling me she could not sacrifice the opportunity of telling me she adored and admired me for my commitments. I was thrilled by her beauty: in a strapless dress, black taffeta all gathered up in the front and all around, she quite overwhelmed me with her pale arms and her face of sincere animation. I quite understood what Ralph Fiennes had said and I would love to meet her again.

NOVEMBER 2012

FRI 2 NOV LEONARD PELTIER FILM

Special. Lorna Tucker came to see me. She spent six months and managed to get permission to see Leonard Peltier for three consecutive days. She is making a film on Leonard and she wanted to film me talking about him. Leonard still hopes to get out and

Leonard Peltier at Leavenworth prison, 1992.

not die in jail. Lorna brought me up to date with his chances. It was heartbreaking to listen to her telling all the things he'd like to do – the enthusiasm and the frustration of a man so powerfully caring about living a good life. I felt so upset when she told me that when Clinton promised to let him out with his presidential prerogative on leaving office, Leonard didn't believe it at first but at last he did and bought a new suit. Clinton changed his mind. Lorna is hoping to be able to film Leonard.

Dear Leonard, I will say this on your film: the reason Leonard Peltier is still in jail is because he will not admit to a crime he didn't do. If they keep you in jail you are guilty. 'America is never wrong'. If they let you out then you are *innocent* and the FBI is guilty.

 SAT 3 NOV ISLAMIC ART AT THE V&A

We are going to India tomorrow for Naomi Campbell's party for her boyfriend, Vlad, and I wanted to look at Indian art before I go. I have not visited India before because I have not yet been impressed by their art. The printed fabrics which they exported to Europe during the eighteenth century are very fine, very attractive. Apart from that, I know photos of the erotic sculptures and bas-reliefs from their temples, and I would love to see the temple dancing, but generally in a museum I pass through collections of Indian art without attraction. The Hindu gods and the Buddhas just haven't lit a spark. They might.

I met my son, Ben, and his girlfriend at the V&A. However, I did not see Indian art because I stopped at Islamic art and it was fascinating. So meticulous: brocades, tiles, ceramics, carpets, metal inlays – mind-bogglingly, beautifully crammed with the finest detail (it must have taken years to make a bowl), pierced metals and a wooden minbar made with little stars and crosses of wood fitted together; geometric but also lots of figurative work. The Arabs were great fans of Chinese ceramics and were inspired by them (the vases as well). What makes Chinese art so great is its spontaneity: the artist studies and absorbs and practices and then does it in one go.

The greatest expressions of the spirit ever achieved. I must come back for the Indian art.

SUN 4 – THURS 8 NOV NAOMI'S PARTY IN JODHPUR

To India. We are not in the main hotel (enormous) but in a smaller one where Andreas chose our rooms – a little house at tree level, one of several with Indian-themed individual decor. Andreas especially loves getting up (before me), opening the door, letting in the sun and sitting on the balcony, making notes, drinking tea and listening to the chirping of the sparrows as they hop from branch to branch in the bougainvillea vines.

A visit to the market, thronging with people – women in bright saris or full Rajasthani skirts. This dress lends women such grace. I love the way the end of the wrapped cloth veils their head and shoulders from the sun as they move; hold this with their expressive hands and then look up with their eyes so animated. They are buying Indian bling and cheap mass-produced rubbish, everything brightly coloured – it was a special festival day. Then up to the Mehrangarh fort which stands on a great outcrop of rock towering over Jodhpur.

On the way up we branched off onto another hill to look at a mausoleum of the famous fifteenth-century fighter who had built the fort. Walking up to it, you see a lake ringed by hills with a wall all along the ridge. I have never been in a more quiet and peaceful situation. I stood a long time overlooking the lake with its dragonflies and swallows and waterfowl. The air was so still.

Then up to the fort which was being decorated for Vlad's party: flowers everywhere, on strings and garlands and hanging like tassels, and amongst the columns of flowers mounds of chillies; in a large courtyard were cushions and couches and carpets, where later that night all we guests would sit feasting and drinking. We continued our journey through the rooms with the other tourists and I can't remember one room or artefact because I saw nothing to like amongst all the ancient paraphernalia. So far in India I've

Mehrangarh fort, Jodhpur, lit up for a party.

seen only bling. The architecture of the fort relied on patterned permutations of pierced brickwork. It was a mess.

For the party nights, we were all dressed in Indian costumes. Michael Howard, the creative director for Dior, must have worked for weeks. The lighting and décor of the fort and the events were amazing: up along the internal ramps leading to the courtyard were dozens of drummers, horses, camels caparisoned in mirrors and tassels, dancers, acrobats, fire-eaters, ladies throwing rose petals; great posters painted by people from the Indian film industry. Vlad was Bond and Naomi was his Bond girl, the title 'Bond is Back'. Part of the attraction of their romance must be the idea of the glamorous couple. And, because of the thronging festivities, we felt like we were in a film set. Diana Ross took a fancy to Andreas and he politely got on stage with her for a minute or two.

Naomi mentioned that she's going to do some charity work in India about waste recycling. I talked to David X Prutting, who was the official photographer. He told me that when he first visited India, he went to photograph and meet the lowest class, who clean up the shit. He loved them; they were the only people who never asked him for money. Like everyone, he found it hard to cope with the poverty. David said, 'The way to deal with it is to accept it for yourself, to take it into yourself, to say yes, this is a life, to respect.'

Thank you, Naomi, for the invitation.

FRI 9 – TUES 13 NOV DRAWING SNAKES

Caught up with our designs, had jet-lag for twenty-four hours (Saturday), tidied up the Climate Revolution charter and drew the snakes which eat each other's tails.

WEDS 14 – THURS 15 NOV ROME CONFERENCE

To Rome for a conference on luxury goods hosted by the *International Herald Tribune* fashion editor, Suzy Menkes. Suzy is so inspired by our project designing bags which are made in Africa that she really wanted us at this conference, which was focused on

CLIMATE REVOLUTION CHARTER

Climate Revolution really is evolution, nothing more nor less than changing the world order so that the human race can survive + evolve, toppling the global financial rulers who cause poverty + Climate Change: Debt + Destruction

Everything is Connected

Economic crisis + climate crisis are the cause + effect of eachother; they are like serpents who eat eachother's tails. The only way out of this double crisis is to fight the Climate Revolution. WHAT'S GOOD FOR THE PLANET IS GOOD FOR THE ECONOMY WHAT'S BAD FOR THE PLANET IS BAD FOR THE ECONOMY Everything is connected — all NGO's are connected. Fight for Chelsea Manning + you fight for the bees. Save the Arctic + you save the small farmers. Culture is connected: know the past to know the present. Ready go to art galleries + know the names of trees + you cultivate lasting values instead of short-term consumption.

You are connected — by following the site

Everything you think + say + do makes a difference. Information is power, "ALL FOR ONE + ONE FOR ALL. By exposing the lies of present governments to the true facts our whistleblowers may help us to build new government. Democracy through the social media

Climate Revolution. ♡

Africa. We met some of our dear friends from the project there. Andreas and I were supposed to talk at 4.30 p.m. on Thursday. I went first. I talked about climate change, which I hope punctured the complacency of some of the speakers who seemed to focus their hopes for the future on the emerging middle-class consumer in Africa. My speech turned out to be popular and Suzy responded to the applause by dramatically finishing it there and moving onto the next speaker. I was sorry not to hear Andreas. He had wanted to talk about the people we met in Africa.

SAT 17 NOV TO PERU WITH COOL EARTH

To Peru. We are visiting the Ashaninka communities in the rainforest with Cool Earth. Andreas and I left the house at 6 a.m., having had 3½ hours' sleep. We met at the airport with Cynthia. the Times journalist Deborah Ross, and Mark Ellingham, a Cool Earth Trustee, who founded the *Rough Guide* travel books.

The Cool Earth team were waiting for us in Lima: Matthew Owen, the director, and Dilwyn Jenkins, an anthropologist who has known and helped the Ashaninka for thirty years. Dilwyn writes the *Rough Guide to Peru* and, after Mark introduced him to Cool Earth, he had set up the project with the Ashaninka council. Of the other members of our party, Carlos and Raphaelle are based in Lima and work with Dilwyn on their NGO, Eco-Tribal, which supports the work of Cool Earth. Jemma and Kitty work with Matthew at Cool Earth in Cornwall but travel to Peru two or three times a year. A good thing about our trip was that we were all great company; everybody so kind, so sweet – clever, intelligent, funny; we became good friends.

Lima is a big city, perhaps bigger than London – population eight million. We stayed in a vast and decrepit hotel in the old centre. Andreas and I were tired; we hadn't slept on the plane. I slept now but Andreas, hardly at all. We had the choice of gurgling water and an air-conditioning plant in the rooms at the back or traffic noise at the front. We chose the traffic.

SUN 18 – WEDS 21 NOV WITH THE ASHANINKA

We set off for the forest early in the morning: taxi, a small plane, jeep and finally a four-hour boat ride. Moving down the river, Andreas became happy and forgot his troubles and worrying about leaving our work on the collections. He had a nap. We arrived at Cutivireni in the Rio Ené Valley where people of this Ashaninka community were waiting for us on the river bank. The Ashaninka are the second-largest indigenous group in Peru (25–45,000 people).

César Bustamante is just about the most important person in the community. It was he who got in touch with Dilwyn (in Wales!) when they needed help. They were under threat from loggers wanting to move in and from drug traffickers wanting to use their little airstrip. Fortunately, Dilwyn was able to link up with Cool Earth, who have helped the Ashaninka in protecting and controlling their own forest. They were the third community Cool Earth worked with.

From 1980 to 1994 there was war in Peru and in this part of the rainforest. A movement called Shining Path, led by a messianic leader, Abimael Guzmán, who saw himself as the political heir of Mao and Stalin, tried to take over. César and the Ashaninka fought them – 10,000 Ashaninka were displaced, 6,000 killed and 30–40 villages disappeared. Although most of the Shining Path fighters gave up in 1994 after the arrest and imprisonment of Guzmán, pockets still exist which are now mixed up with drug trafficking.

The Ashaninka we visited in Cutivireni and neighbouring Tinkareni have gardens around the villages and beyond that the immediate forest is a mix of low and high forest canopy. Matthew says that this depends on the type of ground, rocks and soil. It is a paradise. The staple diet is manioc and maize. They have fish and wild game and lots of fruit. Because three of us were vegetarian, our party ate vegetables, which we brought with us, and we ate fruit: papaya, mango, banana (many delicious different kinds), grapefruit, oranges, coconut. The Ashaninka are now entering the market economy (exporting coffee, chocolate, some of their jewellery made from seeds and bows and arrows which Dilwyn will sell on eBay). The coffee and cacao grow wild among the forest trees.

Crossing the river to Cutivireni.

An Ashaninka woman called Chabuca took me to see the plant whose seeds they grind for their red make-up. She speaks Spanish as well as Ashaninka and stopped often on the way to sweep her arm over the landscape, saying 'Bonito (beautiful), Señora Vivienne'. The Ashaninka are the most casual people. Some of the men and women wear make-up, some not. They rub the red paste on their faces or make little marks and patterns which express their dreams and visions from the native drug, ayahuasca, or simply their present state of mind. There is no marriage ceremony – the kids build a new house and the couple move in together. When people die, they used to lay them on a rock in the river so that the bones were picked and then, I guess, they just disposed of the bones in the forest. Since the 1960s they bury people in unmarked graves in the forest – but they know where the bodies are.

The Ashaninka have one house to sleep in, with a bed which is a wooden table, two or three changes of clothes; they have another house, open-sided, which is the kitchen and 'women's house', with some pots and pans and a bag for collecting. They wash in the river, walk barefoot, and put their head through a giant banana leaf to protect them when it rains. The women's hair is the chic-est on earth – a ragged thinned-out cut. I noticed on a film Dilwyn made in 1970, and showed on his laptop, that their hair was then more of a fringed bouffant bob and the men's hair was long, whereas now it's short. They keep up with the times.

Dilwyn is great friends with one of the villagers, Jaime Pene, whom he has known since Jaime was a child. Jaime has visited Dilwyn's home in Wales but said he was glad to get back to the forest again. He's been mapping the community and its trees on Google maps – which helps them protect their forest.

We fell in love with Cladys, so elegant, a little queen of five or six years old, who is the adopted daughter of Ana, César's wife. The girls wear the same envelope of cloth as a dress as their mothers do – it always drops off one shoulder. Cladys looked at and listened to everything we did and said; she seemed the last to go to bed. One day, I was sitting in the river when she came and splashed me to have a game. Often she was shy but her curiosity got the better of her; the expressions on her face from serious to laughing went full circle through the whole range of human beauty.

Ana's youngest child, Coakiti, is three; his name means 'Little Hawk' (they have Ashaninka and Spanish names). There are the most wonderful butterflies, especially down by the river where we were. We admired a black, white and iridescent green beauty. Andreas saw Coakiti catch it and with triumphal glee rip it apart. Andreas had to kill, with a stone, the half that was still left flying. Andreas saw this as an example of children's natural cruelty. I told Coakiti off. He always holds his hands to his cheek, wringing them when he doesn't know what to do. This little naked thing. I shook his hand and patted his head and said seriously that he was forgiven, miming the poor butterfly.

I should have got Dilwyn to take me to the school so he could translate, but I didn't. Next to the school is a boarding house for children who live far away. It can take them as much as six hours to walk to school and they go home at the weekends. I asked a

Cladys – one of our Ashaninka companions.

girl of about ten to show me her exercise book; it was history and geography with beautiful writing, maps and drawings. The teachers are supplied by the state – all teaching is in Spanish and they discourage the taking of ayahuasca.

Dilwyn said that in this altered state the Ashaninka experience a universal continuity which they think includes their ancestors. Chabuca's grandmother is Noemi, who is my age, a village elder who is one of the few remaining female shamans in the area. I might have asked her to give me the chance of this experience but I was feeling a bit rough – my legs were still swollen from travelling and I felt a bit sick, maybe from our malaria pills but probably from a three-hour walk in the sun between two villages (for a special celebration where the villages came together to mark the end of the fighting with the Shining Path and also in our honour). I missed most of it because

Walking to the village – the Ashaninka use forest leaves as ponchos.

I was lying down. Cynthia said there was a very dramatic poetry recitation by the schoolteacher, the children did a traditional dance about life in the village, and there were archery competitions (they laughed at Andreas for going too near the target and cheating).

THURS 22 – SUN 25 NOV BACK TO LIMA

At our point of departure from Cutivireni, Ana brought a feather headdress she had made for me. I felt I had to give a present so I picked one of the kids who was always around, wanting to know everything, and I gave him my AR badge. I explained through Dilwyn: AR means Active Resistance to Propaganda, means don't always believe what you're told – especially by the government – think for yourself; the man with the beret on the badge is Rembrandt, a great artist and figure of culture. This means that knowledge is power, so take advantage of your education and learn as much as you can. The women were all nodding approval and the kid was grinning all over the place to receive this honour.

Half our party had already left by boat but a few of us were privileged to go in a tiny aeroplane. By the time it touched down on the short runway all the children from the school were there – they came running down the path through the high gardens to send us off. We flew over the wonder of the rainforest to a small town, Satipo, then joined our friends for the flight back to Lima. The air conditioning on this plane was extremely cold and Andreas caught a chill.

Back in Lima, I went with Matthew, Dilwyn, Andreas and Cynthia to see the Vice Minister of the Strategic Development of Natural Resources for Peru. Señor Acosta sat there listening, understanding English, sometimes replying in Spanish. When I asked him questions designed to discover his commitment to saving the rainforest, he gave warm support. We felt that Cool Earth had established a friendship for continuing a dialogue and Matthew hopes his support will help Cool Earth's application to the World Bank for finance.

In the Chinese horoscope, Andreas is a horse (I am a snake). Like a horse, a draught enflames him. That night, the chill had transformed into a raging fever. He burned and I applied ice-cold cloths to his forehead (wet facecloths placed in the fridge). He was two days in the hotel bed and on the second day the fever broke into a sweat. On the third day, he was still weak but we went to the wonderful Museo Larco. The things that struck me most were the gold masks and the reflective plates sewn all over a garment. They moved and must have been constantly reflecting the sun. The people must have looked like gods who came from the sun.

We had planned to go to Cusco and Machu Picchu, with Cynthia and Dilwyn, but on Sunday we caught the plane home.

MON 26 NOV – SAT 1 DEC MICHAEL HANEKE

Back to London inspired by the commitment of Cool Earth and the Ashaninka people to save the precious rainforest for us all. It's their forest and they'll fight for it. Andreas says, 'I feel very privileged to have met the people of the Ashaninka, people whose values are different from our own. I think in ten years' time it will be different.' I, too, am glad.

I stayed home for two days, jet-lagged. Couldn't do anything. Certainly you must suffer to travel. On Thursday and Friday I went to work but did not manage to work much on the collection. Too many daily bits and pieces to catch up with.

I go to the cinema only about once a year but the films of Michael Haneke have made a big impression on Andreas and on Friday we went to see his latest, *Amour*. It is about an old couple and the end of life and it impressed on my memory step by step. The selection of detail and which bits of a lifetime's experience and impressions to use; by using the external to show the internal. Economy: everything included, nothing not needed. Acting truthful, not sentimental.

The film and yoga brought me back to life and by Saturday I'm my old cheery self.

DECEMBER 2012

 SUN 2 DEC **AN ARAB FEELING IN THE NEW COLLECTION**

Iris, our visiting angel pattern cutter, arrived for the week. Not only does Iris create new patterns from our newly dreamed-up cutting principles but she's very important at the fittings with us, helping us to bring to a finish the toiles of our other pattern cutters. So this is a week when we really concentrate on the collection.

There is something rather Arab in the collection at the moment. This happened because of two things: I was interested in the theme of fighting, because of the Climate Revolution, and I am looking at fashion in the illuminated manuscripts of the Middle Ages. The Crusaders brought these Arab fashion influences back. The soldiers in the illuminations are supposed to be Romans but the monks imagined something more Arab. I don't say that I have adopted any specific details, only that the collection has an Arab feeling.

Although the Climate Revolution is a non-violent revolution – an evolution – which we hope to win, there looms the horror of a hot world of violence, death and destruction if we don't. By the way, the Crusaders were the aggressors (yobs), not the Muslims.

I like our current collections to have a mix of new cuts, standard cuts, historical cuts and simple envelopes or cloths thrown on in a theatrical way.

TUES 4 DEC MY NEW DRESS AND GEORGE SOROS

I am wearing a long dress like an apron for special occasions at the moment. I wear it on top of a T-shirt which says 'Climate Revolution' on the back. The dress is in a ravishing green silk satin shot with rainbow stripes which shine through from the back of the green. It has a matching cloak and my green feather headdress from the rainforest matches it perfectly.

I wore it to a dinner in support of the Fortune Forum Summit's Real Aid Campaign, founded by Renu Mehta to raise $100 billion to combat global poverty, disease and climate change. This is an

Wearing the dress again (and a feather tiara from Peru – a present from Ana of the Ashaninka) at New Year's eve, with Pamela Anderson and Andreas (in his kilt).

incredible amount of money. The star speaker was billionaire philanthropist George Soros. Ken Roth, Executive Director of Human Rights Watch, presented a short film showing their work. They have been colleagues for many years, since the time when Roth asked Soros for $50 million so they could hire more investigators; they had one investigator trying to monitor abuses in three countries, and wished to have one per country where violations take place. Soros gave them a $100-million ten-year grant.

Roth then interviewed Soros. He spoke of the 'Open Society' according to Karl Popper, whose philosophy has influenced him enormously. The open society is the opposite of an autocratic state. As I listened, I got the idea that it is a truly democratic and just society, involving free speech and flexibility through discussion so that change can happen.

My own thoughts on this are that democracy can't be mob rule. Mob rule bursts out through prejudice and ignorance and takes the law into its own hands; it never brings progress; it causes a backlash – conservative forces become more clever at controlling opinion. (This happened after the French Revolution but the great thing was that through the activity and ideas of the French salons, culture flourished, keeping conservative forces at bay until World War I, when conservatism finally won.) Now what if the vested interests of the status quo (rule by psychopaths), using the media and advertising (consumption being a part of the advertising) manipulates the public to resort to their base instincts? Isn't this a controlled mob rule? Prejudice and ignorance kept simmering. Gareth Peirce makes the point in *Dispatches from the Dark Side*: the law is a reflection of the just sentiment of the people. When people are emotionally manipulated they are also intellectually blocked. The authorities get away with their state-sponsored crimes.

George Soros grew up in Nazi-occupied Hungary. That's where he learned about risk. Sometimes it is safer to take a risk than not to. He has been placing his money where it will promote the freedom of the open society. Renu, the organiser and our hostess, who was sitting between me and Soros, is a very clever woman at putting

$ Our financial structure is a major cause of C.C.

The world is run for cheap labour + exhaustion of natural resources

Driven by competition + war mentality
(Arms Trade creates→ war, creates→ jobs)

Proof that our system has failed: the financial crisis is a symptom of the ecological crisis — There is less to exploit, the earth's resources are drying up.

We have until 2020 (TOCK TICK) Runaway CLIMATE CHANGE

Loss of habitat (HOT!) + extinction on a massive scale.
Why do we accept Climate Change? STOP it!

PLAN WAKE UP

① Nucleus of the avant garde, Freedom Fighters ♡ for a better world → activate ② public opinion → pressure ③ Gov.t policy
= PRIORITY CLIMATE CHANGE

Stopping Climate Change is the answer to all our problems. In the process we could build a different value system / ☒ / human values / human genius.

Why can't a person ♀ be as valuable as a BOMB ▷ ?

people together and making things happen. She turned to him and asked him what he thought, 'Vivienne says our financial system is the cause of climate change and that in turn has helped cause the financial crisis.' I know him to be conservative on this point so I was delighted to hear him say, 'Hurricane Sandy in the US was caused by climate change.'

Hooray for Michael Bloomberg, the New York mayor, who published this connection in press conferences and through his extensive media holdings (Bloomberg TV, Businessweek and various digital platforms). This has made a hole in the dyke of denial. I think it is one of the significant acts of the year.

 WEDS 5 DEC BRONZE AT THE ROYAL ACADEMY

On Wednesday, we met with the Lush team – Tamsin Omond, Hilary Jones and the company's co-founder, Mo Constantine – to plan the New Year Climate Revolution campaign for the windows of Lush shops. We're planning more events for 2013.

The next day to Nopi restaurant with Cynthia to meet Michael Stein, Julia Groves and Matt Mellen of the Trillion Fund. We are helping. I had to be at the Barbican by 7 p.m., so after lunch I stayed in the West End and rushed along to *Bronze*, the exhibition at the Royal Academy. Stunning! Life-changing! The presentation was genius – one marvel after another – and every effort was made to show them in the round. And the bronze itself! The strength of bronze allows the sculpture to live in its space without support; bronze technique provides the potential to master size and detail; and the range of finish from hard shine to crusted patina bears witness to a metamorphosis from its hot liquid flux. You remember I had never looked at Indian Buddhas and Hindu gods. There were beautiful examples of both. It was interesting that when the Chinese became interested in bronze they made utensils for offerings to ancestors and ceremonial bells and not figure sculpture – because they did not worship gods. (There were eventually sculptures – Hindu and Buddhist – because China was tolerant of religion.)

Early Ming dynasty bronze of Kapala-Hevajra and Nairatmya, 1403–24.

Among the highlights for me were Donatello's *Putto with Tambourine*, which I know well as it belongs to the Gemaldegalerie in Berlin where I used to teach. Whenever I see him, he fills me with awe and gladness; he's the essence of the human spirit. Also a Chinese early Ming dynasty *Buddha and his consort*: the fullness of him with his multiple heads, arms and legs and the gaze that locks them together. I have never before experienced such sexual transmission of feelings from a work of art. And Matisse's *Backs*. In his painting, Matisse so often wiped the paint away and overpainted: a labour of simplification to get at the truth; every decision, every stroke of the brush has to be uncompromising, spontaneous. In the case of his bronzes we can think of the brush as an arrow, released by the imagination and guided by the hand. In his four 'Backs' all are true.

In the evening, I opened the Barbican's new Cinemas 2 & 3 on Beech Street (across from the Barbican Centre) and also took part in the Barbican's 'Seven Deadly Sins' series of films. I was asked to choose a film on Gluttony after which there was a Q&A and late dinner for a group of guests. The film, *La Grande Bouffe* (*Blow Out*), from the 1970s, is about four friends (gourmands) who meet for the weekend in a private house owned by one of them and cook and eat themselves to death. It was their way of escape from pressures conforming to the false values of their age. High class call girls were called in to help with the death/food/sex orgy. There was so much meat being delivered that a kind of school mistress who accepted a duty to help them achieve their end told the delivery man to hang the carcasses in the trees.

FRI 14 DEC THE CHANGELING

This week I did the usual things – fittings, working out knitwear, four interviews, one photo shoot, and talking to Cynthia plotting the Climate Revolution. Lorna came to talk to me and film a bit about Leonard. I think she might be able to do something for him through the film because of the influential people she's meeting.

I went to two classical music concerts and one play – Middleton's *The Changeling* at the Young Vic. This was shit because a clever production meant you couldn't hear the words – the audience on four sides so actors talked with their backs to you. A great actor must always be fully in touch with the audience. The main actor, Zubin Varla, was an exception; he somehow used his head and body to reverberate his voice full circle. There was also writing Christmas cards, which often included mini letters – keeping in touch with all my friends.

Christmas with family and friends. I was reading the *Bronze* exhibition catalogue and re-reading Gareth Peirce's book, which has helped shape my thoughts on the way the US and Britain control public opinion. America keeps its legal activity in the open or, put more accurately, it attempts to legalise its illegal activities. At the moment it has created a new legal regime which nevertheless is illegal according to previous principles of justice. For example, it is illegal to declare war on an idea (no state, no enemy – it's like you have declared war on the whole world), and it is one reason why the US is so keen to use force on the people it designates 'Terrorists'. Trying to make illegality legal is carried to the extreme (e.g. terrorists are not given legal POW status because they don't have a uniform!), which, therefore, permits inhuman treatment and denies the prisoner access to law. The US attorney general has redefined a number of practices for which no immunity exists under domestic or international law: waterboarding, sleep deprivation, forced standing and the like.

As for America's Freedom of Information Act, judge for yourself. There are still 150,000 documents pertaining to Leonard Peltier withheld under claims of national security (it would expose the government's dirty work). The US government went to enormous lengths to frame Leonard. They don't have to frame people anymore. If they have illegal laws, they can just kidnap them.

Britain avoids transparency, except that we, like the US, have a Freedom of Information (FoI) act, which our governments obviously regret because they are now trying to get rid of it. Gareth speaks of a small window 'opened by chance through accidents of litigation in which government communiques were required to be disclosed.' They show that Britain's method is to ignore legal obstacles and lie, e.g. a draft for an official statement on the conditions of Britons in Guantanamo – 'Officials confirmed that the three detainees are being treated humanely and according to international norms. Our team was able to verify that this was the case' – drafted before any UK visit to Guantanamo had taken place. The message coming loud and clear from Blair was that there was no need for legal or moral restraint. David Blunkett, the then UK Home Secretary, recorded, 'The longer they stay in Cuba/Afghanistan the better.'

It is now known that the UK tipped off the US as to Arabs who would make suitable 'terrorists'. One such person, Shaker Aamer, was kidnapped and subjected to appalling beatings in the unprotesting presence of a UK intelligence officer to get a confession out of him (false) that he was part of al-Qaeda and under the directive of Bin Laden. He is still in Guantanamo although he has been cleared for release by US authorities.

The people of the UK have not yet accepted the present government's attempt to set up secret courts (shame on Ken Clarke for trying). They did not accept the previous government's attempt to establish imprisonment for forty-two days without trial – it's still twenty-eight days and higher than any other country. Shall we propose a petition to 38 Degrees? Can we campaign for the release of Shaker Aamer?

JANUARY 2013

TUES 1 JAN YVES SAINT LAURENT

Andreas and I went to work. If we are to get our Gold Label show by the end of February, I will have to concentrate on fashion only. Cynthia will have to deal with all the wonderful things that are coming to us and starting to happen around Climate Revolution.

Andreas and I work separately at first when we start a new collection but then we come together to start fixing things. I had suggested that he look to Yves Saint Laurent for inspiration and he is ever more astonished. As a child, Andreas had a deep attraction to fashion and when as a teenager he discovered Saint Laurent, the attraction was transformed into a passion. I don't believe anyone has ever appreciated Saint Laurent as much. Andreas is an extremely visual person; he is a see-er – seeing, he understands. He is a perfectionist and by experience he knows in advance the effort each undertaking will cost. It looks easy but it is the most difficult thing in the world.

We are both getting a feeling for the collection. We seem each to have grasped something of the elegance and adventure of the fashion of the Middle Ages from our book of reproductions of illuminated manuscripts – these illuminations were of course the most profuse artistic expression of the time. We are excited but we have so far chosen only half the fabrics.

TUES 8 JAN MAN AT HARRODS DEPOT

Our yoga class has been on holiday and I was so glad to treat myself again. At 4 p.m. we went to the English pre-collection presentation of our MAN collection which will catwalk in Milan. It was sponsored by Harrods in their depot where their big green lorries were parked around an installation of Joe Rush's Mutoid Waste Company stuff (my favourite, the horse, was there) and models posed. We were right next to the Ecuadorian Embassy (Julian wakes up at 4 a.m. when the Harrods depot grills roll up and the depot jumps into noisy life), so I was wearing my *I am Julian Assange* T-shirt.

I was interviewed about Climate Revolution and, of course, Julian. The young models did not know about Julian or WikiLeaks. I told them, 'Get a Life! Engage with the world.' And I gave them the two spare T-shirts I had with me; friends who wear them tell me they create a load of interest.

Our MAN pre-collection event at Harrods depot.

SUN 13 JAN MAN IN MILAN – AND PUNK

We had our MAN fashion show in Milan and in the evening, my friend Gian Mauro again hosted a party in his penthouse. I talked to some of the boys who had modelled and came along – Jimmy, Lawson, Duncan and Miles. I was so impressed. They really did know what was going on in the world.

They made me think again about punk. The Metropolitan Museum in New York will put on an exhibition about punk this year and people want my opinion. Since punk collapsed for me with the death of Sid Vicious and the break-up of the Sex Pistols, I have been contemptuous of the movement in general and in particular of its token rebels and career gurus who claim social significance for it. I think they're all posers. I realised that it wasn't enough, jumping around wearing safety pins and a 'Destroy' T-shirt. You need ideas to be subversive. That is why the movement folded: the punks didn't have any because ideas don't come on a plate – you have to get them yourself by becoming engaged with the world and its past.

After punk, Malcolm and I did our *Pirate* collection. The idea was 'get off the island' (insular mentality of England) and plunder the world and its past for ideas. I see how our clothes, our fashion, represented our aspirations. We changed the look of the urban guerrilla with black bondage for the pirate, gold teeth, ringlets and historical dress.

Talking to my new friends in Milan – at the moment they take advantage of their good looks to model – through them I see now how effective the punk message had been. Punk planted an attitude: *Don't Trust Governments, Ever.* The punk stance gave young people a political focus. It was a stand against the mismanagement of the world and the corruption of power and the destruction it causes. That's what punk was for me. And that's what anarchy meant to me – that people would have more control of their lives and more control of government. It is the same reason I write this diary.

By the way, my friends really care about what they wear in defiance of conformity.

WEDS 16 – WEDS 23 JAN THE ROSE, SNOW AND JUERGEN

Andreas and I went to the fifth birthday celebration and fundraising dinner for the Rose Theatre, held at the Hurlingham Club. Judi Dench's costume from *A Midsummer Night's Dream* was auctioned and we contributed a prize of two fashion show tickets.

I was sitting with other theatregoers, talking to journalist and author Mihir Bose, who made the following point (which he put so well that I asked him to email it to me): 'The major problem for the environment is that the world has just one economic model. A consequence of the Western reshaping of the world using this model is that every family now wants to have a lifestyle similar to America, with two cars and innumerable gadgets. The rising middle classes of China and India also aspire to this. The planet's resources cannot sustain such growth, but there are no viable alternative models.'

Climate Revolution is working towards a new ethic, one which involves a hierarchy of cultural values. Particularly, it challenges the idea that wealth = consumption and acquisition. We need quality and less quantity of crap manufactures, we need more carers, teachers and thinkers, then money will circulate in beneficial ways.

We had snow. I loved it. We had a short blackout and my phone was cut off the whole weekend. Andreas went to Paris to check venues for our coming fashion show and he couldn't contact me because I don't have a mobile. I took a real break and stayed in the whole weekend.

I went to my friend Juergen Teller's photo exhibition which opened with three giant nudes of me! Juergen is a splendid photographer, it's a big honour.

MON 28 JAN TRILLION FUND

Meeting with Michael Stein of the Trillion Fund – one of the core members of the Climate Revolution cabinet. How do we get clean energy up and running and make the switch from fossil fuels? Answer: It depends on the scale of investment. The fund has begun and will soon be available to thousands of small investors, who can buy a bond for as little as £100. The Trillion funds acts like a bank – a new bank – because it can give a good interest rate to small investors, the reason being the limitless security of supply for the investment: the sun's energy won't run out like fossil fuels and because it's clean it won't incur the costs of environmental damage.

Talking to Michael, it seems that his studies and career changes have brought him to this idea; the people he has worked with, the contacts he has made seem serendipitous and designed to help him. I am particularly impressed by how well he knows the internet and by the potential of his vast and useful databases to help create a new responsibly human economy.

WEDS 30 JAN EMBROIDERY, HATS AND DEBORAH ROSS

Fashion is a daily job, sometimes from 10 a.m. to 10 p.m., including weekends. All those thousands of decisions, all those fittings; you go through stages where you just don't want to see another toile, correcting it with our dedicated pattern cutters. I say this because fashion students think it's just drawing, filling boards with collages for inspiration! And then somehow you make the design – which will never turn out as you thought it would because you have no idea in the first place of what your drawing means.

Anyway, one of the things I did was four pieces of artwork for embroidery – for four garments (two dresses, a jacket and a long skirt) – using the drawings from the beautiful borders of illuminated manuscripts. Even though I got students to help me copy them out onto full-size templates for the dress patterns, this took a good week. This work is pleasant, easy and therapeutic and I felt guilty for doing it and taking so long because I was leaving all the hard slog up to Andreas. We have to delegate our work and unless we check constantly it will take a wrong turn, people will work for nothing and we will have to begin again.

I can't believe how amongst all this Andreas manages to time, prepare and follow all the details for the final presentation so that it all finally happens – the venue, the lighting, who will do the music, the hats. He asked me to help choose what gloves to get made. I was busy and told him I couldn't be bothered right then. 'What!' he cried. 'There is nothing more beautiful than the arm of a woman, and the legs – and the face. What's in between I don't care!'

When my friend Deborah Ross came to visit us (she is the journalist who came with us to Peru), I was delighted to see her and took time off chatting. She asked what career I would have chosen if I had not been a fashion designer. My passions are reading and art, and I usually answer this question by saying I would like to write plays and design and produce theatre. This time, thinking of my therapeutic experience doing my artwork for embroidery, I answered that I would have liked to have been a painter. I realise I have a real talent for graphic design and a strong direct transmission from feelings and sensations to hand. I feel I could have done something, transmitted a vision of the world. It is true also that each fashion collection, though ephemeral, is a vision of the world and I'm looking forward to our Gold Label show. It will be beautiful. I feel as if I've been mining for treasure.

Thinking how I would like to spend more time with my friends, I told Deborah of a perfect situation, an idyll of friendship I had read of in a book by Marcel Aymé, *Le Confort Intellectuel*. Two men who each have a reason to stay away from Paris meet in a village on the outskirts. The book is an excuse for a highly original attack on the complacency of intellectuals, but it is the setting for their conversations that so appeals to me. They have made a temporary escape from the worries of the world; they come across each other in their walks in the winter woods and repair to the warmth of the village bar or their apartments. Security is a necessity for the intellectual life.

FEBRUARY 2013

WEDS 20 FEB LONDON FASHION WEEK AND JULIAN

For London Fashion Week, Joe Rush did a Climate Revolution artwork for our shop window in Conduit Street. In one half of the

Joe Rush's window for London Fashion Week.

window he represents his view of the world: an iron cage with a man inside (though the door is open for whenever he wants to leave); a tree and a bird and a crab live outside the cage. These sculptures are re-made from rusty scrap metal. In the other half is a shining metal heart of 'Victory for the Climate Revolution' made from two recycled petrol tanks from a Triumph motorbike.

I wore my 'I am Julian Assange' T-shirt at the Red Label show. Since before Christmas, I have wanted to find a way to address the confusion swimming around Julian. I believe that misapplied feminism is holding him in legal limbo; women living in the privileged world who blindly support feminism, not seeing the wood for the trees. The woman in question says she 'did not want to accuse Julian of anything'; that it was the police who made up the allegations. Do women really want an innocent man to satisfy their wish and vindicate himself by spending the rest of his life in a US Supermax jail?

So I was sad and puzzled when my friend Jemima Khan joined the ranks of these irresponsible women, or as John Pilger puts it, 'the pathetic animus of a few who claim the right to guard the limits of informed public debate.' I phoned Jemima. I hope she will change her mind. I will see her when we are less busy. Pilger completely exploded Jemima's opinions in the *New Statesman* one week later but by then her opinions had run through the global press.

WEDS 27 FEB SAVE THE ARCTIC

We go to Paris to prepare for our show, which is on Saturday. We are calling it 'Save the Arctic' and are using a design we did for Greenpeace's campaign. It was Andreas's idea to use the heart-shaped globe. The design says it all: save the Arctic now and we might save the world; the white flag of truce is blank, signifying that the Arctic belongs to everyone. Greenpeace is thrilled. It's part of Climate Revolution!

MARCH 2013

FRI 1 MARCH LEONARD PELTIER

The really best news this month is that Leonard is to be transferred to a softer prison. After forty years in jail. We hope he will now receive treatment for his medical problems. Perhaps this move will be the first step towards greater freedom; perhaps he'll be able to live on the Rez. He hasn't moved yet but we are all keen to hear from him as soon as he does.

SAT 2 MARCH GOLD LABEL SHOW IN PARIS

We had our Gold Label show. It was at the Musée de l'Art Moderne in Paris, in a room too small and narrow for decor. Andreas decided to have it as just a black tunnel. The theme was 'Medieval' and the black allowed great focus and concentration. Lighting (misty, time travellers), as usual, by Toni, Andreas's friend from his village. The models looked so beautiful (hair, Sam McKnight; make-up, Val Garland) and they loved the clothes; they were so happy. The music: we spoke by phone to a young composer, Dominik Emrich, 'Medieval, not religious, troubadours, triumph, another world,' we told him. He sent a CD: beautiful, timeless, modern. That was it.

It's wonderful the help we get: the whole is more than the sum of its parts. I must mention the Scottish mill – Begg Scotland – who made our blankets. I sent them the designs late. Their machines were in full use so they got people to come in to work at night. I adore our Climate Revolution blanket-cloak. Thank you.

SUN 3 MARCH ADRIAN CHENG

Paris showroom. I got involved in the presentation of the collection to the buyers. I have to secure all the links down the chain of our

Our Climate Revolution blanket cloak at the Gold Label show.

enterprise if I am to push for greater and greater quality. Whilst in Paris I met up with Adrian Cheng to discuss how we can launch Climate Revolution in China. Adrian's into modern art. He himself paints – quickly: 23 minutes is his record. (Anyone can be an artist.) He wants to help art students. I wish he would give his money to the rainforests. I should have introduced him to my friend, Franz, who in his *hôtel particulier* houses his collection of modern art. At dinner, Franz told us he's selling the house. The French government wishes to tax private art collections.

FRI 8 MARCH GREENPEACE, PAMELA AND PETA

Back from Paris. I have managed to see one or two friends, read, caught up on stuff and I've been busy, mostly to do with Climate Revolution. The most concentrated day was Friday, working with Greenpeace using the graphics we designed for 'Save the Arctic'. Meanwhile, there has been a competition for anyone from six to twenty-six, organised by the Girl Guides, to design an Arctic flag and we were here to judge it in my office/workroom – myself and two young women, very clever and articulate. We agreed on the winner, thirteen-year-old Sarah Batrisyia from Malaysia, and I had to phone her at home to tell her she had won. I felt quite emotional.

The winning flag and a time capsule containing millions of signatures (including Pamela Anderson, Andreas and me) protesting commercial exploitation of the Arctic, will be planted at the North Pole by a team of skiers on 7 April. Pamela had popped in to have her photo taken in our 'Save the Arctic' T-shirt. She came with her friend, Dan Mathews from PETA, who's so passionate about his work that he's done really outrageous stunts. When he was a kid, he was on the floor, winded in a fight, couldn't breathe, other kids looking down at him, laughing. Soon after, his dad took him fishing and he was looking down at a flounder, just hooked and on the deck, gasping for oxygen, looking up with its two funny eyes and people looking down, laughing.

He told us that PETA has just stopped the culling of baby seals in Russia. Pamela went to see Putin's lot and they won't import the pelts. She's full of relief. The fate of Paul Watson, founder of Sea Shepherd, which is committed to saving ocean wildlife worldwide, is another of Pamela's major concerns. Since skipping bail in Germany, where he was arrested for a confrontation with Costa Rica over shark finning, Paul is now confined to a Sea Shepherd ship that is unable to dock. Along with Julian Assange, he has been awarded an Original Nation passport by the Aboriginal people of Australia.

WEDS 13 – SAT 16 MARCH FERNANDO MONTAÑO

I woke on Wednesday with a head cold. It's awful. I felt as if two stones had been hammered into my temples; stayed in bed but dragged myself out on Thursday night for the Friends of the Earth fundraising dinner to launch their latest initiative to put the onus on suppliers to offer shoppers green choices. I hate these auction dinners but the high point, of course, is the people you're with, and that was all our important member friends of Climate Revolution, the first time so many of us had met. We all got on extremely well and there has been quite a bit of communication between us since.

By Saturday I was feeling well enough to read instead of just lying there in pain. So I re-read John Pilger's terrifying *The New Rulers of the World*. In the evening I went to the Café de Paris to the Latin UK Awards. My friend, Fernando Montaño, was Personality of the Year and I presented him with his award. I really enjoyed myself; such good-looking people, all dressed up. My speech went like this:

Fernando is a wonderful personality because he is the loveliest person, but he deserves the award because he is a ballerina and in presenting him I'd like to acknowledge the others – Tamara and Carlos, they're here – because traditional ballet is one of the high art forms of human achievement – along with Japanese Noh theatre and I think the temple dancing of South India – I long to see it. The training, the 'turning out' which makes possible the 'line' in three dimensions and which lends itself to a completed expression through dance. So many art forms come together in ballet. This is surely human evolution at its highest point.

Secondly, with the weakening of the US (the US may not look weak because it continues to boost its arms sales but it can no longer underwrite the destruction of the earth through war). It is so great to see the countries of Latin America take more control of their countries and face up to the US. *(Huge enthusiasm!)* In particular, I'd like to thank Ecuador for standing up to the US and protecting free speech in the person of Julian Assange.

TUES 19 MARCH DAVID BOWIE AT THE V&A

I started work on next season's Gold Label and in the evening went with Andreas to see the David Bowie exhibition at the V&A.

I don't know much about Bowie because at the time I was working with the Sex Pistols. It is possible he got his hairstyle from me as his then wife, Angie, used to come into our shop. He became famous very quickly. I first knew that because all at once people began to call after me in the street – David Bowie!

Bowie was a phenomenon: studying mime with Lindsay Kemp, terrific style, androgyny, each song a concept. I learnt about him tonight – it's a very good exhibition. I liked best his acting in *Elephant Man* and the suits for a man of perfect proportions with a 28-inch waist. At the dinner I sat between the photographer, Terry O'Neill, and Kansai Yamamoto, who designed many Bowie outfits. I enjoyed myself but great as Bowie is, I'm not so interested in popular culture.

WEDS 20 MARCH BRADLEY MANNING

On February 28th at a military hearing Bradley Manning admitted leaking the biggest cache of classified material in US history – State Department cables that documented back-door deals and war crimes – to WikiLeaks. He said he was disturbed by the seeming disregard by American troops for the lives of ordinary people, being 'obsessed with capturing and killing human targets on lists'; he was appalled by a combat video of a helicopter assault which killed eleven men including a Reuters photographer and his driver – 'the seeming delightful bloodlust the aerial weapons team happened to have … similar to a child torturing ants with a magnifying glass.'

It is worth noting that Bradley first approached the *New York Times* (who didn't return his call) and the *Washington Post* (who didn't take him seriously) with the Afghan and Iraq material. Then he turned to WikiLeaks. How brave that young soldier was for making those calls and then exposing the cover-ups of the war propaganda. He has been nominated for the Nobel Peace Prize. It's worth comparing Bradley's statements with what Prince Harry said, comparing killing people to playing video games. Harry said that he was 'good with his thumbs'.

THURS 21 MARCH PEACE SILK AND SIDDHARTHA

Andreas and I are at work everyday but we are not under pressure at the moment. We are working separately on the other collections and we have begun to choose the fabrics for the next Gold Label. I am clearing up bits and pieces and dealing with requests for all kinds of things that until now I didn't have time to look at. Cynthia is working hard on Climate Revolution, connecting relationships and discussing events. I think it is so important for other NGOs we wish to work with to always state their policy from the platform: 'What's good/bad for the planet is good/bad for the economy'. If we can get the public to see our main message which is staring them in the face we will win the Climate Revolution.

We just had a note from Samata Angel, from Red Carpet Green Dress, the fashion competition we collaborate on, telling us why the 'peace silk' they use is better for the environment. She says it allows the worms to live out their nature cycle. 'Normally silk worms are boiled to kill them and extract their silk (without them breaking the cocoon) as a single strand. With peace silk, it is only after they have shed their cocoon naturally that it is taken and used to make silk. This is why it is slightly 'broken' in appearance, unlike normal silk, as the cocoon has been broken when the worm emerged.'

I have been reading *Siddhartha* by Hermann Hesse, because Andreas, whose senses are so keen, praised the beauty and originality of the writing. He couldn't get over that someone could write like that, do what Hesse did: think it and find a way to say it; say so much in just over a hundred pages. The story moves along like the song of a river, repeating itself but always telling something new. The observations are tremendous. The Buddhist believes in the indestructibility of life and in reincarnation. He desires to escape from this cycle by losing his individuality in the universal life. Underlying this is the belief that the material world is an illusion – this probably accounts for the religious beliefs of half the people who ever lived.

I am not a Buddhist and don't believe in re-incarnation or the life of individuals after death – I have no interest in it. Also what doesn't appeal to me is that in acknowledging the unity of the world we therefore accept and love the good and the bad, the newborn baby and the murderer – for example a Buddhist once told me off for talking politics, telling me that the only thing you can change is yourself. I want to help make a better world.

WEDS 27 MARCH CELEBRATING WANGARI MAATHAI

Andreas and I went at 9.30 a.m. to an event at Kew Gardens to celebrate the life of Wangari Maathai. It was wonderful because we hadn't been to Kew for so long. The magnolia were still waiting for the spring because of the freak cold weather and we had coffee in the orangery where we saw many friends from Wangari's achievement, the Green Belt Movement. Speeches were by Wangari's daughter, Wanjira, Prince Charles and Shirin Ebadi, Nobel Laureate. High points were songs by the Revival House Choir and *Hummingbird*, a play performed by the children of Stoneygate College, Leicester. This was so well composed

Wangari Maathai

and conceived by the teachers – words, song, music, costumes. The chorus wore black tracksuits, and half of them were trees – green satin leaves sewn onto the front of the costume and green umbrellas; half were a forest fire with fiery ribbons sewn on and a bunch in the hand to shake. When the fire attacked the trees they put the umbrellas down and turned their backs to us and twisted their bodies into black shapes. The strong animals didn't know how to use their strength but the hummingbird brought water in her beak, 'Doing what I can'.

What really made it wonderful is the wonderful Wangari and her life. The best I can do is recommend a multi-award-winning film: *Taking Root* tells her dramatic story: her simple act of planting trees grew into a nationwide movement to safeguard the environment, protect human rights and defend democracy.

GOOD FRIDAY 29 MARCH BACH'S ST JOHN'S PASSION

Andreas had organised tickets at the Barbican for Bach's St John's Passion. I don't know when it was – say fifteen years ago – that I would not go to hear this work because I was anti-religious but now I treat the story of Christ as a myth whose purpose is moral regeneration. I was brought up in the Anglican religion and know the Bible well. Part of the satisfaction from the work is that the audience gets very involved in the story.

When I finally did go, I was carried away. I have been several times. The underlying rhythm hypnotises you, supports you, lifts you up with the harmonies and the shifting forms into the ether: you fly. It is glorious and tragic as well as exquisitely beautiful, tender and, above all, light as air: Pure Joy!

APRIL 2013

FRI 5 APRIL **MANET AT THE ROYAL ACADEMY**

Manet exhibition at the Royal Academy. Unbelievable! It was exclusively portraits. As I went round I became more and more astonished at the vitality of his work; life caught by strokes of paint. You can get something from a reproduction but you have to experience the physical painting. The economy was overwhelming: 'Truth is fiction where the fiction's true'. Monet told him that he did not need to spend so long being meticulous. Andreas told me to

Manet's portrait of his wife, Suzanne, at the piano.

always look at the frames. He's right, artists themselves knew they were as important as the painting. He also pointed out the hair: 'It's like sugar. He's the best painter of hair ever.' On *Madame Manet*, Andreas said: 'The blood in the skin. This image is filled with love. Have you ever seen a kinder person?'

SAT 13 APRIL THE ARREST OF AI WEIWEI

We have just heard that Leonard's transfer to a softer prison has been stopped by high authority (just one person on the panel) in the power hierarchy. Two days later an email came via Leonard's Defence Committee: 'Courage!'

Hampstead Theatre: *The Arrest of Ai Weiwei* by Howard Brenton. Ai's interrogators thought they had to deal with a murderer, as they always did murderers. But then they looked him up on the internet and got back to him with new accusations: he was rich, not a real artist, and a fraud. The interrogators studied the art world to build a case against him; they confronted him with Duchamp's urinal and with his own work, which they claimed insulted the Chinese state. Gradually Ai converted them until they finally got it: Ai's art was for them. The art itself was not important: important was what they thought of it. 'Yes!' shouted Ai.

I don't agree. With the enactment of this statement, the play identified the crisis in art which happened at the beginning of the twentieth century with the launch of the abstract art which smashed tradition. Abstract art denies the need for subject matter. By this you deny the value of the work in itself – because there is no way to begin to judge it – as representing reality, as an Imitation. As an art lover, you are cut off from reality and left to your own devising, meditating on your own. Cut off from each other of course we can't share in the work of art. We've all got a different idea. We can only come together by taking part in the same experience. This is culture.

Once you are cut off from tradition and the traditional view of art there is no need for skill, as Duchamp demonstrated with his urinal. This could have alerted people to the need for skill and sent artists

Ai Weiwei's *Remembering* – 9,000 backpacks in five different colours, composing the sentence 'For seven years she lived happily on this earth' – a quote from the mother of a young girl victim of the Sichuan earthquake.

back to work but they preferred the easy (but impossible) option, to repeat the shock: the shock can't happen twice and 'something different' is always a bore – especially when it has to be explained. Simply choosing things and presenting them in a gallery or space (conceptual art) is not enough. It is certainly not original.

When I say there is no progress in art I mean that, through the test of time, the new art fits in, makes its own space in the tradition, and yes, the new art makes the world a better place. Art is timeless and can never be obsolete. Ai thinks that past art is inadequate to express today's world. How does he know that?

I do accept that Ai's installation *Remembering* – 9,000 backpacks on the facade of a Munich art gallery in memory of dead children whose poorly constructed school buildings had collapsed in the Sichuan earthquake – succeeded with its sad message in exposing the Chinese cover-up. He had previously been beaten up for his activism. There is no doubt he is brave and sincere. In this case conceptual art worked, with its political subject matter, in communicating to our Best Self. And yes, he communicated his fanatical rejection of the past by filming himself as he smashed a precious (old) Chinese vase. No one could ever have made that vase or make it again but the man who produced it. It was perfect. This rejection of the past is the received theory of our age. [*At Ai's exhibition at the Royal Acedemy, the point made was that by breaking up traditional furniture and smashing the vase, we are made to appreciate them*].

The play closed with Ai the actor telling off the audience for not thinking. I agree, as they had approved throughout his theory on art. He said that freedom of speech is the most important thing in the world. I agree, especially if you have something to say, as he does.

SUN 14 APRIL MURRAY PERAHIA

Iris came for a week so Andreas and I spent time working with her and our other pattern cutters. I worked on the Red Carpet collection and got her opinions regarding fabrics and fit, which is so valuable. She has such an eye. It's important to know what she likes.

During the week I squeezed in a concert with Andreas at the Barbican by the great pianist Murray Perahia. By the end of the last piece – Chopin – I wish we could have heard it all again (especially because sometimes I don't settle down at the beginning). I would have if the concert had begun with Chopin – every note carries you with it.

THURS 18 APRIL GREENPEACE

John Sauven from Greenpeace came to talk to us about 'Save the Arctic' and about the rainforest. John explained how Greenpeace are funded by the public (they need donations) and their credibility rests on not accepting donations from governments or corporations. To save the Arctic they need, as well as public support, to lobby governments and corporations and hopefully to get support from the UN. If you look on their website you can see what would happen if oil spilled in the Arctic. It is so crazy that the description left me with an image of not a white Arctic but a black one.

John gave me a present – a piece of intense blue canvas from the sail of the *Rainbow Warrior II* – which is now a hospital ship in Bangladesh. We did cut a bit off the sail to get the colour copied – very special – for dyeing.

SAT 20 APRIL BAROCCI AND BALLET

Barocci exhibition at the National Gallery. He is not so well known to the frequenter of art galleries because his work is mostly in situ in Italian churches where he painted altarpieces. Marvellous facility, very special.

Then I met Andreas, my friend Giselle, my son Ben and his fiancée, Tomoka, at the English National Ballet, where Tamara (Rojo) has recently become director. It was the middle one of the three ballets that knocked us out! It had a story and ballet has to have one or it isn't complete (the exception is *Les Sylphides*, which blends for ever with an orchestration of Chopin's music).

What a tour de force was this ballet, *Le Jeune Homme et la Mort*. It had an existentialist feel but it projected right up to each moment as we watched. It was so original, we were in suspense. It was the creation of two geniuses: Jean Cocteau

Tamara Rojo and Nicolas Le Riche in ENO's *Le Jeune Homme et La Mort.*

(the idea and costumes, the stage effects) and Roland Petit (choreographer and husband of Zizi Jeanmaire, who made famous the role of The Girl). I'm so glad Giselle saw it, she is French and appreciates so well the great ideas of the French (some ideas can only be French, like, for example, Duchamp's urinal which summed up an age).

Andreas loved so much the yellow dress, I think he will copy it.

SUN 21 APRIL JUAN DIEGO FLOREZ

Andreas and I went to work – still choosing fabrics.

Evening. Lucky again: Andreas had got us concert tickets for the Peruvian tenor Juan Diego Florez and friends. Handsome, sweet, powerful, sexy, his voice and his persona expanded so that he controlled the whole space and everything in it.

FRI 26 APRIL BEE WISE

11 a.m.: went to demonstration to save the bees from neonicotinoid pesticides. The EU has put a ban on these substances for two years to monitor their harm. England has opted out saying the evidence against is not clear – they prefer to wait till it's too late. I accompanied Katharine Hamnett to hand in a petition of 700,000 names. Katharine said she was honoured to represent so many.

SAT 27 APRIL CAN FASHION CHANGE THE WORLD?

Vogue conference. I was on a panel of four with Livia Firth, Katharine Hamnett and photographer Dick Page. Subject: *Can fashion change the world?* Had I looked properly at the programme I wouldn't have gone as they gave us only 45 mintues between us and there wasn't time to say anything. How silly to propose such a momentous question and then ask you to give the solution in ten minutes each. There was no time for questions and for me it was a waste of time, though I think the other panellists got their main points across.

When I was unlocking my bike to come home a young teenage boy came to me and asked if we could have a photo and when would the Climate Revolution T-shirts be back in the shop. He was quite thrilled to meet me and said, 'Gosh, I think you're my most favourite person in the world'. Of all the thousands of people who have asked me for a photo this boy touched me with his youth and his sincerity. His appreciation I shall never forget, it will fortify me.

MON 29 APRIL BEN AND TOMOKA GET MARRIED

My son Ben married Tomoka. I am sure they will be happy. I was very pleased to see my first husband, Derek, with his wife, Jean, and family. A good man.

Tomoka and Ben at their wedding, Chelsea Town Hall.

TUES 30 APRIL SAM BRANSON AND LEONARD

Sam Branson came to talk to Cynthia and me. It is good to meet up with people who are doing stuff. Discuss mutual support, join the dots. I'm interested in what his dad is doing. I didn't know about Richard's big idea, The Elders, which includes Mandela. If we could get Mandela to reiterate the support he has previously spoken of for Leonard – the Mandela of the Indians – that would be ace. Mandela and Peltier were both targeted for the same reason. The ruling power wanted to suppress their claims for justice. We must hang on to the idea, like Siddhartha, so that we reach our aim as easily as a stone falling through water.

Later Lorna came and we spoke to Leonard on the phone – he's allowed to phone her. I worry about what to say to him, I can only tell him how he inspires us with his courage. It was lovely talking to him; he has a rich full voice.

MAY 2013

SAT 4 MAY THE MET'S PUNK EXHIBITION

4 p.m. plane for New York. Slept. Arrived evening. Hotel Carlyle (near the Metropolitan Museum of Art).

We kept changing our minds about going to New York for the Met's punk exhibiton (*Punk: Chaos to Couture*), because I'm not very interested in the punk past, though I love the clothes. But we finally decided 'yes' – because we wanted to be polite to the Met and express our thanks to them, and also to Anna Wintour. And an important purpose was to express support for Bradley Manning. Bradley is a danger to the Power Structure. Blowing the whistle on war crimes is not a crime but Bradley now faces life in prison for sharing a video with WikiLeaks of a US helicopter attack that killed eleven civilians and wounded two children in Baghdad.

SUN 5 MAY NEW YORK GALLERIES

Interviews: 11 a.m. at CNN, a four-minute piece with host Alina Cho. Then 1 p.m. with *Vanity Fair* back at the Carlyle.

Immediately after, I walked to the Met. The Chinese painting gallery was closed so I looked at the Japanese paintings. Chinese culture was a major influence on Japan from the introduction of Buddhism in 552AD. They mastered the Chinese technique of painting and for centuries you can't tell the difference, the paintings are as good. I was carried away: there's just you, a white heron and the grey calligraphic stem of a lotus pod.

Went for an hour to the hotel bar with Andreas. He is fascinated by the taste in dress of rich old American gentlemen, eccentric and super-chic. My friend Gene from Brooklyn, now living in Japan and fashion editor of *Vogue Nippon* and *Korean Vogue* – though not so old – has the same taste. Andreas had been to the flea market (near the Natural History Museum) with our friend Sabina, originally from Vienna (she was a pupil of mine in the same class as Andreas), now a stylist in New York. He told me of the old ladies (probably my age) taking tea at the market who all look like Raine Spencer – hair and make-up. You don't find them except in America. Eccentric. Why? Could be because of American isolation.

Andreas had also been to the Frick Collection. Frick was a coal baron who visited Europe around 1900 and was inspired by the London Wallace Collection to form an art collection – not only paintings but furniture etc. He built a mansion on Fifth Avenue to house it – now open to the public. Andreas says that experiencing art in someone's house is different, walking on carpets. The art is tremendous. Frick achieved his aim of buying the best. His mansion is the only one standing on Fifth Avenue, other people demolished theirs and built giant blocks of expensive apartments – families who had once made their money from industry, turned to real estate.

With Andreas and Lily Cole at the Met Ball for the opening of their *Chaos to Couture* exhibition. I wore a photo of Bradley Manning on my dress.

MON 6 MAY THE MET BALL

I met my friend Terry Doctor but only for an hour. We got coffee to take away and sat on a wall in the street. He knows everything about fashion and politics. He and his wife Louise were part of the fashion crowd when fashion was at the King's Rd in the 1960s. Then I walked to the Met for an interview at the punk exhibition. The clothes inspired by punk didn't work; exceptions were Gianni Versace and Hussein Chalayan.

Then, though the museum was closed, Andreas and I were allowed to look at the *Impressionism, Fashion and Modernity* exhibition, which included one or two sensational Worth gowns. Worth is the first creator of fashion – others had trimmed and decorated existing shapes which changed slowly over time. By dynamic cutting, Worth changed the silhouettes and movement of gowns according to their rapport with the body. We also saw a so-great painting by Manet of Berthe Morisot in a white dress, getting up from a sofa and saying something: totally engaging. Its originality had shocked at the time; 'she's not sitting, not standing', they scorned.

Evening at the Met ball. It was glamorous because of all the actors and models who were there. Andreas found Linda Evangelista, who he adores. She gave us a lot when she did the shows.

And what about Bradley? Mostly people didn't recognise the photo on my dress. When I said the name then one or two knew him; when I said WikiLeaks they all did. The reaction was guilt that they didn't know already but glad to know when I explained; all these people know American justice is a travesty and they were all sympathetic to Bradley. The people who did recognise him were democrats who still believed in Obama even though he is personally responsible for deciding Bradley's trial is in secret court.

TUES 7 MAY BILL MCKIBBEN

Bill McKibben came to see me at the hotel. He wrote the article in *Rolling Stones* magazine, 'Do the Math' naming the fossil fuel industry as Enemy Number 1. I had invited my friend Irina, and Bill arrived with JB, a lady I shan't say anything about until the day I tell you what she and the NGOs she works with have been doing. One of the things she said which stayed in my mind was that to continue campaigning for justice and to hang on to your initial outrage and live with it is (morally) an act of courage.

Because of the urgent need to hold back climate change we all feel the need of mass protest. On his laptop, Bill showed me photos of protest events where 350.org has linked with people in every country in the world except North Korea to stage protests and to maintain contact. It's jaw-dropping what can one man do. Bill's wife told him he's been in jail for more days than at home this year.

Irina is so pretty – the more serious she looks, the more pretty she looks. Bill liked her, especially as she came from Lake Baikal, the largest freshwater lake in the world, and one of his favourite places on earth. She is Inuit, an author, a model and an activist. Her focus is on precious water and she told us of the environmental destruction to the Lake Baikal area, enforced by Putin, who has put his own men into the local government. She is too scared to protest even from New York because she has family there.

Later, I had three hours to spare, so went to the Met and looked at Chinese vases and Buddhist sculptures. You feel affection for the Met because everything about humans that we know of is housed in one building. In London our vast buildings with their enormous collections specialise. With the Met you feel that if you came once a week for a year you would know everything in it, then you could keep going back and know it all better. And in London we don't have a collection of Chinese painting. Their bookshop is also the best art bookshop in the world.

WEDS 8 MAY THE CENTURY CLUB

Morning – arrived home from New York. Evening to the Century Club for a panel discussion, Q&A and a video link to Julian

Assange. The focus of the event was support for Bradley Manning. Human rights campaigner, Peter Tatchell, spoke. As you know, Peter is active in gay rights and gays are building support for Brad. Also on the panel was journalist Andy Worthington, author of *The Guantanamo Files*. I was particularly interested that he helped get 25,000 people on to the streets of Lewisham to protest the closure of the local hospital as I'm interested in protesting the evictions of people from their homes in Clapham, where I live, so the council (Lambeth) can sell the houses as part of their economic squeeze (short-term madness, storing up trouble for the future).

THURS 9 MAY TAI MISSONI

Tai Missoni died. A big romance, a lovely family, a good business with knits loved throughout the world. They lost their son, Vittorio, in January. Rosita, you have all always been so nice. Bless you all.

TUES 14 MAY NUCLEAR ENERGY AND LEDERHOSEN

Olivier from the French magazine *Purple* popped in for half an hour to interview me. He is passionately against nuclear energy. I don't know what to think – it is supposed to be the cleanest in comparison to fossil fuels; the greatest killer is carbon but there is a great body of anecdotal evidence for death from nuclear. The hope lies in solar and fusion. Dams cause untold destruction, which isn't great; we need efficient national grids.

Olivier left for New York with a travel bag not much bigger than a washbag. He doesn't need clothes, just underwear, because he's always in black leather – like Joe Rush. When Joe washes his shirt he's bare-chested under his leather jacket. And me – in this usually cold and changing weather chaos I wear every day my lederhosen.

Henri Rousseau – *Surprised!* at the National Gallery. You have to see it in real life..

A view of my back garden. Andreas said, 'I want to show you, it's the same as Rousseau.' It was the same – the thriving manifold abundance.

WEDS 15 MAY RANKIN AND ANDY GOTTS

Photo by Rankin for *Marie Claire* interview. This is for a green issue so that's why I agreed. I don't do interviews on just fashion.

Rankin's studio is very busy – of course it's the headquarters of his fashion magazine *Hunger* (he also set up *Dazed and Confused* with Jefferson Hack). Lovely breakfast, then lovely lunch; lots – help yourself. I was worried it would get wasted. No, it's never wasted, they cook for fifty people each day.

Then on for another photo, by Andy Gotts (same outfit means I only have to prepare once). Andy's doing a book on fashion people and pop stars with the proceeds going to Elton John's charity. In the quiet of a suite in the St James Hotel there is just him; it's comfortable, no fuss and he uses the same lighting. Hence his popularity: 'People don't like having their photos taken, I make it simple.' It was a pleasure to have him take my photo. He offered his service to me for any charity work.

I had time to walk over to the National Gallery for an hour. I had a cup of tea then looked at Henri Rousseau. You have to see Rousseau in real life (and don't forget to look at the frame). There is nowhere a more thriving representation of nature. I bought a good little book on him. Then got the bus home.

THURS 16 MAY JAMES HANSEN AT THE LSE

I went to LSE in the early evening to hear James Hansen, the most respected scientist in the world. He told his story. He was the fifth of seven children of itinerant farmers – good business in the 1950s – before going to university and then to NASA.

By applying his studies of Venus to earth he discovered the dangerous rate of global warming in relation to CO_2 emissions. In the 1970s he spoke out and was attacked by the scientific and political authorities. He wasn't good at dealing with this so he stepped back from debate and continued his work. But when Sophie, his grandchild, was born he stepped back into the public arena: he said, one day when the world was destroyed his grandchildren would ask, 'Why didn't grandfather try to do something?'

He showed photos of the monarch butterfly which migrates from one mountain top in Mexico to his home in California, where they flock to the milkweed bushes his family plants for them; he made the point that if earth gets hotter they will have to plant higher up his home mountain until they reach the top.

James's idea is to price carbon. It's a very simple idea: fossil fuel companies would pay a pollution tax at source before fuel enters the market. This tax would be passed on to the customer, who would realise the effect, e.g. when a gallon of petrol cost $1 more. However, all the tax collected would be paid direct to the citizen. Each US citizen would receive $3,000 per annum paid into their bank account in monthly instalments; children would receive $1,500 so a family with two kids would receive

James Hansen being handcuffed.

£9,000. People who had no car (or a green car) would make a profit. The tax would increase each year. This scheme would put money into circulation and stimulate the green economy. Governments are interested. James was on his way to testify to the EU. He had another idea: to prosecute the US government.

One of the questions James was asked was, 'How do we get more people engaged in activism?' He didn't know, he said: 'Bill McKibben got 35,000 people on the streets recently in Washington to protest the pipeline from the tar sands. It wasn't enough.' James was among the people arrested.

WEDS 22 MAY GERGIEV AT THE BARBICAN

Concert at the Barbican to mark Gergiev's 60th birthday. It blew me away as usual. Gergiev is artistic director of the St Petersburg Mariinsky Theatre, home of the legendary Kirov ballet. Among his worldwide activities he is Principal Conductor of the London Symphony Orchestra (home, the Barbican). Russia has already rewarded him with a new concert hall and now a new Mariinsky opera house. I hear he is a pal of Putin – he must be – and although I have very much enjoyed meeting him once or twice I haven't broached the topic of politics; but I would like to – so I will if I get the chance. Barbican concert tickets start at £10. Great value, great acoustics, no tricks – just people power and centuries of skill.

FRI 24 MAY A TULIP NAMED FOR ME

A special treat to mark the honour of having a tulip named after me: tea at the Dutch Embassy. I was asked to invite thirty guests and Tizer was clever – why didn't I invite our couture customers, those who were around? And our pattern cutters and sewers.

The ambassador's speech touched me. She felt that I appreciated the importance to culture of Dutch painting and spoke of this often and that my fight for the environment, along with true human values is shared by the best that is Dutch. Ligthart Bloembollen, the man who invented my tulip, presented me with a bunch. It takes twenty-five years to create a new one. The tulips are a fiery, burnt orange with yellow lights inside and purple lights outside; their petals are framed with a tough little fringe. I love them.

I spoke on the importance of culture. If people only bought beautiful things that would be Climate Revolution. I enjoyed meeting and being with everyone, and pianist Nelly Akopian-Tamarina – who looked so chic in our dress of black Cluny lace framed with a navy Cluny lace which also bordered its diagonal cut – played a little piece of Chopin. Yes, I am a fan of seventeenth-century Dutch painting. There is no progress in art and this is the

The Vivienne Westwood tulip, which blooms around my birthday in April.

place to start if you wish to love art. Its small format and original and intimate subject matter is intended to hang in houses with smaller rooms. Starting from here you can go forward and back in time to know painting but if you start at, say, the Impressionists, you might go on in time, to Picasso, but after that there are only birthday cards. You might get stuck there and never discover the past.

SAT 25 – SUN 26 MAY **TO MEGAN'S IN KENT**

We drove to the country with our friend Robert. He has a workshop in the Kent Weald, which he thinks is the most luscious country landscape in Britain. He used to be a tree surgeon and can build anything – furniture, wood sculpture and sets for our catwalk shows: he built a forest on the third floor in Harrods. Robert told us we could stay with Megan who rents a lodge in the deer park of an estate belonging to a family descended from the Nevills (it must be the family who fought in the War of the Roses). We travelled down with Rema, who lives in Hastings. I know her father, Craig. There was a period when my children were very young that I did not work but lived on Malcolm's student grant and my precious family allowance. I was studying to go to university but my plans changed when I borrowed £100 from my mother and Malcolm and opened *Let it Rock* in the back half of a shop which is now *World's End*. For a few years, our diet was macrobiotic and I bought brown rice etc from Craig's shop in the Portobello Road – there were very few wholefood shops then. Craig headed the Soil Association for many years.

May is the crown of the year and because nature is late this year we were in perfect time: everything in leaf and in blossom, bursting, steaming and swaying into the big blue sky. Highlights: a visit to the cottage of the mothman, whose private collection of moths is an important one. He is a third generation of moth specialists and instead of collecting them he traps moths, records them and sets them free. He was an important spy during World War II. He is descended from Nelson.

Megan happens to be a friend of Julian Assange and among her guests for dinner were some of the activists for Bradley whom I'd met, including Emma from Century Club and her young daughter, who live nearby. She had made a delicious Thai curry – I had it again at breakfast.

Sunday: late morning visit to the house of the Nevills' estate and its gorgeous garden: a stunning old cedar and a giant oak standing squat on a mound heaving up its too many arms like a basket till its fingers scratched the sky. And the lawn leading down to a view of May in all its green glory, rolling in a ring of hills, while Andreas and I entered the warmth of grass paths walled by bushes of every kind, many in flower, especially the fiery azaleas.

JUNE 2013

SAT 1 JUNE BRADLEY MANNING DEMONSTRATION

I went to the Bradley Manning demonstration. You remember our plan to ask NGOs to go on each other's demonstrations because everything is connected under the banner of Climate Revolution. Well, we phoned around and emailed but I didn't see anyone I knew from among the NGOs. Our company did very well – there were thirty-four of us – but there were only 300–400 people altogether. I was shocked. I thought there would be at least a couple of thousand.

It was a fantastic event with great speakers and singers. Wonderful people. We really care about Bradley Manning and we care about the poor people who were shot down by soldiers who treat killing people as a game. The most important thing we learnt is the case the prosecution intend to push for: Bradley has admitted leaking information on war crimes; he will not be allowed to submit his motives or claim that no one has been harmed or bring witnesses to prove it. People say the court will give him twenty years. But the prosecution wants more than that; they say if a whistle-blower gives information to any media outlet and the outlet publishes then that information is in the public domain and the public includes terrorists, therefore the whistle-blower has helped the enemy. This is a capital offence and they will ask for life imprisonment without parole.

After the demonstration some of us went to a café where we discussed reasons why we in the privileged part of the world don't get out on the streets like we used to. Some cite the anti-Iraq demonstration when two million people (official figure one million) massed in Hyde Park – but the British government ignored them and declared war on Iraq straightaway, so now people think demonstrations aren't effective. For sure it matters how directly you are affected, for example during the Vietnam War, which led to the hippie movement. There was conscription in the US; it could be you or your son that got killed. I heard that today there is only one American politician who has a soldier son.

SAT 15 JUNE YOKO ONO'S MELTDOWN

I did an interview with Julian Assange as part of Yoko Ono's Meltdown Festival at the Southbank. I asked him: The petitions people sign on the internet (Avaaz, etc.), how important are they? It's easy for people to click on a button but how committed are they? These petitions can be effective. How important are they in comparison to public demonstrations?

I asked Julian to speak from his own experience and he said that when *Time* magazine conducted a readers' poll for 'Person of the Year 2010', he won twice as many votes as the person who came second. But *Time* rejected the vote and decided on one of the other candidates as winner. In their 'Person of the Year' poll in 2012 the *Guardian* heavily promoted the case of Malala Yousafzai, the girl who was shot by the Taliban, but Bradley Manning won overwhelmingly. The *Guardian* published the result discreetly. The point Julian was making is that there is mass support for people and for policies which the official media ignores and that social media is a more accurate consensus – 'Body Politic', he calls it – of opinion. Due to WikiLeaks and other online outlets, people can now see the difference between the official media and the truth of what really happens.

This new Body Politic already gives power to the people (perhaps it gave power to the witnesses who refused to be intimidated by prosecutors of Bradley Manning) and it must affect our rulers. The necessary thing is to work out a structure for this new Body Politic (a cabinet of respected people we could vote for, a new government that could be truly democratic). The internet offers us a new franchise, a true body politic. So public demonstrations are a driver and a back-up of people's real opinion on the internet. It is the aim of Climate Revolution to build that public assembly.

Julian next made me aware of a tremendously important fact. My way to explain it is: when President Eisenhower warned politicians to beware the 'military-industrial complex' he saw that the economy was being driven by the vast profits which tied these two interests so intricately together. However, the politicians backed it completely. The resulting 'political–military-industrial' complex became so enmeshed that no-one could have separated it out. It has a life of its own and it is now growing like a cancer: more tax is being allocated to it and away from social needs (health, education, etc.).

Now we come to the importance of the whistle-blower Edward Snowden. We heard about his leaks this week and this information is probably the most important that has ever been leaked – because it affects everybody. **It makes clear that to our rulers the public is the enemy.** The privacy of all people has now been invaded. This is bad for society; people will self-censor and be scared to speak freely, express themselves or criticise in case they are discriminated against.

What about Orwell's *1984* – 'Big Brother is watching you'? That book is about power for the sake of power. Is this the logic of our rulers? Is this our world?

 SUN 23 JUNE OUR MAN SHOW IN MILAN

I carry a scrap of paper around in my purse. It is my advance diary for the month – just a list of appointments and events. Then every two or three weeks I refer back to it, and pull out the main events for this diary. Now I report less on a daily basis and concentrate more on the big issues and ideas – tell you what I'm thinking. Regarding my daily life and work you know how it goes and how we are constantly building a collection. On Thursday the 20th we shot our publicity campaign with photographer Jack Pearson and on Sunday the 23rd we did our MAN catwalk show in Milan.

Our MAN show was inspired by India and Bradley Manning. I don't have direct experience of India. I have only my romantic impressions. So our inspiration came from museums and photos: Hindu gods and dancing and colour and flowers and spices and tigers and the jungle and the Ganges; temples and saris worn by the most elegant women, beauty and grace.

We knew we had to have colour but we began with whites – white that shines in the sun and white that looks dusty; cream and black

Our Bradley Manning TRUTH T-shirt – part of the MAN Spring/Summer 2014 collection that we launched in Milan.

with texture and pattern and mixed with indigo. Then checks and prints, then some colour and colour degrade. I think the overall colour effect belongs in the light of the sun. A few motifs from Persia or Morocco crept in. There was a feeling of being in an oriental garden.

Does sunshine disguise poverty to the English outsider? In a recent essay Noam Chomsky summed up what's happening in the world: the rich are racing as fast as they can to destroy the world, the poor are fighting to stop them. India is the most extreme example of this. The government is selling the country's mineral rights to corporations and consortiums (these huge profits by the corporations can pay for corruption). When the land is ruined the people have nowhere to go. I have been reading Arundhati Roy's book, about how Maoist organisations fight the evictions – and when people have nowhere to go except the forest, or squat on the pavements of cities, they are considered Maoists. The police are allowed to kill anyone if they call them a Marxist. The government is purposely creating war. Why? Because they want the people off the land. Why? Because most of the minerals the government is selling are still in the ground.

Why is Bradley Manning featured in a collection about India (no turbans but military berets)? Well, I always hijack my collections to talk politics and Bradley is there because everything is connected. The depredation in India is caused by the global political financial war machine (political-military-industrial complex). Bradley stood in the path of this great juggernaut. He told the truth by exposing war crimes and releasing documents which revealed that the purpose of our wars is total plunder.

SUN 30 JUNE ST-PAUL-DE-VENCE

I have had several speaking engagements (fees to Cool Earth) focused on Climate Revolution – one of them in Cannes, where we met Brandon, Pamela's son, who was working on the city's Lions Festival). Prior to that, Andreas and I stayed two days with his aunt

Miro wall fountain – Fondation Maeght.

and uncle, Cristel and Otmar, who have a house on the neighbouring hillside leading up from Nice to St-Paul-de-Vence. They are a really glamorous couple and I so much enjoy their company.

St-Paul is famous because so many artists stayed there, like Matisse. We visited the Fondation Maeght – modern art. Half the garden sculpture was by Miro, who bores me (one wall fountain was good). I liked a painting by Braque. I find cubism uninteresting and I had never looked at him but this painting was less formulaic and quite beautiful. Braque had also contributed a stained-glass window to the restrained decor of a tiny chapel. The wooden crucifixion was donated by Balenciaga. I have never experienced something so complete – austere, sublime, it made the soul quiet. St-Paul itself is full of derivative art reproductions for tourists and the other shops all sell the same stuff, same clothes, same gew-gaws as every place on earth.

JULY 2013

THURS 4 JULY AT THE DOODLE BAR

A Climate Revolution event: we invited colleagues from work and friends for drinks and a film at the Doodle Bar, across the road from our studio in Battersea. The film was Bill McKibben's *Do the Math*, which he had sent to us; it illustrates the content of the article he wrote for *Rolling Stone* about big oil and the fossil fuel industry. It was the best article this year and got far more hits on the internet than Justin Bieber, who was on the cover. We enjoyed ourselves (free drinks) with discussions and suggestions chalked up on Doodle Bar's big blackboard.

SAT 6 JULY JULIAN'S BIRTHDAY PARTY

I went to Julian Assange's birthday party at the Ecuadorian Embassy. He was wearing army camouflage; I was wearing my 'I am Julian Assange' T-shirt. I met some great people, the lady ambassadors from Ecuador and Argentina, and a beautiful girl called Angela, wife of the German artist Daniel Richter. She has written and produced a play on Julian – and just by supporting him she has received hate and threats from feminists, especially Austrian ones. These complacent wrong-headed Furies! My friend Gary used to call such women 'Cunt Fu'.

SAT 13 – TUES 16 JULY WORKING ON GOLD LABEL

Iris came for a week and we really concentrated on the Gold Label collection, working with her on toiles and fittings. Then we had to fill in the charts while our other pattern cutters finished the toiles. To finish the charts means we have to choose the fabric for every design that exists as a toile. Many years ago when I worked on my own with a smaller collection this was not a problem; I designed together with the fabric as I went along. Now, the rush is to develop all the toiles and then choose the fabrics, and if the fabric has arrived we do a prototype. I consider right use of fabric to be the hardest thing – often you're working in the air with just a scrap of fabric. Andreas needs the fabric to hold it and see how it behaves; hard though it is, he is a wizard.

On Tuesday we finished; we had worked Saturday, Sunday and Monday. Sandra took the charts and information to Italy so they could finish the sample collection. We had already sent the toiles and patterns. That was such a relief and for the moment we can take it easy; we have time to work on grand dresses and putting outfits together, styling, telling the story of the collection.

I am doing prints and embroidery designs and I have to finish the knitwear. I am waiting for a few more tests of different stitches – textures and colour combinations from Italy – then I can finish it quickly. I find graphic design easy and therapeutic because it's so intensely absorbing. I keep it in my head at night in bed and don't want to go to sleep. Also, knitwear is something you build from two

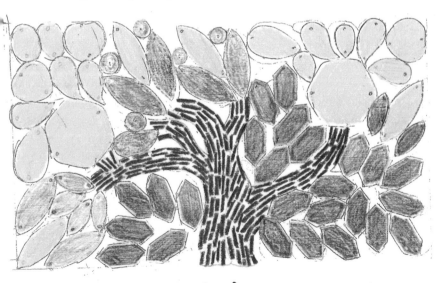

Embroidery design made from plaques cut from re-cycled reflective sunglasses + bugle beads 11½×20

basic stitches – it's binary like a computer – you pass the loop either to the front or the back, you can also knit two loops together or increase by making two loops on one stitch. That's it! The stitches replicate lace or tweed, plain or jacquard, and in the process resolve the 3D-shape of the garment. I feel guilty for having it so easy.

MON 15 JULY ALEXANDRA SHULMAN AND MATTHEW ARNOLD

Andreas and I went to Bryan Adams's for dinner. Bryan is a friend of Alexandra Shulman and as I have never really spent time with her he thinks I should know her better; she came with her partner, David. Bryan's mother, Jane, was over to see him. She was born in Devon, married a Canadian. She loves driving around Vancouver where she sketches and at age eighty she learnt to fly. A lively mind and exuberant love of life, wonderful company.

Alexandra didn't agree with some of my ideas but because she is intelligent and quite open maybe I can half convince her that pop culture gets us nowhere and that if we had true culture we would have different values and we would not have climate change. But she did not accept my point that if we had evolved according to our human potential for true culture we would have been able to eliminate war. That, she could not take; we would never eliminate the 'territorial imperative' meaning we cannot rid ourselves of the instinct to fight for and defend territory. If you read the chapter on Rwanda in Jared Diamond's book *Collapse*, you would be forced to concede her point but people do have the potential for kindness, altruism and self-sacrifice – even some animals do. There was something else involving a rather more personal situation we did not agree upon and when we kissed goodnight Alexandra said, 'We'll have to agree to differ.' I said, 'No, we won't.'

Now we have to go to the thing I've been dying to tell you from the beginning. But it's so important I didn't want to present it cold. I had to warm you up a bit first with something a bit more chit-chat. I have been re-reading Matthew Arnold's *Culture and Anarchy* (1869) and what I am about to tell you is the wisest thing I have ever heard and the greatest advice this diary can pass on. It is a star to live your life by: it is Arnold's concept of the Best Self. This and the concept of Sweetness and Light are ideas I have carried with me since my first reading a good twenty years ago. The concept of sweetness and light (originally put forward in *The Battle of the Books* by Jonathan Swift) prepares the way for understanding the Best Self. These two passions are complements, the dynamics of the Best Self. Sweetness is empathy, our heart: 'all the love of our neighbour, the impulses towards action, help, and beneficence, the desire for removing human error, clearing human confusion, and diminishing human misery, the novel aspiration to leave the world better and happier than we found it – motives eminently such as are called social.' Light is the scientific passion, our mind – 'a desire after the things of the mind simply for their own sakes and for the pleasure of seeing them as they are.'

We all know our Best Self, especially when we compare it to our ordinary self. Our ordinary self does what it likes: feeds on desire and wants immediate gratification, sucking up what it can, childish; it loves to act, often with passion but without much thought; it wants material success, is envious and gets its adrenalin through gossip, causing trouble and the 'culprit' is punished. The cleverest thing to say about the Best Self is that you know it – it's when you're kind and brave and stand up for things.

Arnold elaborates on the passions of the Best Self. Sweetness, the ancient Greeks had it: 'Greece did not err in having the idea of beauty, harmony, and complete human perfection, so present and paramount. It is impossible to have this idea too present and paramount; only, the moral fibre must be braced too.' The moral fibre is Light – that 'desire for the things of the mind for their own sakes and for the pleasure of seeing things as they are'. Not simply as we would like them to be. This is intellectual bravery.

How do we cultivate our Best Self? I give you my own example. As a child I needed information. Although I read it was not until I was eleven and went to grammar school that I discovered literature. Aged eighteen or nineteen, my friend Susan, who I had met at teacher training college, introduced me to theatre. In my late-twenties I started to understand politics, the hippies politicised us, there were 'underground' bookshops. Malcolm introduced me to modern art but no light went on. Then in my late-30s I met Gary Ness. He directed my reading – Bertrand Russell, Huxley, Proust – and introduced me to art and music. I would not be the same person if I had not met Gary, he sparked off my vision of the world. My husband Andreas has an original view, no-one could tell

A self-portrait by my friend Gary Ness.

you what he tells, he seems to see the soul of things. When I was young I absorbed pop culture, which is fine. Teenagers have a great time running around, but it can't last. You need to inform yourself, find what you're looking for. I am self-educated but until those introductions I didn't know where to find it. When the lights switch on and you begin to see, you have to continue. Your authority is your Best Self: it's a moral choice, an attempt to understand the world and be part of the great human drama.

Arnold's talk of the pursuit of our perfection refers to each individual's unique potential for fulfilment, and to our evolution, our ability to become more human, more civilised through culture. Leading up to and throughout the twentieth century the main ethos has been the cultivation of the ordinary self – doing as we like! This ethos is now global. We have been arrested in our development. This is why politicians cannot progress, they're stuck in a trap, glued to the rotten old financial system (Rot$). Progress is measured by consumption. This is why I say we're dangerously short of culture.

If our ethic was that of the Best Self we would have different values, we would not have climate change. It's not that people don't go to art galleries etc. and engage with our great cultural tradition. They do, but this passion is not aspirational for the public at large; it is not supported, not shared by everyone; they have been trained up as consumers. We do not engage with 'the best that has ever been thought or said or shown'. Nevertheless the art lover is a freedom fighter for a better world. Without judges there is no art.

FRI 19 JULY RÉNEE FLEMING'S CHIC

Renée Fleming invited Andreas and me to the Royal Opera House where she was starring in a concert presentation of Richard Strauss's *Capriccio*. We had done her dress and it was the coolest look ever – beyond elegant – and she is one of those few people who really knows how to wear clothes: She uses the dress to express herself emotionally and aesthetically: this is the true meaning of the word, 'chic' – it means what you're wearing has your signature.

Our dress for Renée Fleming.

The opera was unimaginable – meaning I am still astonished that such a thing could exist. How did it happen? Because a genius did it. There was no plot, just an argument about which was more important to an opera, the words or the music. Renée, the heroine, had two lovers – one who wrote the words, and the other the music. There were other arguments, all personified by the role of each singer: bel canto v. plain speaking, elaborate stage effect v. the bare minimum, modernity v. tradition. Andreas marvelled that Renée could remember all these words and in a foreign language, all the shifts and subtleties of argument. No plot, much passion. We were enthralled – for two hours and twenty minutes with no interval. Everything fitted together. It was so delightfully hyperbolic. The music was out of this world.

At the end Renée didn't choose either of the lovers: to choose was too banal. What would she now do?

SAT 20 – TUES 23 JULY LIBERTY

Andreas left home on Saturday for the Tyrol – at 5 a.m. I didn't go back to sleep. I stayed at home because I want to deal with a few outstanding things. Some meetings, some writing. I tried to write; I stayed confused and tired all the hot weekend.

I went to see Shami Chakrabarti. I haven't seen her for ages and I was so excited and so looking forward to it. It was lovely talking to her and I feel affected by having seen her and happy just thinking about her now. I am a trustee of Liberty and I wanted to know its position with Julian Assange. Liberty has to fight within the law (though they can challenge laws). For example, Sweden is legally able to ask for extradition even though this is unprecedented for an alleged offence that even if it were proven would not carry a jail sentence. If Sweden were then to send Julian to America this would break international law – you can't ask for extradition for one reason and then change the goalposts and extradite him for another reason (whistle blowing). And Britain would have to agree. I wouldn't trust them – once they've got you they do what they want.

Liberty cannot acknowledge this danger because if it happened it would contravene international law. If America requested extradition then Liberty would oppose it on the grounds of freedom of speech. Liberty did support Julian's lawyer at his appeal before the European Court. They too were of the opinion that the Swedish prosecutor who signed the European arrest warrant for Julian was not 'judicial authority' entrusted to issue such warrants.

Monday night was a full moon. Now I realise why I have been so sluggish. So on Tuesday I was all fit and active again. I'm at home a bit this week doing my writing for the diary and continuing the embroidery designs.

THURS 25 JULY OUR LIBRARY

Went to visit my neighbour Julian Hall. He's part of a housing co-operative and Lambeth Council want to evict the members and sell their houses. Climate Revolution is about promoting a green economy, it's about short-term policies storing up trouble and cost for the future, in this case breaking up communities and adding to the queue for social housing. I wrote to Lambeth Council.

We have started a library on the window ledge in reception. The fiction includes *Brave New World* and *1984*, two socio-political satires. I have written introductions for them. There are other books there which are just stories. I love these stories because it is like carrying another person's life along with your own, adding to your experience of the world; it could have been you. I included one or two such books, like *The Catcher in the Rye*, but also a humble story by Alison Uttley, *The Country Child*. It has no plot. It is just the experience of a child living on a remote farm in the Pennines in the mid-nineteenth century, one or two generations before Alison Uttley but from the same area and, as it happens, where I come from. I also put it in the library because of the illustrations by C. F.

Farm house amongst the hills of North Derbyshire, where I was born. Illustration by C. F. Tunnicliffe.

Tunnicliffe; today the illustrations in children's books are an insult to the intelligence of a child, trying to keep them infantile.

I remember as a child of eight my dear mother coming home on a Friday from her work at the mill – she made herself ill with asthma worrying about us having to stay with our neighbour until she came home. This was when the aspirations of mothers were to stay at home and look after the family; with her wage she brought us a cake, sometimes a present. I always had a ginger biscuit and one day she brought me a children's book by Alison Uttley – one of her series on Little Grey Rabbit; it must be the most treasured gift I ever received.

I want to finish with a chorus about Alysoun. In the time of Chaucer the name was popular – like Sharon or Tracey are today – and it signified a sweet nubile girl (hot!). Read it fast to get the rhythm – it was sung.

> An hendy hap ichabbe yhent,
> Ichot from hevene it is me sent— 10
> From alle wymmen mi love is lent,
> And lyht on Alysoun.

9. hendy hap, handy happening. **ichabbe yhent,** I have received. **10. Ichot,** I wot, I know. **11. lent,** gone away. **12. lyht,** lit /ich pronounce like German.

AUGUST 2013

MON 5 AUG AMERICA LAND OF THE FREE

I and my friend Frank, who lives in San Francisco, communicate by letter. The stamps on the one he just sent read: *America Land of the Free, God's Country*! Tell that to Leonard Peltier, having spent coming up to forty years in jail, framed and convicted in a travesty of courtroom justice for a crime he didn't do, set up because he was a member of the American Indian Movement (AIM), which was targeted by the US government in its offensive to wipe out the rights of Native Americans and continue the process of centuries of abuse.

It is a bitter irony that America is still able to get away with this propaganda, not only at home but abroad, at the same time as promoting the propaganda of an invincible empire that will not tolerate resistance. In the 1980s, when the countries of Central America tried to rid themselves of American domination, America responded with slaughter and barbarism, creating societies 'affected by terror and panic ... collective intimidation and generalised fear ... and the frequent appearance of tortured bodies' (Noam Chomsky, *Hegemony or Survival*). America wanted them to see the tortured bodies.

This is how the Roman Empire behaved. It wanted people to know it had no mercy and that its cruelty was inhuman; whereas willing subjugation brought the benefits of the Pax Romana. America wants the world to know that its war machine is more than all other weapons put together. How dare you oppose it? We'll just take what we want and we will give you in exchange – the American Dream.

MON 12 AUG THE NEW WEBSITE

So what have I been doing in August?

Lots of our people are away and the factories in Italy are closed but Andreas and I have been going to work making sure everything is sorted out so that our next Gold Label collection can go straight ahead at the end of the month when everybody's back to work. We have edited the shoe collection, worked out how to do the embroidered garments, selected fabrics for the couture evening dresses. I have supervised the Red Carpet collection and next season's Red Label collection.

I wrote the new and final Charter for the new Climate Revolution website (replacing *Active Resistance*). I think it will be the final one because I've reduced it to its essentials. I'm really pleased with it because it is also a working manual e.g. my son Ben wanted to write a piece for the site on the plight of elephants. I said, you can talk about elephants if you explain how the danger they're in is linked to the fact that everything is connected, because 'Everything is connected' is a basic tenet of Climate Revolution. That's what he's going to do.

I also wrote an introduction, for our library, on Steinbeck's *The Grapes of Wrath*. I read the book all in one go – it's really best to read fiction like that. I gave myself a day or two holiday. I have seen friends, and lingered in the glorious weather a little – I picked some blackberries from Battersea Park and stewed them with some apples, still a little bit sour, that fell off a tree on our roof at work.

TUES 13 AUG THE WORLD NEEDS POETS

I went to meet the young poets who were taking part in YOUYOU Mentoring, a London-based not-for-profit scheme that aims to give young people the opportunity to work with high-profile/successful mentors in their chosen field. In today's difficult job market, and with so many falling into the NEET category (Not in Education, Employment or Training), these opportunities are proving to be invaluable experiences for young people developing their craft and needing that 'something extra' on their CV. I was asked for a quote to publicise the project. I said: 'I am pleased to be patron because the world needs poets.'

I talked to them about the importance of culture in the Climate Revolution – saying of course that if we had true culture we would have different values and therefore we would not have climate change. I told them that Gore Vidal said 'the Nobel prize should be given to readers not writers; everybody's writing a book but nobody is reading.' By that he meant that the fit reader is someone who reads the best writers throughout time, those who tell the universal truths, and that is why I hardly read fiction from the last few decades, it's so cheap and ephemeral. I said that today art education is generally a negative experience and represses the fact that inspiration comes from the past and absorption in its ideas and preaches the nonsense that it all starts from here i.e. you/the tabula rasa. **'Ignore the past, express yourself!'** Therefore people don't communicate – if it makes sense to them it's good enough – or, their ideas are too banal for anyone to be interested. I explained to these kids, 'You have to supply the stepping stones so we can both get across the stream, they have to be there even though they might be hard to find.'

I liked Greta Bellamacina, the poet who has chaperoned the project. She is a serious person.

FRI 16 AUG FLY LESS, STAY LONGER – AND BALCOMBE

Andreas went for a long weekend to see our friends Rosita and Paula, who produce for us in Italy. They have a little holiday flat in the great old city of Viareggio near Carrara – famous for Michelangelo. Andreas is in his element on the beach and you know the Italians – how different enterprises own each strip of the beach down to the sea, and they provide everything: showers, towels, robes, sunbeds, beach restaurants and service.

I didn't want to go: 'Fly less, stay longer'. It's too short a visit to bother hanging around in airports. I prefer to stay with myself at home and read. However, my son Joe had asked me to go to Balcombe, where the government want to start fracking.

On the train with Ben, Joe, Tomoka and friends, Joe showed me an article in the *Financial Times* where energy companies had issued a threat to the government amounting to: we can't make profit from renewable energy (unlimited). We can make profit from fossil fuels (limited). Unless governments support fossil fuels we will have to close plants and investment will plummet. Such an admission! Joe said he'd never read anything like it. He was so excoriating about fracking that I said, 'Oh Joe, I wish I was a ventriloquist and you could talk to the press.' When we arrived the press were asking me how long I was staying and what I felt about civil disobedience. I hadn't realised that today was the start of the drilling and that the protesters intended to stop it. And as it happened Cuadrilla laid off

The Balcombe anti-fracking protest.

because the police had said they couldn't protect them. I was really pleased to hold the sign, 'Lock the Gate'.

One of the protest groups camping in a field donated by a local farmer is 'Reclaim the Power'. I talked to Cara (a stunning beauty with freckles and blonde rasta hairdo). I said, 'I'm all for *Claim the Power* but as for *Reclaim*, I don't think people ever had the power, people have always been manipulated or made stupid by every form of government and the present plutocracy has been the most successful.' I thought next day: this is it. Climate Revolution starts in Balcombe. Climate Revolution has to join in. We will establish the revolution by fighting fracking in this country. We will take our model from 350.org.

SAT 17 – SUN 18 AUG KNITWEAR

Saturday: yoga and reading. Sunday: to work from 10 a.m. to 10 p.m. on the knitwear. I finally cracked it. I had worked out a scheme which depended on samples from Italy – I needed to check

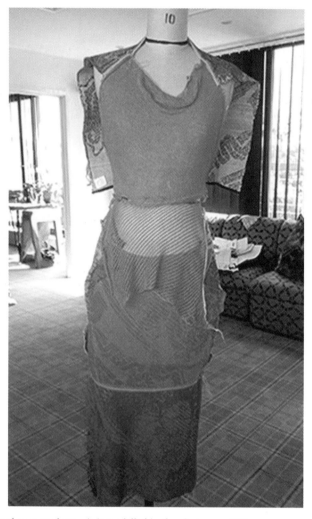

The knitted-squares dress – it is modelled in the photo on p.239.

weights and degree of firmness and colours. Having just received samples, I had loads because every time they had never been quite right – they kept changing from what I had asked for. I started from scratch – just keeping my scheme in mind – pinning this wonderful mix of knitted squares on the stand. I got what I wanted – the possibility of combining different textures and colours and looking like it had been thrown together – which it had.

WEDS 21 AUG CHELSEA MANNING SENTENCE

The day of the Chelsea (Bradley) Manning sentence: thirty-five years, speculation of parole after twelve years. There's an appeal. We went to the American Embassy to meet up with support groups, then a bunch of us, including Andreas, went to the pub. I did enjoy talking to all my friends.

Now the guess is that Chelsea Manning might get parole in seven years. What a strong character Chelsea has – true to herself! And I think she will become even more popular now. Public opinion is so important. I think her popularity will help Edward Snowden.

SAT 24 – SAT 31 AUG FRIDA KAHLO

Andreas went to Corsica for a week. Once again I preferred to stay at home. All week we had worked hard and I needed to keep in touch with myself so this bank holiday weekend I began by writing up the diary and it took most of the weekend, though I did pop out on Saturday to have dinner with my friend, Giselle.

On Tuesday, I went in to work to make sure the last important information is relayed to our manufacturers in Italy now that they are back from holidays. The other things I have to do are sort outfits for this season's Red Label presentation for London Fashion Week and check the content and look for the launch of the Climate Revolution site.

At the weekend, I had time for myself and met Shami and her son at the Royal Academy's exhibition of Mexico's 1910 Revolution. Photos and paintings: very intense. The photographs left an indelible impression on me, so skilfull was their composition, but the greatest thing was a tiny self-portrait by Frida Kahlo.

SEPTEMBER 2013

MON 2 SEPT BEN'S GOT ART

My son Ben writes the *World's End* shop website and he was explaining the origins of a man's suit – one of our favourite classics, which we have just reintroduced. It is from a portrait of a man called Krall by Otto Dix and Ben found out more about the work of Dix and talked to Andreas. Then Andreas came to me, really excited, and he made me excited because he said, 'I think Ben's got art!' If this happens to you it's a gift out of the blue – you enter the parallel universe (where everything is perfectly expressed). Andreas has got art, he gets it immediately – and I'm sure Andreas is right about Ben. I talked to Ben, who said, 'I'm very alive to the subject matter.' I don't know if I get art. I know I love paintings; I stand in front of them for ages and I don't want to leave. I think you'd call it worship – or meditation. I marvel and I'm completely grateful they exist.

They have found a new Titian. Andreas showed it to me on his computer. It's been 120 years since the last discovery and this one has been in a private family collection. Titian painted it when he was young, around twenty-five. It's a Resurrection. Andreas said,

'It's obvious, of course it's competitive, he is showing off his power. It's very important. An interesting face – someone he knew. Intellectual. The loincloth (shroud) is the greatest ever painted, its swathes include every possibility but it doesn't exist in real life.'

I don't know how big the painting is. It could be life-size or more. Jesus fills all the space; he fills the world, the clouds are the horizon, the sunrise is low down, level with Jesus's legs. The composition gives confidence, in Jesus and in the world – a feeling of security. 'Christ' means the 'anointed one'. Christ has saved us for everlasting life by dying for us on the cross. We can share in his divinity: 'I am the way, the truth and the life.' This is what I read in his expression: *I've done it, I have fulfilled my destiny.* Contemplation of this all-embracing icon gives peace and confirms heaven.

Though I have no religious belief I can share in the power of this painting, put myself in Titian's shoes, go back in time and understand the solidity and confidence that this religious outlook gave to one's view of the world. Jesus's face is full of health in the prime of life. His flag is the victory over death (the dragon of St George).

SUN 15 SEPT RED LABEL SHOW

We kept postponing our decision as to how to present Red Label, our very important second line. Were we going to do a catwalk show or ... our marketing people explored the idea of a film combined with a presentation. Time ran out and Andreas rang up Lily Cole and asked her, 'Lily, you're an activist for the environment, can you think of a way to use a presentation of Red Label?'

Lily was interested to know that we wished to focus attention on Environmental Justice Foundation's campaign (EJF) to help climate refugees. She herself is already a passionate supporter of this. EJF are distributing postcards for people to send to Ban Ki-moon to get the UN to give official recognition to this human crisis. There are more than thirty million climate refugees (compared to ten million war refugees). We could put these postcards on seats and help distribute them in other ways.

Lily talked to a friend from her schooldays, Lorna Tucker, who makes films. Lorna is also my friend and at the moment is making a film on Leonard Peltier. They came up with an idea. Lily (I didn't know this) is a dancer. She would dance Hans Christian Andersen's story of 'The Red Shoes'. The girl cannot stop dancing unless she

Red Label make-up for the show.

can rid herself of the shoes. This would be a metaphor for climate refugees who must escape their hostile environment. The dance of death must end. Trapped in its hostile environment an animal will die. It will try to leave. It will leave but there is nowhere to go. Lorna made a ten minute film of Lily's dance which we will send to Ban Ki-moon and for the Red Label presentation Lily danced live for three minutes and then the fashion show took place. We somehow wanted the models to look like animals who die due to degraded environments. Andreas gave the brief to make-up and hair, Val Garland and Mark Hampton: *imagine an animal caught in headlights.*

The postcards ask us to write about home.

I wrote: 'Anyone who gets home late from work and finds she's forgotten the key. What a disaster! My home is my refuge.'

Lily wrote: 'Planet earth is our home. Yet climate change now makes someone homeless every second.'

MON 16 SEPT GRAPES OF WRATH

The library at work now has a selection of eight books with six copies of each, enough so that some of us can get together and discuss them. The book of the month is Steinbeck's *Grapes of Wrath* and we decided to launch the library with a showing of the film, starring Henry Fonda and directed by John Ford.

We did this in the Doodle Bar, across the road from our studio in Battersea. It was really nice. Prior to going over, Tizer had organised people to each bring a dish of food and then there were free drinks at the bar. I was disappointed that mostly the same people came – the ones who get involved, come on demonstrations. The others? I know people need to get home after a long day but it is really a question of habit; they could say, yes, I'll go, and if that means I have to make arrangements at home, I'll do it. It's so important to engage with the world.

Grapes of Wrath is a great film. Henry Fonda wanted that role so badly – he is a hero and all the casting is shrewd – and the sets – the way it looks is graphic and timeless. It succeeds in condensing Steinbeck's message and it ends at a good point for a film – on a note of optimism. The advantage of the book is (of course) more words, words that flow and ideas that build. More time to introduce us to the aspirations of all the individual characters who belong to this rich story of human kinship. The book continues beyond the point where the film stops and though the chances of survival for the family are precarious the pathos of the final scene is unsurpassed in literature.

WEDS 25 SEPT A VEGGIE RECIPE

I've been working on next season's Red Label as well as preparing stuff for the Climate Revolution site for when the site structure is ready. And of course Gold Label. The last week has been lovely; seeing all the designs become reality, receiving the last of the embroideries, the hats, the jewellery. I was trying to put the show together – draw it out on paper, outfits, what goes with what – tops and bottoms. It seemed quite difficult and somehow we will have to do it in Paris with all the actual clothes when they arrive. This will make us rather later than usual. It's always a good thing to have a provisional run to work from.

Andreas always buys flowers for the studio. He is so excited, he said: 'The feeling I have, I can only compare it to the harvest.' Johannes, who works on *Worlds' End* (an ex-student of mine from when I taught in Berlin), takes it upon himself to cook because we all work late. Here is one of his recipes (vegetarian).

For 8–10 people:

2 small Hokkaido squash/pumpkins, 1 onion, 1 leek, 5 sticks celery, 2 carrots, 1 big piece of ginger, 2 cubes vegetable stock (yeast free), 1 chilli (red), 1 lemon grass, 1 can of coconut cream, ½ bottle of white wine, juice from 1 lime, fresh coriander.

Cut all the vegetables into small pieces. You can use the Hokkaido squash with its peel, which makes it a lot quicker to prepare than butternut squash. Put everything into a big pot, fill up with water and bring to boil; use less water if you want a thicker soup. Add salt and soup stock and cook for 10 mins. Now add the spices (cut very small) and the wine and cook for another 5 mins. Take it off the heat, add the coconut cream and mix it with a hand blender until it is smooth and creamy. Add lime juice and coriander topping.

THURS 25 – FRI 26 SEPT PARIS PILGRIMS

I left with Andreas for Paris. Our Gold Label show is on Saturday and we don't have a title yet – and even more than this I need to tell the story of the collection, for a press release and for when I do my interviews. So I just wrote everything down, hoping the title would grow out of the process, and it did. This is far too long and complicated for a press release but I was able to pick out a few paragraphs. Here is the full version:

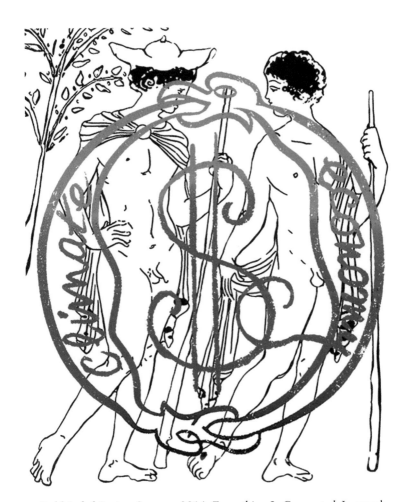

Gold Label Spring–Summer 2014. Everything Is Connected. In search of a title. Now that our world is at the chaos point I want to know more about the world order of the medieval community. My interest in these people deepens.

A couple of years ago I went with Andreas to Canterbury. There was a service in the cathedral and we weren't allowed into the splendour of the nave and altar. I'm so glad because instead we gained another experience; we explored the cloisters and vaults and I felt that I was wandering in the presence of ordinary people who lived in a different world to mine and I thought of the specialists – the alchemists of those days who aspired to become more spirit than flesh because they believed in a divine order of things.

I thought also of pilgrims throughout time and it became a working title for this collection. How did they dress? They would try to balance the need for humility and austerity with a display of their importance in this world. In those ordered earlier worlds you dressed accordingly to your status. I thought of the pagan Greek, a young male pilgrim walking to the shrine of Apollo in his noble nakedness, his cloak, hat and staff. Only young men of the priveleged class were allowed to walk around naked. We used this image in our invitation.

Our medieval pilgrims on their journey must be austere, serious and festive, each wearing her most important clothes.

Their colours begin with un-dyed cloths (perhaps this mark of piety implies wealth – poorer people would try to show off more) and colours and tints of vegetable dyes. There is always a way to show wealth, for example scholars and clerks dressed in 'austere' black but in those days the process of achieving a black dye cost a fortune.

Amongst the travellers would be important people from the countryside wearing their most festive traditional dress. I love the way that folk costume carries its wealth: an apron can be the most costly item, an example of the finest, most perfect or most elaborate spinning and weaving; a belt could have taken a skilled member of a village a year of his spare time; scarves and cloaks and jewellery can be pinned flat, transposing the refinement of their decoration into an overall panache.

Frida Kahlo began to inspire our collection. We visited the Royal Academy's current exhibition on the Mexican revolution which happened at the same time as World War I. Frida was one of the artists who grouped together to celebrate through their work the new power of the people. She wore the Mexican folk costume. You may think anyone could look like her by doing that but they couldn't. She had the keenest sense of style – the way each day she just fixed her hair, sometimes adding ribbons or flowers. You would think that Sam McKnight had just flown in to do it. She made the look so spontaneous, so her, so chic, and she wore it all her life. A great fashion icon and a great artist.

Pilgrims is not a big enough idea for a whole collection – as a title it is too limited. Now that it's finished it's sexy, even kinky – you could style it like a sexy nun. To Andreas it looks Arab with clothes from a strange charity shop thrown in; Arab, that is, of the Middle East, as we British refer to it, and of north Africa; Arab as we imagine it before the global war machine largely smashed this culture. I would like to connect the idea of the collection and the show to Climate Revolution, my main preoccupation.

Gold Label Paris show. She is a pilgrim spattered with mud from the road. This dress is an accident, worked from the squares of knitting stiches which were never quite right (see p.230).

To review: the ethos of the medieval world is the complete opposite of our's. Its structure is a hierarchy of different classes and functions, striving for harmony through reciprocal duties and help. However the hierarchy is unjust and ruled by dogma. It is swept away by scepticism which arrived with the Renaissance. The Renaissance is the re-discovery of the pagan Greek mind. The modern world embraced scepticism – diverse opinion, scientific enquiry, knowledge based on experience – but it came to ignore the Greek concerns of harmony, form, proportion and balance, of giving back what you take out, of not going too far, of over-weaning pride. Nature will always be our master. We are men not gods.

Shakespeare saw the disaster we were heading for. In the quotation below (from *Measure For Measure*) it is useful to know that glass means mirror, the picture it gives us is of man holding up his own image to challenge God. I am going to call the show 'Everything Is Connected' because so many influences of the last six months and of the past went into it. This tallies with our message as activists: Everything is connected. The most horrific connections between climate change and the rotten financial system (**CC & Rot$**).

Shakespeare understood where we were heading:

> but man, proud man,
> Dress'd in a little brief authority,
> Most ignorant of what he's most assur'd –
> His glassy essence – like an angry ape
> Plays such fantastic tricks before high heaven
> As makes the angels weep;

Andreas added this P.S. to the press release:

Dear Clothes Lover:

This season I would like to draw your attention especially to the knitwear. I am very fond of it and if I were a girl, for sure it would be my absolute must-have. Its fine netty yarns and burnt colours are perfect to show off my sun-kissed 'super body'! It's just like being naked and is going to be a great friend on my next holiday. Most pieces are enhanced with recycled mirrored sunglass lenses cut into special shapes and motifs. Again, I can so very much imagine the sun reflecting on them and causing quite a stir at the beach bar. You can put those knits into little bundles and take loads of them with you without paying excess luggage.

I love Vivienne's sense for yarns and what she does with it.

Thanks darling – Your Andreas x

SAT 28 SEPT GOLD LABEL SHOW AT LE CENTORIAL

It was a beautiful show. The venue, Le Centorial, is a bank during the week. It is all wrought-iron and glass. The models came up and down escalators to an arena on the top floor and we had large mirrors reflecting their progress. This gave more feeling of space and travelling. Sam McKnight and Val Garland again for hair and make-up. They are the best. Dominik Emrich composed the music specially. Very beautiful, we really appreciate him. And the models – every one gorgeous, beautiful black girls having fun, strong characters, strong image.

Pamela came to the show and in the evening we met for dinner. She is travelling with her friend and ex-husband, Rick. He travels in the course of earning his living. He's a professional gambler and they are living a life of high adventure – both surf as well. We really liked him, we're all vegetarian and, like Pamela, Rick cares about the environment and supports various activists. Wherever they travel (next stop is Biarritz) Pamela runs – fifteen miles a day but not every day. She is training for the New York Marathon, raising money for Haiti. Pamela is always concerned.

Pamela with Ellen DeGeneres, raising sponsorship for her marathon for Haiti.

SUN 29 SEPT BUY LESS, CHOOSE WELL, MAKE IT LAST

Sunday: at 10.30 a.m. I was in our Paris showroom to present the collection to the buyers. I gave a talk about the clothes. They are really easy to combine and to buy – easy to understand.

Andreas and I then met our friend Lawrence for lunch. He works for the Gates Foundation and has high-level contacts. His work is all about empowering women in poor countries – involves mobile phones and facilities for saving which didn't exist for them before. He is impressed by our slogan, 'Buy less, choose well, make it last', thinks it could have a big effect on changing people's aspirations and could be a most important tool in Climate Revolution. He really gets into you, caring and spiritual.

OCTOBER 2013

 ## TUES 1 OCT WE'RE LATE AGAIN FOR THE GOLD COLLECTION

Our Gold Label show was the culmination of our fashion season and now we're already late with next season's Gold – our most important collection. Why are we late? Because Gold depends so completely on Andreas and me. Of course, we have people to help us, we delegate. But we initiate. Our team has work to do for the production of the last collection, meanwhile we choose the fabric (samples from the factories are waiting in boxes); but we don't, we are too taken up with all the daily business of running a company and its public face – interviews, etc.

Our people and design teams want Andreas's input, opinion, approval. He did work with Iris for a week on new toiles. And he has an inspiration for the new Gold – his all-time favourite designer, Frederick Worth. Every dress Worth ever made is different, one from the other. Andreas went to study him in the new V&A archive in Olympia where they keep all their historical costumes, fabrics and images. He was extremely impressed by the building and archive –

the way it's been done. He said he had had the happiest day of his life from what they had shown him, from what he had seen (nobody sees like Andreas).

I have managed to choose the knitwear yarn for Gold and ask for tests – samples of stitches and differences in handle for the designs I have worked out. Choosing the Gold fabric can take hours and days because you're having to think what to do with it so that you're getting a feeling for the collection. I have also been working on Red Label. I love this collection and I had some strong ideas. I want it to be really archetypal Westwood, I want to epitomise it more and more.

SAT 5 OCT FREE THE ARCTIC 30

Andreas and I went to the Greenpeace 'Free the Arctic 30' demonstration outside the Russian Embassy in Notting Hill. It was really great, lots of people on both sides of the Bayswater Road and all the traffic hooting and people on the buses waving. Do go on demonstrations – the more people turn up the more fun you have, the more friends you meet and who you can then go to the pub with, after. We know Frank Hewetson, one of the 30. We talk to Nina, his wife, and their daughter Nell who is there with her friend Cora, my granddaughter. Frank has been with Greenpeace for over twenty years, always at the front of the action. Once, when protesting against bad practice in tuna fishing in the Mediterranean, a fisherman harpooned him through the calf and, by the connecting line held by the man who shot him, he and his boat were being dragged at speed by

Frank Hewetson in jail in Russia.

the fishermen's boat; each time Frank tried to pull on the line to get some slack, the man pulled it tight. Eventually, Frank managed to rip the barbed weapon out of his calf. Frank did a lot of diplomatic work for Greenpeace: e.g. persuading companies to buy soya from growers with well-managed soil instead of those who cut down the forest and move the crop in there.

Greenpeace are fundraising for lawyers to work on the release of the Arctic 30. They come from eighteen different countries, so need eighteen lawyers. The Greenpeace activists must have been terrified when the Russian helicopters came over their boat and let down special forces on ropes, with their heavy guns and balaclavas over their faces, coming on deck to arrest them. They were focusing world attention on a drilling operation which will endanger the lives of all people and Putin's response was full military aggression. Now he's hiding behind the 'law' (ha!) saying he can't interfere. No doubt Greenpeace will build up pressure on Shell, the equal partner in Russia's lethal Arctic operation.

MON 7 OCT VOGUE PHOTOS

I was invited with four hours' notice to *Channel 4 News* to speak on behalf of the Arctic 30. So great is my respect for the importance of Greenpeace and for the danger posed by exploitation of the Arctic of tipping over into runaway climate change that I think I used the opportunity well. After this I went on to to Daphne's restaurant in Fulham where my friend Linda Watson was expecting me. It was the launch of a book of *Vogue* photos of our fashion since the 1970s. Linda wrote the text.

THURS 10 OCT THE CHEAPSIDE HOARD AND CLERKENWELL

Andreas and I met my son Joe at the London Museum for the opening of 'The Cheapside Hoard' – the stock of a seller of jewellery from Elizabethan times which had been discovered by complete and lucky accident during a 'normal' digging operation (anyone who travels appreciates the distinction between London and any other town: roadworks – the streets are constantly dug up). Elizabethan jewellery hardly survives except for this stash. The exhibition gave you a feeling of the importance of the streets of a London that was thriving and commercial.

We walked over to Clerkenwell Green. Joe, who lives in this part of London, took us for something to eat. As we walked, he told us some of the history. Lying just outside the city walls, Clerkenwell became the natural home for those wishing to live outside the law. He talked about Jack Sheppard and Bess Lyon's escape from Newgate Prison. A hero of the poor, Sheppard escaped from prison four times before being hanged at Tyburn, aged twenty-two. A third of London's population came to his execution. Joe's latest fashion collection is called Jack Sheppard.

When Charles Dickens wrote *Oliver Twist* and cast Clerkenwell Green as the training ground for Fagin's crew of pick-pocketers, the area was commonly known in the press as 'the headquarters

The Cheapside Hoard at the London Museum – and Jack Sheppard and Bess Lyon's escape from Newgate prison, Clerkenwell.

of republicanism, revolution and ultra-non-conformity'. Vladimir Ilyich Lenin drank beer and discussed revolution in the Crown and Anchor pub (now the Crown Tavern on Clerkenwell Green). From revolting peasants to revolutionary Communists, Clerkenwell has a long history of political radicalism and religious non-conformity. Perhaps the most significant demonstration occurred in 1890, when the green was the gathering point for London's first May Day March – a left-wing tradition that continues into the twenty-first century.

Everywhere was packed even though it was a Thursday and we ended up sitting outside on a cold night with a glass of wine and a packet of chips.

SAT 12 OCT KEATS HOUSE FOR YOUYOU

To Keats House in Hampstead and the latest project of Brenda Ramsey's YOUYOU mentoring. Brenda is passionately dedicated and she must have managed to get sponsorship and free mentoring at every stage of her project, which now culminated in the poets reading their work to an audience.

I'm sure she was disappointed in me. For though I encouraged the poets to continue I did not praise them just because they're young. The poems were good but not yet good enough. I thought they had been too easily satisfied with themselves, even self-indulgent and therefore not quite honest, and we attempted a public discussion which I hoped was better for them than patronising praise: if the poem didn't touch the poet, how could it touch us?

One of the poets, Laura O'Driscoll, was very good. What I like about her is her courage; she wants to be the voice of the world. Her poems were about climate change: 'The Last Sunset'.

WEDS 16 OCT ANTI-FRACKING AND JOCHEN ZEITZ

Andreas is in Italy working on our menswear. I went to Joe's office where he and Cynthia had put together a meeting of anti-fracking

NGOs and friends. Jane Thomas from Friends of the Earth, who had fought the frackers in Blackpool, was really impressive – said only what was important, understood everything it was possible to do. Cynthia pointed out to me that she and Jamie from Reclaim the Power were from Occupy; every time they had a good idea they did a little two hands wave in the air.

In the evening I went to a reception to mark a CNBC film on the philanthropic projects of Jochen Zeitz (he spent his career building up Puma), one of which is Segera in Kenya which Andreas and I visited and for which we are now ambassadors. I am also ambassador for the school there – which had nothing, it didn't even have a door. I was amazed to see what the Zeitz foundation has done to improve the school and the health of the children. The school just won a Greenest School on Earth award.

SUN 20 OCT ELIZABETHANS

I meet my friend Shami Chakrabarti and her eleven-year-old son Christian. We plan to go to the National Portrait Gallery's exhibition *Elizabeth and Her People*, as Christian is studying the Elizabethans at school, but first we got to lunch in the National Gallery restaurant. In Trafalgar Square I bump into the villagers of Balcombe who mean to stop the fracking there. They are dancing to attract people and gain public support.

I worried that the portraits of Elizabethans might be too formal for Christian to appreciate. You just have to imagine what they would look like in real life – from another planet, Elizabeth, her dress covered in embroidery and jewels, dazzling in the light, flickering in candlelight, her white face in an aura of soft frizzy hair lit with jewels, presented in a ruff and transparent veils, her beautiful hands. The exhibition has objects as well. It shows the different pins she would need to get dressed, starting with small fine pins for the ruff. Getting dressed was a big deal. Elizabeth's most impressive dress is one where she is being carried through the streets on show to her people. First of all, it's all one colour and that colour

Elizabeth's most impressive dress – and a copy made for me for the Venice Carnival by a student when I was teaching in Berlin.

is white, architectural and plain but for the fact that it is covered all over with the one uniform decorative effect, which is studded with jewels. It's the most minimal dress; it acts like a heraldic shield with just one great badge of a jewel on the sleeve: I am the monarch.

When I look at paintings I notice the age of the painter – and in portraits the age of the sitter. Half of them die around forty and death from old age is sixty-five, though one sitter, Bess of Hardwick, lived into her eighties and survived four husbands. In one family the young wife, aged about twenty-four, already had five children. And this is in a family rich enough to have their portraits painted. You married young, women died in childbirth, child mortality was high.

Youth must have been so short, children brought up with the idea that they would soon be married and live the same life as their parents. Courting was very important, the most lovely time of your life if you were lucky, truly springtime.

Like in Shakespeare's *As You Like It*:

It was a lover and his lass,
    With a hey, and a ho, and a hey nonino,
That o'er the green corn-field did pass,
    In the spring time, the only pretty ring time,
When birds do sing, hey ding a ding, ding;   5
Sweet lovers love the spring.

WEDS 23 OCT MASTERPIECES OF CHINESE PAINTING

Our friend Bruno invited us to the opening of *Masterpieces of Chinese Painting* at the V&A. You know my passion for Chinese painting and this exhibition is possibly the most high-level ever mounted. It has the originals of some of the most famous paintings we have seen in reproduction. You have to see it to realise the height of genius that human civilisation has been capable of. It is going to have an earth-shattering impact on the values of those who visit. My son Joe went; he came out shaking. I went five times.

After the opening about forty people went to Bruno's house for sit-down dinner – beautiful tableware and prime-quality food.

Bruno is Chinese and I think his family are Chinese American investors. He is cultivated and has some sensational Chinese objects and paintings. He also had some modern abstract paintings – churned up colour, paint as thick as possible applied to canvas. I was sitting next to Patrik Schumacher, the creative and business partner of Zaha Hadid. He made a statement some of you may be interested in: abstract art had a radical influence on design, it freed up architecture.

It was late so we left before the pudding – I was happy, I had filled up on kimchi – Andreas had to go early in the morning to Vienna, because he has designed the costumes for the ballet interlude of the Vienna Philharmonic New Year's concert – televised for millions.

Andreas's ballet costumes for Vienna's New Year's concert.

SUN 27 OCT MAZELTOV: MRS PURCELL AND MAUREEN

Like everybody, I spend time with family and friends – and their troubles and joys – but I seem to have less time than ever. I don't mention them often because that's not what I want to talk about. I mention Pamela often because she's well known.

But I just wanted to show this photo of Mrs Purcell on her 100th birthday. Well done, Celia. She is the mother of my friend Maureen, from Glossop, where I went to school. Maureen's family kept a hardware store and lived at the back. Celia changed the light fittings

Me (lef0 and Maureen (third from left).

often, putting them back to sell in the shop. When I first went to Maureen's home after school and met her mother the first thing she said was, 'Hello Vivienne. Do you like my new light fitting? Put some coal on, love, it's out the back.' The family was one of two Jewish families in Glossop; I loved them, they were so lively. Maureen stayed with her cousins some weekends in Manchester, twelve miles away. She had to go dancing there so she would find a Jewish husband.

Maureen later went to live in South Africa. She was a hairdresser and developed products for black people's hair; no one did this at the time, and others took her idea and these same products were then used for white people everywhere – volume boosters, etc. When Maureen trained, no one mentioned that perm lotions could ruin your lungs but that's what happened to Maureen: she had asthma, then emphysema and tuberculosis, from which she died.

NOVEMBER 2013

FRI 1 NOV LESLIE WINER

We did our publicity campaign with Juergen Teller. The idea is Leslie Winer. I knew her when young. She came to Paris and immediately became a top model; we were hanging out at the *Bains Douches* club the first night it opened. Andreas saw her now in Paris and was struck by her and the power of her beauty. She agrees to do it. Juergen is so excited. Wait and see.

Leslie Winer (third left) in a spread for the Buffalo Girls collection when she first came to Paris in 1982.

MON 11 NOV WHO ARE OUR RULERS?

It takes time to do a website and AR (Active Resistance) has now become incorporated into CR (Climate Revolution). By the time these diaries are published CR will be merged with the main Vivienne Westwood website.

You remember I said my job as an activist – communicating through my website – is to analyse the problem, epitomise and give the complete picture all in one go. Well, this MAP is it. This is our world and it is happening already. Because we refuse to engage with it, the result is inevitable and we will die. We are global! Don't you realise what that means? It means a few thousand people control seven billion.

I copied the map about a year ago from maps supplied by NASA which predict the results of climate change according to current increasing temperatures. Their images are presented more photographically. By using the computer, we turned this into a simple graphic.

This is the best thing I have ever done.

The other most important thing I have ever done is to take the information from 'Who are our Rulers' and reduce it to a list of bullet points which set out how the Rotten Financial System works. We call it – neoliberalism.

I have used the map as a graphic on clothes and publicity posters, etc. I also carry a single sheet A5 leaflet in my bag to give to people who stop me in the street. On one side is the map and on the other the Rot$ which causes climate change.

+5°

<u>Uninhabitable</u> <u>Land</u>

Once the rising temperature goes beyond
the tipping point it will run away to +5°
= Only 1 billion people left by the end
of this Century

The Rotten Financial System

The central banks control the world's economy. They do this by creating debt.

The central banks are private banks. The US Federal Bank is one, the Bank of England another. They are organised by the Bank for International Settlements (BIS) in Zurich.

These central banks print money. Today, they do this by pressing buttons. They create virtual money out of nothing.

This money is loaned to other banks, monopolies and governments. It has now become a debt.

The central banks prefer it if the loans are never paid because what they want is the interest – which accumulates out of all proportion to reality.

This means they always have fantastic amounts of money to lend and they don't have to print virtual money except in an emergency. It also means that central banks come to own everything – because they own the debt. How often have we heard of a poor country selling its assets and natural resources just to keep up with interest payments on the debt it has been forced to borrow?

The monopolies work this system for the central banks. They do the actual job of wrecking the planet and exploiting its people. They suck up small businesses.

Politicians serve the central banks and the monopolies. They promote Big Business and its speculators and investors – through tax cuts, deregulation and selling off national assets and through the war machine; they pay for it by squeezing the taxpayer and reducing public services so that everyone is in debt (Austerity).

Rot$ aka Neoliberalism.

WEDS 13 NOV EL DORADO

I meet my son, Joe, who has lived for many years within walking distance of the British Museum – and goes often. We go to see *El Dorado*, an exhibition of golden treasure from the tribes of Peru living at the same time as the Incas. The name El Dorado (The Gilded) refers to a legendary rich king – or his kingdom – abounding in gold. This idea might have come from a tribe that performed a ceremony each year in which the king was taken on a raft to the middle of a deep lake in the mountains and gold objects were thrown into the lake as a sacrifice. No one has retrieved the objects. (Anyway, the Europeans found that there was very little gold to be extracted from such precious objects, as they were gilded, not solid).

The larger objects, such as crowns and masks and breast plaques, were beautiful. The exhibition was so incredibly researched and resourced that the presentation was able to display the different methods, crafts and interests of different tribes. It showed examples of the same animals, so there were glass cases full of gold bats, frogs, snakes, fish, birds, crabs and spiders, most six inches high or less. These and the small spiritual/magical figures were powerfully intense. Jewellery! The methods of making the artefacts made it fascinating.

Afterwards, Joe and I walked through Soho and he took me to Andrew Edmunds's club in Lexington Street. Andrew is a print expert, especially on Hogarth, and his premises comprise a print shop, club and restaurant. The interior is old, which makes you feel comfortable. How nice to sit down with a soup and a glass of wine and sit and talk without distraction. We talked quite a bit about Climate Revolution. Joe is really good on strategy.

THURS 14 NOV IAN KELLY AND CAROL ANN DUFFY

In the evening we go to the King's Head in Dalston (since then, two or three times people have mentioned to me, do you know this club where there are all these stuffed animals – it seems to be the latest place to go). Picador Books are introducing the books they will launch in late summer/autumn and Ian Kelly is writing my biography. He gives a good speech and I think he will do a good job. He wants to be true to who I think I am. Then I speak and, of course, I talk about fashion because the book has to be about fashion – but first, I crash right in telling everyone about 'Who are our rulers?' because it's so important to get this fact of the fragile economy clear to everyone – and that we're letting it (it's a pyramid scheme that must collapse) destroy life by causing climate change.

I enjoyed listening to the other authors and one in particular could interest me but I have such a queue of books I want to read first. Then we came to the end and Carol Ann Duffy, the Poet Laureate, read some of her poems from her coming book. I liked very much one about English counties, and another about the person whose job it is to pollinate because there are no bees, 'The Human Bee'. Carol Ann has a great voice; she's one in a million who can connect things and put them into words.

FRI 15 NOV BARRY HUMPHRIES

We went to the opening night of Barry Humphries's farewell tour (we hope it's not). I was once on the Dame Edna show and I wore a red button-up cardigan and a pair of flesh tights with an applique green mirror fig leaf at the crotch. Barry wasn't quick enough. He told me after, if only you'd told me, I could have checked my lipstick in the mirror. Whah!

The show was so original. I've never seen Les Patterson before and the characters who are part of his life – part of him. The main sketch was 'Les Get Cookin'!' – a supposed pilot for TV – done with the help of four dancers – two men, two pin-up posing women – 'The Condiments'. It took place on his back-garden lawn and he was often rushing into the toilet with chronic diarrhoea then back to his hamburgers. It was so astonishingly lewd (it made one gasp and stretch one's eyes) but so fast that he got away with it. Andreas had a pain – he hardly stopped bending up and down, rocking with laughter. Behind us were Siegfried and Roy, the stage magicians from Las Vegas. Roy, who had surgery after an accident with one of their tigers, was too impressed by the in your face daring of it all to laugh, just telling me and others how amazing it was.

I can't tell the second half. That was Dame Edna – I couldn't do her justice and, anyway, she works with the audience and it changes every time. Her confidence in her petty (non)talent and achievement is so monolithic it's exhilarating. It tells us so much about what the spoilt little child inside us would like to be.

SAT 16 NOV ROMEO AND JULIET

Fernando Montaño invited Andreas and me to the Royal Ballet to see him dance *Romeo and Juliet*. He looks after us, he's so generous, and it can't be easy for him to afford. I compensate by sending him our square T-shirts. He loves to practice in them. Champagne and sandwiches then supper in between acts; we imbibe the festive atmosphere of people coming together to celebrate the arts in this big beautiful space of glass architecture. It really is a grand occasion. This is the greatest love story in the world and the most tragic. There is nothing greater than this music by Prokofiev. The phenomenal Rupert Pennefather was Romeo and a beautiful one. Fernando was one of his mates, Benvolio. The opera are giving him the roles. We all believe in him.

THURS 21 NOV PROTESTING SHELL

Greenpeace pick me up at 7.30 a.m. at my house along with *iD*, who are making a film about whatever it is we're going to do – secret up until now. Cynthia and Laura, who does our press, come along, too. In the car John Sauven from Greenpeace tells me we're going to the Shell building at the Southbank to protest the arrest of the Arctic 30. John is on the phone to someone called Rachel, who

I think is in the law court in Russia, and to Nina, Frank Hewetson's wife, trying to get a copy passport so that Frank can ask for bail. John suddenly tells me, 'Frank is just before the court'.

As we arrive, the Greenpeace team are unloading ten-foot-high wooden boxes covered with portrait photos of the 30. They line up the boxes along the front of the Shell Building to create a display. The idea is to hand out leaflets to the Shell workers as they arrive so they know the full implications of what their bosses are doing. The press are there and I do some interviews. I am chatting to Frank's colleague when we get the news that Frank got bail. After two months with two Russian chain-smoking prisoners. I say, 'I don't think he even had a book.' 'Oh that's alright, he can't read,' his friend jokes.

The Shell security people don't try to stop the demonstration. It would cause more publicity. It's cold; Cynthia is blue. We are waiting for something, so I answer some questions for the *iD* film (young people always want to know about punk – what was I

Protesting against Shell on the South Bank.

fighting for then?). John is on the phone; whatever we're waiting for, it's taking ages. Another ten minutes. He points through the window to a space in the short distance between where we are and the river. 'Do you see that flag pole – we've been waiting for a security person to move out of the area. Emily is going to climb it to a point where we can fix our flag to the rope.' Now he tells me: I'm gonna hoist the flag!

We go over. Emily is smiling down at us. It's taking longer than we thought. She has to throw the rope, which is fastened to a belt at her waist, around the tree and catch it, and the flag pole is really fat so she keeps missing. But she finally hitches it up high enough. They get me a ladder; two men hidden behind me let out the rope, the wind is too strong for one person (me).

I hoist the flag. Done!

FRI 29 NOV FIRST NATION UTOPIA

Andreas and I were invited by Julian Assange to the Ecuadorian Embassy to see John Pilger's latest documentary film, *Utopia*, about the Australian First Nation people. There were three of my heroes there: Julian, John, and lawyer Gareth Peirce (Gareth is a woman), whose work and latest book, *Dispatches from the Dark Side*, I have written about before. Julian and John are both Australian. I really appreciate the impact on British society and the world some of these Australians have had: Richard Neville in the 1970s with *Oz*, Germaine Greer, Barry Humphries, Julian, of course, and John who worked as a war journalist in Vietnam and elsewhere, analysing the facts, witness to unbearable horror and mounting atrocity. He revealed the crimes of Pol Pot in Cambodia to the world. He has continued since the 1970s to bring world attention to the plight of the First Nation people of Australia. Along with Noam Chomsky, Arundhati Roy and other monumental writers, he continues to expose the global political/economic/social SCAM.

Andreas was impressed with John, his clarity and humanity – no ego. I'm glad Andreas came as we have been able to talk about the film at home. It is fair and very well done. John interviews white and aboriginal people who are trying to deal with the problem – the neglect and inhumanity, the absence of justice. To the minister who said he was proud of certain incentives, John asked how in all the long years he'd had the job, he could be proud when nothing, absolutely nothing, had changed? John got involved in the 1970s (he includes some footage from this time) and since then nothing has improved. And this is the really shocking thing: what are we doing on this earth if we continue these abuses unabated? The First Nation people are a small percentage of the population, it would be possible to restore them their rights.

The film begins with an official person – I think a politician – who says that he can tolerate the ones who fit in, not the others. And here you have it, the real problem that no one can solve: the right of people to be different, have different values; not the values of our civilisation whose ethic is leading to self-destruction. This difference I think, is what the white Australians are afraid of, why they ignore the problem. Recently there was a press campaign against the First Nation people falsely claiming that they were paedophiles. Why? To prove that they are different and therefore barbaric? To harden people in preparation for future abuse?

Other ways to deal with difference: there is a gross disproportion of First Nation people in jail and John cites examples of a complete lack of care, which has caused shocking deaths in custody and for which no-one has been prosecuted. And I mention one last fact which you won't believe could happen today: First Nation mothers have their new babies snatched from them in the hospitals by government forces without explanation, never to see them again.

I told Julian about the article 'Who are our Rulers?' from the Climate Revolution site. He wants a print-out and also of the diary. He said it's more relaxing for him to have it in this form than reading on the computer. He said that our real rulers are probably the secret services, who are a law unto themselves, though they serve the highest bidder.

DECEMBER 2013

SUN 1 DEC FABRICS FOR THE GOLD COLLECTION

Iris arrives for a week. Our resident pattern cutter, Barbara, has also become a real tour-de-force. Both she and Iris are German – you can still get proper training in Germany. Their capabilities would not be possible without it. They really know tailoring.

Andreas is getting very excited by the Gold collection. He's so happy with the fabrics – they're so odd! Inflation is rocketing: the main fabrics for this collection were up to £20 a metre a couple of seasons ago, now they are £20–50. Andreas says he wants to make clothes that nobody can wear; meaning, I hope, that whoever does choose something will look beyond special.

TUES 3 DEC REPRIEVE AND EGYPTIAN PUPPETS

We bought a table at an event to support Reprieve. It was a quiz night and Jon Snow was there supporting. He's a man who knows what's going on in the world and does what he can. The questions were good last year but this time they were just popular trivia, which I know nothing about; indeed the team who came second was *Harper's*! Sara Stockbridge ('such naff questions but I'm so competitive') and my son Ben took it seriously. However, it was a treat to be in the Serpentine Gallery, where there was an exhibition of puppets by Egyptian puppet master, Wael Shawky. His film used puppets who were more riveting in the close-ups, as they spoke, than people.

FRI 6 DEC CHRISTMAS PARTY

Our Christmas party. Entertainment: Northern Lights Symphony Orchestra, Abigail Iverson, The Carnabys, Fernando Montaño of the Royal Ballet, Nadine Shah. All really good. Nadine Shah is good-looking – masculine, powerful, sexy, good voice, own material. Fernando – very classy, a tango – had combined two pieces of music for his own fast and furious choreography, riveting and ravishing. Amazing the stamina these dancers have.

SAT 7 – WEDS 11 DEC ITALY WITH WITH ROSITA AND PAOLA

Andreas and I went to Italy. We stay with Rosita and Paola, our best friends, who produce Gold Label. I would never have been able to pin down the knitwear and communicate the ideas in time if I hadn't gone. The knitwear is unisex, done for the men's collection in mid-January and for the Gold Label, which is end February. It looks good on a woman – I like the look of wearing your old man's sweater. It's a good trick because now from this base I can just add a few garments exclusive to women for the coming Gold. It's lovely to stay with our friends, and Rosita's mother, who lives in the country nearby, cooks for us. She grows and makes everything herself.

SAT 14 DEC MASTERPIECES OF CHINESE PAINTING

I've been back to the *Masterpieces of Chinese Painting* three times and I have been in bliss just reading and looking at the catalogue. I am so interested in the scholar-officials, the literati. Every painting tells the story of the painter's life. Bertrand Russell's book *The Problem of China* gives the background. For 4,000 years China was an empire (the dynasties changed) until Western depredations finally sabotaged it. China – so unlike any other civilisation! Respect for others and for learning was already embedded in the

This is our Christmas card, back and front. Back: we gave this idea to Greenpeace, who campaign against Shell – oil spill in the Arctic causes black snow. They made a short film of it. Super. Front: Leslie Winer in our 'Save the Arctic' vest.

Zheng Sixiao (1241–1318), Ink Orchid. I'm sure each leaf was done with one stroke of the brush.

culture when Confucius (c.500 BC) edited the mythical annals of the Golden Age (supposed to be c.3000 BC). They tell of the legendary emperor, Yao:

> He was reverential, intelligent, accomplished and thoughtful – naturally and without effort. He was sincerely courteous, and capable of all complaisance. The display of these qualities reached to the four extremities of the empire, and extended from earth to heaven. He was able able to make the able and virtuous distinguished, and thence proceeded to the love of the nine classes of his kindred, who all became harmonious. He also regulated and polished the people of his domain, who all became brightly intelligent. Finally, he united and harmonised the myriad States of the empire; and lo! the black haired people were transformed. The result was universal concord.

I find this incredible. I've never heard anything like it. Think of Homer's *Iliad*, one of the West's earliest mythical stories (c.1200 BC) – it's mostly a catalogue of gory details of how heroes killed each other.

By the time of the Tang dynasty (c.600–900 AD), the scholars (*literati*) administered the country. There was no state religion, though religion was tolerated – no religious liars as in the West. The scholar-painters were either administrators who painted in their spare time or professionals. What I love about them is that they lived by the Confucian ethic. They had pride in living an honourable life; this made them true to themselves, they lived up to their own standards. Painting was a means of telling the truth, it affirmed and reflected back to them their own value in living the best life possible to them. Often the subject was a personal metaphor representing individual circumstances. This is really clear when circumstances changed dramatically as when the Mongols overthrew the Song dynasty (the Mongol dynasty is named Yuan and lasted from 1271–1368).

Zheng Sixiao was a man of exceptional literary talent and was on the way to high office when the dynasty fell. He refused an invitation to serve at the Yuan court and as a *yimin* (leftover subject) remained loyal to the fallen Song. He retired to a monastery. He wrote many poems raging against Yuan rule, which he collected in an anthology called *History of the Heart*, sealed in an iron box and threw into a well at a temple. They were discovered 350 years later when the well ran dry. He painted the orchid over and over again to express his bitter feelings – elegant and fluid, without roots (which show above ground in the orchid). When asked about this he replied, 'The soil has been taken by the foreigners. Can you bear it?' He wrote in the poem accompanying the orchid in the exhibition: 'I opened my nostrils before making the painting, And there, floating everywhere in the sky, is the antique fragrance undying.'

Until the twentieth century progress was a concept unthought of by the Chinese, as it still was to us at the time of Elizabeth I. The concept runs parallel with the emerging aggressive trade of the seventeenth century and locks in with the Industrial Revolution. What is progress then but the art of war and aggressive trade? And it brought climate change. The only progress is in the art of living. I just hope the human race can survive. Growth is nothing to do with us – only for banks, business and governments. In my company, I want to expand less but still make beautiful clothes.

TUES 24 DEC **FATHER CHRISTMAS FOREVER**

These are the stamps on my friend Frank's latest letter. Father Christmas ~~Forever~~. Frank crossed it out. Santa is part of our national identity. Every country owns him – and it's important to our rulers that we believe in him just as we believe the propaganda that the world will carry on as normal. Well, 'normal' means death. Not only will Father Christmas die but so will our whole way of life.

I'm at home writing up this diary for December. I think it's cool to write the diary after the events – the events are just as important to me now as the original experience, in fact it's a bonus to live them again. And it's in keeping with the Climate Revolution website; our news doesn't switch from one thing to another like the daily media. We hold onto our facts and our aims.

A note on the Arctic 30: my guess is that Putin painted himself into a corner with their arrest. Whether they were convicted or freed on the charges that were brought against them it would have been bad. He had to free them – and quick – because of the coming Winter Olympics. They are not Russian so there is more international pressure. Therefore, to cover up, he freed the Russian oil tycoon and the girls from Pussy Riot (fucking brave, aren't they just?) as well.

JANUARY 2014

WEDS 1 JAN CHRISTMAS READING – AND FRACKING

A quiet Christmas at home – just Andreas and I. We sometimes went for a walk on Clapham Common – love the time of year especially at twilight time when the weather is miserable, then back to a warm home. He pops out more than me, sometimes to work, though there was no one else there. Andreas was reading a biography of Bernard Berenson, the art historian. He told me a bit about him. How he began by travelling in Italy, looking at art in churches, in homes and public collections and became an authority, authenticating for dealers and buyers in the exodus of European art to America. In particular, Berenson advised the rich widow, Isabella Stewart Gardner, who built a Boston gallery to house her acquisitions. Berenson made money, too, and housed his famous collection of art books in his villa, I Tatti, overlooking Florence. He was one of the models for Swann in Proust's novel. Swann fell in love with his mistress, Odette, because she looked like a Botticelli.

I was reading my beloved Chinese Masterpieces catalogue and going through my papers. I don't use a computer, which I realise must be convenient for storing information. Instead, I sorted through piles of papers – photocopies of articles copied from the internet by Cynthia. I re-read them and keep only the most important ones.

Me in my old flat, around the time of the Buffalo Girls collection, just back from working in Italy. The poster is Botticelli's *Primavera* from the Uffizi gallery.

I have been reading John Pilger's books and articles since 1986 when he published *Heroes*. Its section on the Vietnam war – the lengths America went to in order to impose supremacy, to establish world hegemony – and create hell – is beyond belief, beyond the imagination of the Devil.

John is the same age as me. At forty-five I already had a good grasp of global politics and reading *Heroes* everything fell into place. John had learnt so much by direct contact with the reality of world events; he had done so much.

In *Heroes*, John says: 'As Chomsky has pointed out, American policy was never concerned with Vietnam alone ...' America is supposed to have lost the war in Vietnam. But they achieved their aims; the threat was that Vietnam would have a more communistic financial model instead of the model of capitalism – and that other Asian countries might copy it. 'Far from being vanquished in South-East Asia, the US has devastated, blockaded and isolated Vietnam and its "viruses" and has subordinated to American interests almost every regime in the region.' One thing we need to know – the world is run for cheap labour; the American interest and capitalism has since been able to exploit this densely populated region, especially Indonesia.

On New Year's Eve I woke up about 2.30 a.m. I was thinking: Climate Revolution is working with NGOs, activist groups, organisations and individuals to prevent fracking in the UK; together we will draft a letter as the first step in informing the public of the facts. I worry that despite David Cameron saying nothing would go ahead without fair discussion, what we hear from the government is that it's all going ahead: licences have already been issued and more are in the offing. Everything I've heard the government say is untrue. They want to allow this infrastructure, with its hundreds of test wells, at the risk of ruining our soil, water and our beautiful countryside, so companies and their investors can make a profit. They are locked into destruction. But there is so much opportunity now for cheap green energy.

WEDS 8 JAN ANTI-FRACKING MEETING

To Curtain Road, Old Street, to a photographic studio. When we began our business in the '70s, I spent three days a week driving over London to outworkers. I cut the clothes and took them to machinists; I made the knitting patterns and took the wool to the handknitters; and I went to Greek artisans delivering materials to get tailoring and shoes made. In Curtain Road I visited a trimmings merchant, an enormous warehouse filled from floor to ceiling with treasures. Nowadays we choose trimmings from brochures or send our own designs to companies, usually in Italy and not open to custom from the street. This now was where I did my photos for an interview with Deborah Orr in *The Gentlewoman*. The photographer, Alasdair McLellan, and stylist, Jonathan Kaye, were nice and clever. I enjoyed myself.

Then at 3 p.m. I went on to my son Joe's in Amwell Street to meet the anti-fracking groups. The role of Climate Revolution, with the help of Joe, has been to try to get the various activist groups together. People liked the idea of using the fact, 'the government is behaving irresponsibly'. We discussed the main content of our letter. It's good. Most importantly, it demands the government stop until all our questions have been answered (we will refute their claims). The people we're working with are really impressive regarding the organisation they have in place to physically protest; and we all rely on the climate activists in the camps to keep the focus of the protests.

FRI 10 JAN MILAN FOR THE MENSWEAR SHOW

Andreas and I go to Milan for the preparation and presentation of our menswear collection. The show is on Sunday, and all next week in our Italian showrooms we will begin selling our collections, except Gold Label, to our buyers and to our own shops. Selling then continues in London, Paris and Los Angeles. There are a lot of people in our Italian building. I concentrate on the unisex knitwear, making sure it looks good and making improvements for the production. I also looked at Red Label which had just arrived.

I was, in general, pleased. I want the woman who chooses to wear this collection to look looked-after, warm, adventurous, important and artistic. I left it to Andreas to get on with the MAN collection, styling and casting, with Georg, to whom we gave a lot of freedom to design this season and who worked so hard. The show looked good. I interview on anti-fracking.

This outfit at our Milan menswear show used the CC snakes and a jacquard.

WEDS 15 JAN MAKE ECOCIDE A CRIME

Home from Italy yesterday. This morning I'm on a boat moored near Blackfriars Bridge, for a 10 a.m. press conference where I will speak on 'ecocide'. This is how it happened: The concept of ecocide has been around since the 1970s. Making ecocide a crime against peace was examined within the UN for decades from the 1970s to 1990s. It was shelved at the last minute in 1996 without being put to the vote and despite a number of countries objecting to its exclusion. Polly Higgins, a UK lawyer and an advocate for making ecocide a crime against peace, picked up the idea in 2010, judging that people would again be responsive to it. Her proposed amendment to the Rome Statute reads: 'Ecocide is the extensive damage to, destruction of, or loss of ecosystem(s) of a given territory, whether by human agency or by other causes, to such an extent that peaceful enjoyment by the inhabitants of that territory has been or will be severely diminished.'

Polly gave a talk, after which Prisca Merz, director of 'End Ecocide in the UK', offered to help Climate Revolution in any way she could. It is still only a small organisation but they are doing awfully well. They had a mock trial that found two oil company CEOs guilty on indictments of ecocide of Canada's Athabasca tar sands – an event live-streamed by Sky News. Leading QCs Michael Mansfield and Chris Parker and their teams of lawyers fought for and against the indictments. Although the CEOs were actors and the companies fictional, the evidence was real.

The launch was well attended and reported by the press – and the movement has a real chance of concrete result.

SAT 18 JAN KATE MOSS'S 40TH BIRTHDAY

Andreas and I went to Kate Moss's 40th birthday party out in the Cotswolds. I enjoyed myself so much. I'm so busy that I see these friends rarely. My old friend Chrissie Hynde (we once went everywhere together), and I do like Sadie Frost and her mum (I must invite them to the Red Label show, inspired by a collection Sadie first modelled in sixteen years ago), Stella McCartney, and Rifat Ozbek (he did the decor – psychedelic). And, of course, Kate herself. *'Hello!'* I've said it before, her voice is so sexy and intimate. Everything she says sounds like a conspiracy (to do what? One day I must find out). And then there was Naomi! Andreas loves her. She really is a goddess – she behaves like one, she makes things move.

MON 20 JAN JEAN-YVES THIBAUDET

Another dear friend, Jean-Yves Thibaudet, world-famous pianist. Andreas and I bike to the Wigmore Hall after work where Jean-Yves and mezzo soprano Angelika Kirchlager are in concert together. I love the Wigmore Hall and the concert. We're so lucky. Jean-Yves is sweeter than ever. It's not only his super-talent that makes him a star but because he is also so endearingly nice – and fun. We were all together with his friend Paul.

TUES 21 JAN ANDY GOTTS'S PHOTOS

Tizer and I bike over to Somerset House after work to see the photographic exhibition of stars who have been nominated for BAFTAs – supposed to be the biggest collection of film stars in one place – by Andy Gotts. We want to thank Andy because he has been taking photos of celebrities wearing the 'Save the Arctic' T-shirt we designed for Greenpeace.

THURS 30 JAN A BRIEFING ON FRACKING

Jamie and Tisha come to give us a briefing on fracking, so that we are truly armed with the facts. We will demolish the government's misinformation and win the fight.

9 of Andy Gotts' Save the Arctic photos: top row – Sadie Frost, Stella McCartney, Julian Assange; middle row – Pamela Anderson, Sharon Osbourne, Sienna Miller; bottom row – George Clooney, Andreas Kronthaler, Tracey Emin.

How clean is fracking? The one thing I keep hearing is that fracking is somehow clean/cleaner, that it will cause less pollution than other fuels. Lord Browne, former CEO of BP and now chairman of the shale gas company Cuadrilla, advises the government and is promoting an assumption that it is clean. He makes it feel like it's our duty, telling us on the news that it's a 'national imperative'. If you assume things often enough people will start to believe it. Tisha says we still don't know which is worse, coal or fracking. The University of Minnesota is working on this, comparing it to coal (coal combustion being the worst polluter on earth) and they have yet to come to a decision; it's difficult to choose between them.

I find it interesting that fracking is now not an option in Germany. There has been such an improvement in insulating homes and businesses that gas consumption has gone down to the extent that companies cannot make a profit. In some cases of new houses built with passive insulation and air-sealing, energy bills are really small; the home is kept warm by body heat and normal cooking and baking.

I also think it's good to know the real story of America's energy boom from shale gas; they don't need their coal but are exporting it at a cheap price. The story is that it is short-term economy. Anything short term is bad for the planet. The US is a country with vast areas of low population but with over 80,000 fracking wells operated by different companies, competing and selling cheap. The reports are that the useful life of a well is three to five years. So, new drilling is unlimited in a frenzy of 'make money while you can'. Now the peak is probably past and the damage has not been accounted for.

I am happy to know Jamie and Tisha, such fine people – she having changed her career to focus on what she considers most important. Jamie is passionately supportive of his friends in the climate camp at Barton Moss. His friend Kris O'Donnell had live streaming from his phone when the police came for him. They broke the bone around his eye socket and the picture of his muddy, bleeding face went all over the internet. There are other incidents of police aggression at Barton Moss and Jamie told how one night the police raided the camp under the pretext that someone had seen a flare go up and turfed everyone out of the tents and into the rain and trampled their bedding and possessions into the sludge. These people are so important to our campaign to save the planet.

I'm sorry that the police were so aggressive. I thought things had got better since the 1960s and '70s when we went on demos. People then called the police 'pigs' and we glared at them with enmity. Since then the attitude of the public has changed; neither police nor people are so respectful of governments. So, I don't think the police are as anti-people as they were, especially now that jobs are harder to get. I think of the police in general as having a job to do and that means keeping the peace and they should be protecting people's right to peaceful demonstration.

FRI 31 JAN POSTCARDS FROM THE FRONTLINE

I met Lily Cole and Lorna Tucker at Selfridges for an event organised by the Environmental Justice Foundation. Steve Trent is the NGO's founder and its current task is to send 'Postcards from the Frontline' to Ban Ki-moon asking for UN recognition of the plight of climate refugees. We show the *Red Shoes* film and then we three women answer questions. Steve is the moderator. Lily is a very affectionate woman; she is always pleased to see me.

FEBRUARY 2014

SAT 1 FEB FLOODS AND THE UKRAINE CRISIS

I have been busy with fashion – which is why this diary has got rather late – and it is just too much for me to tell of all the preparation of two collections and two shows, one after the other. I liked them a lot and I'll tell a bit about them later on. While we were working away the main news topics in the wide world were flooding in England (which everyone now accepts as a symptom of climate change) and the crisis in the Ukraine. According to present political policies there is only intermittent solution to conflict, no end to perpetual war. Putin's a macho thug, a criminal, and don't let's forget that his people planted explosives in the basement of flats and killed Russian civilians so they could blame the Chechnyans. He spreads terror whilst trying to develop his own personality cult. The Americans spread global terror but they manage to cover this up to most of the people in their own country.

MON 3 FEB THE MONTEVERDI CHOIR AT THE PALACE

We were invited to a concert and dinner at Buckingham Palace in celebration of the Monteverdi Choir's 50th anniversary; Prince Charles is their patron. The choir and its orchestra are the work of conductor Sir John Eliot Gardiner, who has researched how music sounded in its day and recreates it on similar instruments.

Prince Charles said how he, as a young boy, became aware of how great the paintings on the walls of the palace were (we were looking at them during the reception and dinner) and made a link to the fact that John Eliot had in his home the only portrait of Bach, which had been left there for safekeeping by a young man who fled from the Nazis to England by bicycle; Prince Charles wondered if this might have helped create the passions whereby he formed the choir at the early age of twenty.

The two pieces played were by Bach and Handel, both born in 1685. You are sustained and lifted by the rhythm of Baroque music; you fly. John Eliot had chosen a favourite Handel piece and gave us the image to this composition: Handel as a young man in Rome for the first time – Then! – when Rome was the same size as it is now, when it was so rich – all Baroque, with its cardinals and churches – when the palaces which today are museums or divided up into flats were lived in by the famous families. How Handel showed off in this piece of music! He wanted to out-dazzle the dazzle.

We met really nice people. Isabella, John Eliot's wife, wearing one of our gowns in ice blue, was so animated and friendly. I said to Andreas that I'm sorry we're so busy that we don't cultivate new friendships. I would like to see them again. Lo and behold, the next day arrived a present of a small box of CDs – the collected recordings of the Monteverdi Choir and orchestra with very special sleeves, the photos of (mostly) arresting faces by Steve McCurry – Isabella's idea – and an invitation to dinner. I am so pleased. Isabella's interested in Climate Revolution, perhaps she'd like to help us.

WEDS 5 FEB VANESSA THORPE

I did an interview with Vanessa Thorpe for the *Observer*, about the famous people wearing our 'Save the Arctic' T-shirts, photographed by Andy Gotts. Vanessa seemed serious and lovely and I thought I'd like to know her more and in person. I always trust journalists but you can sometimes be wrong. When the article came out I couldn't have wished it better – chatty about the celebrities but she found a way to include every important thing I said. Thank you, dear.

SAT 8 FEB HANDEL'S THEODORA

To the Barbican to hear Handel's *Theodora* oratorio. Handel's 'victory oratorios' were prompted by the Duke of Cumberland's brutal crushing of the Jacobite rebellion in 1745 and matched the bellicose national mood. But *Theodora* cut right against audience expectations, 'emphasising the power of the Holy Spirit to change lives and sanctioning religious tolerance and freedom of thought'.

WEDS 12 FEB JUDE LAW IN HENRY V

Jude Law in *Henry V*. Loved it. I know the play quite well and can quote the prologue, 'Oh for a muse of fire ...'. Shakespeare's

Jude Law in Henry V. Loved it.

craft is forever original, no matter how many times you hear it. I discovered my favourite scene was Henry wooing the French princess: she is talking in French all the time and he in English but you understand everything. Sexy! Jude Law has such a physical presence. (Agincourt was truly a terrible battle, fought in mud and rain, with the English archers slaughtering the French knights as their horses skidded. English deaths a few hundred, French 10,000. The two-fingered 'Fuck Off' gesture is rumoured to be that of the English archers – their fingers which drew back the bowstring when they shot the arrow. These fingers were chopped off if they were captured.)

It was so well done. Everything just fell into place. Unfussy, down-to-earth, especially the scene changes, which I remember as just carrying the props on and off, and changes in lighting. The actors did the same, just moved around, or on and off, and you immediately accepted the changed scene. The costumes suggested the period in history but suited the characters; true to cliché – in the play and now – the French were dressed more decoratively – more silk and velvet, made to seem more effeminate and inconstant by comparison with the manly Henry in his leather jerkin and solid crown and at the time of battle his heraldic tabard. The Welsh windbag Fluellen was a little turkey-cock in a wide-brimmed felt hat, and very smart in boots and breeches, which I think were called galligaskins. Everything considered but it looked so natural.

MON 17 FEB KLAUS

Klaus is here again with us. He, Iris and Kai are three great pattern cutters, all so different – you can tell who did which pattern. (Kai teaches in Hamburg now.) All our pattern cutters are German – that's where the training is. They learn so much more working with us – they will learn from Klaus – and Andreas's original approach and our innovative cutting systems.

MARCH 2014

SAT 1 MARCH GOLD LABEL SHOW, PARIS

Gold Label show, Paris. Andreas and I arrived on Wednesday at noon. He went straight to the showroom for the casting. I went to the hotel and stayed in bed till noon the next day, reading.

Then I went to the showroom where most of the collection had arrived. Now I could see all the clothes in their proper fabrics and put all the outfits together. I knew it would be strange: I am used to us mixing things, from tabards to togas to tailoring, including our signature cutting principles and historical cuts and with innovative use of fabric. There is always some hint of a story, theatre; a way of dressing up to express more of yourself. But with this collection I feel I've never seen anything like it. It's pure fantasy, the character of each outfit has not yet been identified. It's waiting for whoever wears it to invent it. I will choose something and I will feel the freedom to be anything! Even anonymous or at least incognito. I will feel very self-aware.

The Gold Label show – inspired by the Ashaninka of Peru's rainforest.

I told you Andreas was inspired by Worth and beside that we were also inspired by the quite different world of our friends from the rainforest, the Ashaninka. They sent us some garments and beads and we designed workware/battledress in forest green. (The Ashaninka have fought many years for their forest. Many died in the last war with the Shining Path.) I love their woven or painted garments – a simple bag – shape, beads and red face paint. I respect people who until now have need of so few clothes and possessions, and who identify with their elegant traditional attire. It keeps you more at one with the world. Sam and Val did cool stuff as usual. Sam took away the hair by plastering it flat around the head but also did five girls' hair in belle époque styles. And Val used the Ashaninka face paint.

Venue: beautiful deconsecrated church of the Oratoire de Louvre St-Honore. Lighting: cool (Tony). Music: cool (Dominik). We put presents of chocolate from the Ashaninka on the seats. The plan to save the rainforest is on track.

SUN 2 MARCH NOBUKO

Still in Paris. Such a treat being with our best friend, Yasmine Eslami (French stylist and lingerie designer), who worked on the show. And at dinner I enjoyed talking to Jonathan the stylist who did the shoot for *The Gentlewoman*, who was there with their editor Penny Martin. Of course I talked about 'Who are our Rulers?' and the danger we face from climate change. My friend Frank came all the way from San Francisco. I managed to spend time with him. But I hugged my friend Nobuko, who came from Japan and who I haven't seen for a few years, and then missed her before she went back, she having hurried across London to visit the beautiful pots of Steve Harrison. Nobuko is fantastic. Very beautiful with no make-up. She usually wears black and has long, slightly wavy, black hair down to her waist. She used to wear the most perfect make-up when we first met her; she introduced us to Japanese partners more than twenty years ago and worked with us in Japan. Then she changed her career, wore kimonos, and learnt to work with leather, against taboo. In Japan, leather-working is considered filthy work and done by men of low rank.

WEDS 5 MARCH HOUSING THEFTS

Scandal in Lambeth. I join the local protest outside a house under threat near to my home. Kate Hoey the Vauxhall MP was there; she's great. Lambeth Council are picking off the members of the housing co-op one by one. Must fight them. I heard that at Elephant and Castle the council intend to demolish half the council housing and build posh apartments, adding to the waiting lists of people who can't afford a home. Andreas likes a cup of tea of a morning in the café across the road. He's noticed in the last year the women who meet there after dropping off their children at school – all in smart, keep-fit gear with expensive bags. They have bought houses for £2 million on this south side of the river and sold their houses on the other side (Chelsea), which they've had handed down to them, for £10 to £12 million.

WEDS 12 MARCH DOING THEATRE DIFFERENTLY

In the evening I went with my friend Peter Olive to a discussion at Battersea Arts Centre on 'The future of text' in theatre. There was a panel of two women director-managers and a woman who improvised drama on a night bus, chaired by an actor who performed his own material. The audience was a small group of supporters of this theatre. I am a trustee and I like it because it's local and it's also an important theatre. I was interested to hear the discussion because a lot of theatre has a problem with text. You can't hear the actors. They talk as if they're doing TV or film.

The panel talked (to each other) for 45 minutes and managed to say nothing. What they did over and again was to repeat, 'We do things differently', without saying what it was that they did differently. One of them said that in a play something happens (that was the important thing) and you can say that differently (she must have meant mime it or change the meaning or the words). Yes, you can, but then the whole play must change. Why would you want to change the words of Shakespeare halfway through the play, then rewrite the rest? They talked about audiences, too, and I could see where they were coming from; they didn't want to cater for a privileged class. (Is text a problem for the less privileged?) They were anti-intellectual because they confuse that with being anti-people.

Peter and I had wanted to leave but we didn't because it seemed so rude – we were such a small gathering. However, when question time came I told them that we had been bored from beginning to end because they had nothing to say on the subject proposed for the discussion. The chairman told me I had a right to my opinion to which I agreed because it was more than an opinion but a fact. The audience were angry with me and told the panel it had been interesting; they couldn't say why. Presumably they had sat there as complacently as the speakers, happy supporters of people who said they did things differently. We must assume that these two women speakers, who each ran very prestigious theatres, put on good plays.

At the end, David, who runs the Centre, brought the evening smoothly to a close by telling us that the thing you think of last is often the best idea. I've heard this before but it's an empty, useless statement; it rather encourages people to think you can pull an idea out of a bag – whereas an idea is built; it grows and develops. It is formed. Every now and again I cannot make an idea work and when I've really had enough I go back to the beginning and aim for what seems like the only solution – but this is part of the work.

Theatre is, I think, the greatest art form for communicating ideas and it can be used to criticise the status quo. It is affecting; it gets to you much more than film because you have to supply the imagination. You can't be passive. I was lucky when I first went to the theatre, aged nineteen, to see Robert Bolt's *A Man for All Seasons* starring Paul Scofield. It is the story of Henry VIII's cardinal, Sir Thomas More, who opposed Henry's wish to divorce his first queen, Catherine of Aragon, and was burnt. The scene changes were minimal and magical: banners dropped from the ceiling and More's home was transformed into a court of law. A character called the Common Man rushed in with a long bench with eleven poles stuck in it, put a hat on each and sat down, completing the jury. That's what I mean about imagination being an active collaborator; we willingly take part in the pretence. We just love the play for showing us the trickery, giving us the gesture, and we supply the rest.

Theatre is larger than life. It does this by representing a thing by its essentials. It is artificial; artificial = made by art.

I think it would be great to reintroduce the artificial declamation of text into some of our plays. Laurence Olivier was larger than life but his style was too artificial on film, it looked contrived. How powerful the text in Peter Hall's Greek dramas which use the convention of masks! The actors never turn their backs and when they walk on from the side they twist to face us, full on. They talk to each other by facing the audience, talking to you in turn as if you were the one each was holding a conversation with. Aristotle says the end or purpose of a play is the plot, the thing that happens, 'for it is in the action that happiness or unhappiness lies ... according to their actions men are either fortunate or the reverse.' And, of course, men's actions depend on their character and how that character might behave in certain circumstances or in response to the behaviour of others. He must stay in character. Text is part of the drama, it moves the play along.

TUES 18 MARCH SHOWERING FOR PETA

Press launch of the video I did with Dan Mathews and PETA: I was filmed taking a shower. It's about being a vegetarian and saving water. It takes four million gallons to make one ton of beef. Nicely shot, good idea.

Pamela came. She does such a lot for animal rights. Whenever she travels Dan sets it up for her to talk to important people and they

have changed laws and practices. Imagine doing that every time you travel. It takes a lot.

WEDS 19 MARCH FRACKED FUTURE CARNIVAL

Our Big Day! The Fracked Future Carnival with Climate Revolution and Friends of the Earth, Frack Off London, Ecocide, Fuel Poverty Action, Reclaim the Power, and many community groups. It is scheduled for today so that we can protest the conference of conspirators, those business and government officials who are meeting to force fracking through against the public interest and before the public have been warned of the danger. Officials who

At the Fracked Future Carnival with Sadie Frost.

have their head in a box and are prepared to destroy the world for profit.

We know they have relocated their conference for fear of us and we know where it is. We will stick to our original plan: meet at our Battersea studio, march over the bridge to the King's Road, join fellow protestors at Knightsbridge tube then move to the original location of the conference, by the Jumeirah Hotel. We will give our speeches outside and then go to the secret location.

At Battersea we were ready. I had given all our workmates the day off. Cindy, the youngest member of Climate Revolution, had done a great job mustering the troops and organising our students to make placards. Others who joined us were in carnival mood, dressed as zombies and ghouls. I hadn't wanted a carnival. It's a matter of life and death and I didn't wear my warpaint. We want to attract 'ordinary people' and by that we mean people who aren't normally political. But our activist colleagues were right – we needed the carnival. We looked great. There was lots of press. I was asked to lead the procession. I bowed and put my hands together in prayer, as you would before a battle. Then off we went!

At the Jumeirah Hotel was a little square where we gave our speeches and thanked the fighters in the anti-fracking camps. Vanessa Vine from Balcombe is an inspiring speaker and full of powerful information. She's been fighting fracking for three years and is just back from America. The queen of it all was engineer Tisha who was responsible for much of the organisation; she is the prettiest ghoul you ever saw but stays anonymous, so you can't see a photo of her. Then some of us got on Nigel's bus and went to the 'secret location' at Armoury House on City Road. The press asked me, 'How do you feel that the pro-frackers have come here to escape you, protected by the army?' It's so important to demonstrate for your beliefs. We will win because we have to.

Evening dinner with the Gardiners. Our mutual friend Romilly McAlpine was with us and also Ronnie Harwood, screenwriter of *The Pianist*. He was so sweet.

SUN 23 MARCH MOZART AND MUSSORGSKY

Afternoon at the Royal Festival Hall. We got some take-away Egyptian food at the Southbank market and went into the concert. Mozart Violin Concerto No. 3: soloist, Esther Yoo. Chinese, brought up in New York, twenty years old. She was a delight. Tiny, moving her head to the music. Andreas said 'Mozart would have loved her with her swirling ponytail'. Then Mussorgsky's *Pictures at an Exhibition*, orchestrated by Ravel. Hear it before you die!

MON 24 MARCH 1984 AT THE ALMEIDA

To the Almeida for a Headlong/Nottingham Playhouse production of *1984*. I saw it about ten years ago but they've changed it. It was perfect before and it's perfect now. Such skill, such use of theatre. Bravo! The book is one of the greatest importance.

I went with Andreas, Ben and Tomoka. I wanted to cry. Winston was played by the actor Mark Arends, so little and thin. He was actually quite tall but he was being tortured and even then he stuck up for himself, his hopes. You didn't see the torture, you saw what it did to him. He was fighting for his love for Julia and hope for somebody not yet born. And there came the point where he couldn't stand the torture. He had to say, 'Do it to Julia', and then he lost his identity. The whole world had him in its power all the time even when he thought there was a chance.

TUES 25 MARCH TEA WITH MISS PIGGY

Miss Piggy was in London for the premiere of her new film and we are proud to have made her such lovely clothes to wear for it. So this afternoon we went to see her at her hotel where she had invited us for tea. Andreas had met her at the fitting so he introduced me. She couldn't have looked more pretty in her 'Save the Arctic' T-shirt

A chat with Miss Piggy about politics and fashion (we made her wedding dress).

and her tartan mini kilt. We recorded our chat on video so we'll all be able to see it.

FRI 28 MARCH TRILLION FUND

Trillion Fund came to see us – Michael Stein and Julia Groves. They're doing very well. Their aim is to open up banking and make it possible for people to invest in renewable energy: in effect, energy projects can be crowd-funded. Julia has been talking to government ministers (lobbying) and they have now agreed! Small investors will not be restricted; anyone can fund projects. Also we are going to get Green ISAs. Michael seems to know more about energy and energy extraction than anyone. Ask him a question – e.g. about the Severn Barrage scheme – and his face lights up (the scheme's not necessary, disused Welsh harbours are better places to do this). Michael has simple solutions. One idea he mentions could be to work with France and the EU to lease desert in Algeria and Morocco, or Greece, who need the money, and build solar parks. We can use the same pipeline which brings nuclear energy from France to bring us solar. Indeed Trillion Fund could supply a plan for us to have energy security, as clean as possible, and very cheap once the investment is paid back.

No need to frack: Climate Revolution talks only sense for the environment and sense for the economy.

SAT 29 MARCH DINNER AT LIMA

Dinner at Lima, a Peruvian restaurant. Reunion dinner of we friends who went together to the rainforest, invited by Cool Earth. Treat to see journalist Deborah Ross. Plans.

APRIL 2014

TUES 1 APRIL IAN KELLY'S BIOGRAPHY

I had thought after all the work in March for two collections I might have a pause but, no, straight into one last print needed for Red Label and I must read the first draft of Ian Kelly's biography of me and make some notes. One of the things I'm keen to get right are my motivations and what drives me. I have read half of the book and I think it's good. There are a few surprises from people who love me, things I didn't know or realise.

TUES 8 APRIL BIRTHDAY FLOWERS

My birthday. I don't usually celebrate because I don't fancy the fuss. At home, flowers arrive, beautiful, quite a lot by the end of the day.

Thank you. At one o'clock Ian comes and we work through the book. He comes again on Thursday and we work from 10 a.m. to 6.30 p.m. In between the special events this month of April is taken up with some work for Red Label – mainly correcting and finishing the knitwear samples we received from Italy, fittings and fabric choice for Red Carpet. But no work on Gold Label – always left till last though it's our most important collection. Cynthia is snowed under, working with Cindy on Climate Revolution; I manage to join  in some of the discussion especially on our campaign, 'We Need to Talk about Fracking'. I managed to attend only one of our weekly meetings of Q v. Q which aims to concentrate and reduce the size of our company and product. Any spare time is taken up with checking the first draft of my biography with Ian.

WEDS 9 APRIL TALKING ABOUT COMPUTERS

Morning: to Juergen's place to discuss the idea for our next campaign – the most important aspect being who to choose as the model.

Evening: dinner with our friend Lawrence, and a colleague of his called John. They both work on a developement scheme linked to one of the cyber giants. As far as I understand it they locate social groups who could benefit from having mobile phones. Lawrence's main aim is to empower women and phones are a tool for them to control and organise their lives, for example through banking and microfinance. He tells me about a woman who, through using her husband's phone, found a program by which she taught herself to write, then taught other women in her village and is now the head of a communications company.

Inevitably the conversation passed to the evils of computers. I thought of Lila aged five who was sitting next to her mother (she had to bring her to work – with us), killing time before they could go home. Lila had a computer and her task was to organise coloured shapes. I never saw anything so ugly as the neat graphic on her screen. I said, 'That's really boring isn't it? Anybody knows the difference between blue and red, or a star and a circle. I suppose it's a program for a two-year-old.' (God forbid!) 'This is my favourite program,' she responded, activating the standard game of Little Hero avoids or kills all the shit that comes streaming at him. Nadir of human experience, nothing of beauty or aspiration. If I'd been Lila I would have been reading or drawing.

Another inevitable discussion we had is how social media enables protest. This is good and we really need to build on it. And how useful are online petitions? WikiLeaks and other NGOs have revealed the difference between fact and propaganda. People don't swallow the political propaganda so easily anymore. Is this a reason why some of them turn to racist political parties (or radical Islam)?

It's very good talking to Lawrence. He asks the kind of questions that are important to me.

SAT 12 APRIL HOME TO GLOSSOP

After yoga we took a taxi to the home of my brother Gordon and his partner Geraldine and drove to Glossop in the Pennines where we were born. I took one of Geraldine's books, which I began to read on the motorway, a biography of the ballet superstar Rudolf Nureyev. We were on our way to our cousin Edith's Golden Wedding celebration. I haven't seen Edith for many years and when she phoned to invite me she told me something I had heard

Rudolf Nureyev on the set of the ballet film *Le Jeune Homme et La Mort* with Zizi Jeanmaire, December 1966. I wrote a three-part profile of Nurevey for the CR site.

but forgotten. Her husband Ken had a stroke which paralysed him. For the last eight years, Edith's life, except for a game of golf once a week, she has been looking after him. The way she puts it – 'I have to sort him out.' It must be harder for Ken, but how people love life despite difficulties, and of course I had to go. Edith told me that I (aged thirteen) and a little boy were the only two guests in the wedding photo who were still alive.

It was a lovely ceremony, a really good buffet and good speeches. We met our cousins and friends again. We were in the hotel for two nights. My cousin Hazel, her family and my old school friend Mike came to see us. I enjoyed being with Gordon, he's full of information. And I loved talking to his teenage grandchildren – Leigh and Sky and her boyfriend Sean. I told them my philosophy of life, you have to follow your deep interest. I remember when I was at school there, the glamorous job ideas for girls were be a nurse or a teacher, otherwise you had to be a secretary or an accountant; it's the same still. I suggested to Sky that she could study history of art.

My home countryside – around Holmfirth.

Andreas had never been to Glossop. He said he 'did not know England could be like that'. It's very beautiful and it's my home. I think we all love best the place we're born. The Longdendale Valley set amongst hills. From our home we could go in three directions and walk all day, all different: the green hills of the Derbyshire Peak District, the Cheshire woods, the Yorkshire moors. We drove Andreas over the moors to Holmfirth (*Last of the Summer Wine*), a one-time wool town, factories built amongst the hills in the middle of nowhere to access the water power.

On Monday we walked with Hazel and her daughter, Paula, through Swallow's Wood and down to Devil's Bridge, as we used to. The families would stay on the bank of the stream, picnic and talk, while the children played in the water. Andreas loved it and we came back 'over the top' where we were followed by a new lamb who wanted its mother and then found her. It was a boy, so he gets killed soon. Paula said she feels so sorry when the lambs are taken away, you hear the mothers bleating all night. Then we drove over the spectacular bare moors and back down to London.

FRI 18 APRIL BACH'S ST JOHN'S PASSION

To St John's, Smith Square, for Bach's St John's Passion. Orchestra of the Age of Enlightenment. I don't believe in God but I believe in the concept of perfection.

I was brought up in the Anglican religion. Some of the hymn tunes we sang are from this Passion but it's impossible to match exactly which ones because the music is so full: the instruments, the choir with its descants, and the swelling base and culmination of the strains and overlay ever-changing and soaring; the music fills you, you can't pin it down, you don't want to, you're just part of a world which is carrying you away and you're riding up on the hypnotic rhythm of Baroque music. This is the difference between the Protestant religious service, filling yourself with song when you yourself sing with everyone, or the Catholic service and being carried away by the choir. In between are the arias, each different voice partnered by a different instrument and the story told by the recitateur. This one, Jeremy Ovenden, was the best ever. The clarity of his expression, voice and acting!

SAT 19 APRIL MARK SPYE'S BIRTHDAY

Mark Spye's birthday. Mark has worked with me since he was a kid, and now for many years as a main designer. He began as a machinist, then managed our Davies Street shop. We still have customers who remember the days of Mark, who still wear the beautiful clothes he organised for them. Great stylist. His friends organised a surprise for him – we all came. He had a lovely time.

SUN 20 – TUES 22 APRIL AT JOE'S IN CORNWALL

To Cornwall, staying with my son Joe. Family members try to meet around Easter to celebrate the memory of my mother and father. Dora died at this time of year. I finished writing and choosing three

With the family in Cornwall: Ben, me, Joe, Joe's friend Faye, Gordon, Andreas.

excerpts from the Nureyev biography, which I'm posting on the Climate Revolution website. I was still reading it on our way down, driving in Andreas's car, which he hardly ever drives but lends to friends. I wish we could stay another day but we have to get back. It's lovely where we are, talking round the fire, cooking. It's more luscious than the Pennines – I never saw primroses growing when I lived there as a child – just the odd violet and lots of bluebells – but here the banks along the hedgerows are fairy gardens.

SAT 26 APRIL SARA'S PARTY – HENDRIX AND UKIP

Sara (Stockridge) had a house party for her friends – who happened to be our friends as well. We gave her a little scarf, others brought cakes and wine. She had cooked so, so good curry dishes! We all stayed in the kitchen, talking and eating until finally Sara got us upstairs to the living room where we could dance if we wanted and where Cobalt was making cocktails. Cobalt is Sara's husband; his band, Zodiac Mindwarp and The Love Reaction, still gigs, though he works in information security. He gave me his favourite guitar to hold. It was so heavy, I couldn't have held it for more than a minute. I said, 'Hendrix was the greatest R&R Star. Ever.' (That includes Elvis) 'The best,' agreed Cobalt.

No wonder Jimi Hendrix threw that guitar around, slung it away from him so that it lost its weight, then pulled it back like a dancing partner; no wonder he set fire to it like it was his loved one. They say he wore the guitar constantly. I saw a documentary – Andreas called me up to watch TV – but we didn't watch it all because we didn't want to hear about when he died. These stars who only live to be young. I lived all my life as if I'm young but now I'm old I realise not just that youth is precious but that it's actually something else. Jimi was beautiful. And the way he dressed! There was nothing like it at the time, the way he looked and played and moved and sang; he had a method of singing then talking as he breathed – he sang like the wind, Jimi Hendrix.

Something unexpected happened. Our friend Robert got drunk. What was unexpected was what he said. 'Vivienne, we have all got to vote UKIP. If we don't we will have Sharia law in this country.' Nothing we said could make him see the disconnection between these two things. So one by one we ignored him, he slept there and in the morning he told Sara that he wasn't going to vote UKIP. How could he think such a thing when drunk? *In vino veritas?*

The very existence of UKIP is the fault of the two main political parties run by the pathetic Cameron and Miliband. People don't believe them when they say that things will get better. UKIP is the same as these two main parties, the same old formula that is heading for disaster, except it has given us an enemy. Capitalism runs on war mentality, an enemy real or constructed is necessary (read *1984*). Hate and nationalism are the last things we need if we are to save ourselves: not competition but co-operation, a global solution.

We need new politics. We will get them if we apply:

"WHAT'S GOOD FOR THE PLANET IS GOOD FOR THE ECONOMY"
"WHAT'S BAD FOR THE PLANET IS BAD FOR THE ECONOMY"

This is Climate Revolution of course. It is also the agenda of the Green Party. Our politicians are too frightened to change their politics, which support only big business. The trouble is the general public is scared as well. We have been trained up as consumers for two hundred years. Free market capitalism depends on consumption. We agree that business should make unconscionable profits because that gives us 'growth' – no matter that it doesn't trickle down to people. We have to change our values – then we'll have true value for money.

SUN 27 APRIL MAHLER'S SEVENTH SYMPHONY

Barbican: Mahler's Seventh Symphony. I asked Andreas what I should write. He said, 'Who doesn't know him should try to get to know him. It is an incredible experience every time I listen to him. I really think it adds something to life. The first time I heard him of course was in *Death in Venice*, Visconti's film from the novel by Thomas Mann. I was very young. Has anyone ever seen anything better? You would hear talking on the beach and the children playing and the music would take over – that was Visconti.'

MAY 2014

WEDS 14 MAY PRINCE CHARLES

The first draft of my biography has to be in by mid-month so it takes up any spare time I have between my regular work. I've been checking, and sometimes meeting Ian, who comes to my home. Now the first draft is sorted and Juergen did my portrait for the cover. I don't know how he does it, he shows me myself.

Evening: with Andreas to the Almeida Theatre to see *King Charles III*. I love the journey: direct tube from home to Angel, then walk up Upper Street. The Screen on the Green cinema is still there, opened by Roger, who became our friend soon after we began *Let it Rock*. Malcom recommended him to do a Brigitte Bardot season but he could only get a couple of films; no one had kept them all because they didn't think they were any good. My favourite shop, no longer there, sold lingerie.

I went to see the play because I am a big fan of Prince Charles; he has done much good in the world, for example The Prince's Drawing School. Drawing is the basic skill necessary to all expression in the visual arts; it is like seed corn and visual art cannot flourish without it, yet this is the only school because skill in art is unfashionable today – that's why art isn't happening.

Charles campaigns to save the environment and the planet. His position does give him prestige. He uses it to have a voice and people listen. He is criticised on the principle that he is not supposed to voice opinions that might influence people.

How will Prince Charles manage when he becomes King Charles III? How will he cope with having to rubber-stamp the introduction of laws he doesn't agree with? Why does he want this job? This is the matter of the play.

It makes psychological sense to me that the monarchy do this job from duty. The Royal Family must see it as an overriding good. Otherwise who would want this slog of a job? A job where you can't make decisions. The monarchy has value. It gives stability and provides social cement and national identity. This is possible because the monarchy is hereditary. Its preservation depends on it having no political power or voice: this is the deal with democracy.

In the play, even before his coronation, Charles tries to persuade/threaten the prime minister to drop the first bill he will be required to sign, a bill which supresses press freedom and protects the government. The prime minister refuses and the action is set up for constitutional battle: to win Charles will need the support of his family and the public. The play is really impressive, with a feeling of importance and of Shakespeare – it is written in iambic pentameter which gives weight. Staging and costumes fit perfectly and the acting is completely convincing. Tim Pigott-Smith playing Charles is super; they all are. The plot is gripping – until, in the second half, for me the psychological truth fails with one phrase. Charles says he wants to be 'the best king ever'. This doesn't ring true. I don't think the Royal Family do the job for personal aggrandisement. If the play kept to the one motive of duty then Charles's decision between signing away people's freedom and risking the end of the monarchy would have real drama. The idea that somehow he wants it for personal vanity weakens the dilemma. And Kate Cambridge would not have needed to be cast as ambitious and scheming, wanting the monarchy 'for George'.

One last thing. The play gets really Shakespearian with the threat of civil war. I don't think civil war today would get further than the newspapers and the internet. We've begun to swap participation for virtual reality.

THURS 15 MAY RANKIN

To photographer Rankin. Photos of Andreas with me as accessory They are needed for a profile Deborah Ross did on Andreas for *The Times*. I'm glad. I want people to know he's a great designer, doing as much work as me. Also, *Love* magazine wanted a photo of us kissing. O.K.

FRI 16 MAY CANNES FILM FESTIVAL

To Cannes. Pamela and her husband Rick organised a charity event during the film festival: baccarat gambling on a yacht with speeches in between. Pamela, with her short hair, looked more sensational than

THE ★★★ TIMES

07.06.14

BEAUTY
SPECIAL
100 BEST
PRODUCTS

She never lies.

She brings me
coffee in bed.

She's not
materialistic.

She doesn't snore
(often).

The secret life
of Mr and
Mrs Vivienne
Westwood

By Deborah Ross

SEX, FAMILY
FEUDS AND
PARANOIA
Michael Jackson's
last days – by his
bodyguards

Rankin's cover for Deborah Ross's profile of Andreas in *The Times*.

ever. She gave a speech to launch the Pamela Anderson Foundation. At the next break between gaming I gave my speech, 'Who are our Rulers?'. Johan Eliasch, who started Cool Earth, talked about the charity's work and we raised nearly a quarter of a million dollars, mostly for Cool Earth. Brandon, Pamela's son, won the baccarat.

We stayed in Cap d'Antibes in the Belles Rives Hotel, which Scott Fitzgerald, Zelda and daughter Scottie once rented. It was really lovely there among the cliffs. We ate there, down beside the sea.

Next night we went to a dinner hosted by Giorgio Armani for *Vanity Fair*. Pamela wore just a Climate Revolution T-shirt. Didn't try to go to any film premieres. None interested me except the YSL documentary, which is said to be good. Honestly, I didn't fancy paying (a lot); you have to, though usually the money goes to charity.

Stella Schnabel modelling our campaign – photographed by Juergen Teller.

TUES 20 MAY STELLA SCHNABEL

Our publicity campaign shoot with Juergen. We had fitted in three days' preparation, before and after Cannes, so it went smoothly. We did it with actress Stella Schnabel, Julian's daughter; her mother is Belgian so she spoke French as a child, though grew up in America and lives in New York. She is a strong woman, generous and charming, and speaks with definition and focus. I loved the way she said, 'yes': so positive. I couldn't hear it enough.

She thanked me for having directed her to the Wallace Collection while she was here in London; she was very thrilled. It's such a relief to meet people who are intellectually inclined. She's staying with Anita (Pallenberg). We shot in our house. Juergen found a spot where the light was good and special and stayed there. We had prepared food and we all enjoyed ourselves. Stella liked the clothes.

FRI 23 MAY SUSAN AND LELU

My friend Susan came to stay – until Sunday evening. We met when we were eighteen at teacher training college and shared a room in Brixton. This is a real treat for me.

We dined at home with Andreas – a niçoise salad (no tuna). Susan lives in Portland, near Weymouth, and is up in London to check out a Greek pot (do go and look at them) in the British Museum; it's part of a course she's doing for the Open University. She and one of her daughters, Clare, have been running for council election for the Green Party. Clare almost made it. I said I'd go to help them next time. We went to yoga together, then we met Sara (Stockbridge) and Cobalt and Sara's daughter Lelu at the Gate Theatre, Notting Hill, for *Grounded* – about drones. Really well done, theatre at its best. Lelu is just sixteen and I wanted her to come; it's so important for young people to know what's going on.

We all went over the road, after, to *Le Pain Quotidien*, where we met Peter Olive for a chat. Lelu told us that she had helped a young

Indian girl from her school to avoid an arranged marriage to a man living in India whom she had never met. I don't have an opinion against arranged marriage per se but the girl was desperate against it and I think Lelu was good to get involved. Lelu wears the look of girls her age: black footless tights and trainers, nylon blouson, cropped vest worn over bra, and showing midriff. Cleavage. Longish hair, full make-up. She's beautiful, serious.

Susan and I went to the Matisse cut-outs at Tate Modern.

TUES 27 MAY WE NEED TO TALK ABOUT FRACKING

Launch of our *We need to talk about Fracking* campaign. Venue: HMS President on Victoria Embankment; 10 .a.m. Our letter of celebrities, scientists and organisations has just been published. It calls for an independent debate on the possible dangers of fracking to the environment and our health. The public need to know. We do interviews for press and TV and announce our tour of five towns in England, Scotland and Wales. By means of a panel of speakers we aim to discuss all the facts about the potential for fracking in the UK. Government propaganda has avoided this discussion.

Who are we? Having for weeks discussed the problem with charities, NGOs and business people, my son Joe, his charity Humanade and his friends formed this plan with Climate Revolution and backed up by Lush handmade cosmetics shop. Since forming the plan we have also talked to scientists to collect all our facts. Jeremy Leggett of Solar Century will be on the London panel.

THURS 29 – FRI 30 MAY VIENNA AND TEDX

To Vienna for the Life Ball. Stay at the Sacher Hotel. We go to visit our friend Irma, who Andreas has asked to prepare a traditional country dish, a home-made spelt pasta with a sauce of different cheeses. She is a very special cook – Andreas calls her 'immaculate'. All the other things she prepares are immaculate, too: salads and a rhubarb tart. I met Irma at the same time as Andreas when I came to teach here; they were both in my class. She makes home furnishings and I have a patchwork wool cover for the bed from her which I really like. It's immaculate. We are with Ruben, her son (around twenty), and two neighbours and lots of champagne.

Irma's flat is quite big with high ceilings; the rent is controlled, kept low. In London you would have ten people living in the house, each paying what she pays for the lot. There are no school fees. They don't seem to knock down or dig up the roads: easier to live here. We have a shop in Vienna, though sales have been affected because of sanctions and bank account freezes to Russians.

On Friday, an interview with *Falter*. The journalist, Christopher, is kind; he lets me explain step by step 'Who are our Rulers?' and what they do to end life on earth by means of their financial system. This was really good because it was a practice for what I will say later in the afternoon when I am giving a TEDx talk.

When I gave my TEDx talk I felt quite desperate; we heard last week that part of the Antarctic is in irreversible melt. If all its ice melts the sea will rise by *seventy metres*. Can we stop this? I ended up saying, 'Please do something. You can't do it on your own. Get together with a friend and focus on one thing.' I gave examples.

SAT 31 MAY LUNCH IN THE COUNTRY AND THE LIFE BALL

We spent time in our shop with Gregor, who runs it. I had wanted to go to the art gallery but instead we took advantage of a Tesla car which was at our disposal and drove half an hour out of Vienna and into the country with Irma and Andreas's cousin Teddy. On the way the undulating country was so beautifully cultivated. Luscious.

We went for lunch to a very special place. Martin, the owner, introduced himself. All the food is grown there, and the wine and schnapps, and they sell seeds of the old varieties and many different potatoes so that they don't go out of existence. Wonderful tastes you never had before: e.g. slices of raw asparagus marinated for months in pear schnapps served with strawberries and then, among the salad leaves, slices of raw marinated rhubarb. Martin served us twirly crisps all in different colours made from different potatoes.

We sat on couches around a table on the grass and under garden umbrellas when it rained. Martin won't admit people who want to discuss business. He wants people to relax and fully enjoy the experience. You must switch off your mobile and children aren't allowed to press buttons. They can play and climb and there are paddle boats on the big pond.

We got on to art. I told him Matthew Arnold's definition of art and culture and that visual art is a representation of reality – the Greeks called it 'imitation'. Human beings are the only creatures that can do this, abstract something from the flux and fix it in time (timeless). The thing we call 'abstract art' is total rubbish. It has no meaning in itself; each separate person must invent a meaning and that has nothing to do with reality. The traditional Chinese painters refer to representation when they say 'the purpose of painting is to perceive largeness in smallness'.

In the evening was the Life Ball, with first a dinner and auction to raise money. We were part of the fashion show and we were ever so good. The great thing was Courtney Love and I'm so glad that Andreas escorted her, took her hand and presented her to the world. It took three strong men to get her into her dress. Courtney, you are a phenomenon. I've never seen the like. Gary Kessler is the man who began Life Ball twenty-one years ago. We have come so far. AIDS used to be a death sentence. Gary, through his work, has helped save lives. Imagine it. How many people have saved lives?

JUNE 2014

THURS 5 JUNE NUREYEV AND ART AGAINST CONSUMPTION

Andreas in Italy until Tuesday 10th – for work and including the weekend at the beach. We are now starting our Winter 2015 collections at a time when the current ones are being finalised. The current ones go in the shops next spring, but we show them now: MAN this month and our two women's collections, Red and Gold in September/October. My regular work is divided between fashion and Climate Revolution. I have been selecting, for the website, extracts from the biography of Rudolph Nureyev by Julie Kavanagh to show how art serves culture and that culture reveals the human genius. Over time, by reading my diary you will come to a view of true culture. My aim is to introduce you to my heretical point of view and thereby defend you against consumption – so that you will never be infected by this chronic illness. The pursuit of art and culture brings health to body and soul and is the antidote to consumption. You just won't need it when you follow the real thing.

The terrible thing is that people do not know the difference between true culture and popular culture and that popular culture is indeed consumption. Thus generally the human race is not thinking but conforming to the degree that we are almost suffocated by the need to consume (under a blanket just sucking things up and pressing buttons). The dogma of consumption is the most effective propaganda of all time and it is a dogma to which most people now conform. It is the cause of climate change and we must stop that.

NB: Going to an art gallery is not consumption – you engage with the past and therefore engage in the life of the world. You get out what you put in. (And you do not destroy anything.) Put another way, it is sustainable consumption – not just sucking up.

Art Lovers Unite ! ♥

SAT 7 JUNE RECLAIM THE POWER

My son Joe comes to my house to tutor me re fracking, making sure I have the facts right, and to talk about our tour. We planned a debate in five UK towns but it now seems the politicians and business people who are pro-fracking and said they are keen to debate have all pulled out one by one. We can only think they were scared of losing the argument; we have important scientists and campaigners including Liz, a young woman from Philadelphia, who will share her knowledge of the toxic impact fracking has had there, and Tina Louise, who comes from Blackpool and has been campaigning since the earthquakes fracking caused there. She probably knows more about fracking than anybody. The tour has been organised by Joe and our friend Jamie, who belongs to the activist group Reclaim the Power and who I first met at London Occupy. So the tour is now about informing people of the overwhelming disaster fracking could cause here, whilst making clear that the government don't care and probably don't even know what the consequences would be if they try to push it through.

MON 9 – MON 16 JUNE ANTI-FRACKING TOUR

The tour begins in Glasgow. I stayed in London because we had a meeting with Matthew from Cool Earth and some people who were at the Cannes event and are interested to contribute financially to his charity. We haven't yet had their decision. [*Just some rich Arab ladies who were really only interested in me.*]

I join the tour at Nottingham on Tuesday, travelling with Lorna, who is making a film on me, following our work. We do interviews for local media. It is the phenomenon of our age that our campaigns are also amplified by social media. I am not on the panel – I talk at the end. Afterwards, I ask a young man who works in the Nottingham Conference Centre the way to the toilet. He shows me and he says, 'I believed fracking was fine but now I've changed my

A cup of tea at Barton Moss climate camp.

mind because all the people who came tonight really care and the government don't get involved.'

Our team is an organic, collective little bunch; when they met each person just fell into place knowing what to do, Joe says – and Jamie put us together. We're all travelling by van in bunk boxes. Lorna and I go to bed. I thought I wouldn't like being so socially bunched up with people but they are so nice it's the best thing.

Our driver is Brian and on Wednesday, we woke up in Manchester. I was born twelve miles away, and from my village we came on the bus as children to see Father Christmas in Lewis's department store. There was a Christmas tree which went up the central cylindrical stairwell of tiered floors. I went shopping and dancing here – always a special occasion. We visited the Free Trade Hall with our school, all in our uniforms to listen to the Hallé orchestra – and to walk round in the interval looking at all the young teenagers from other schools in their different uniforms, especially the boys. This, now changed into a hotel, is where tonight's meeting will be.

However, in the daytime we drove out to visit the people in the climate camp at Barton Moss. These people are our base, holding the ground in protest against the intentions of the government. If you go to visit them you can have a real chat, learn a lot and they will make you a cup of tea. You will help them in their determination to stop any fracking. John McNamara, who began the Barton Moss group, is wearing one of our shirts. He started a garden at the camp. I enjoyed our companionship.

Ki Price's photo of me dressed in a Welsh flag.

The event in Manchester was really crowded and finally we had two people who did not agree with us on everything. Unfortunately, members of the audience harangued them; we were grateful to the two and one of them did contribute to the facts. Later, our group discussed how we could keep things more calm in future. I don't know what they decided, I went to bed.

Next day was Swansea. A glorious day and an unbelievable beach in a horseshoe bay. They say the beaches of South Wales are all a knockout. (I chose the word because you get blown away and then just to stand there brings you back to life, restores you straight away.) No wonder the resort was once so rich, with people coming for holidays. We explored George Hall: grand and immaculate art deco venue for our event. In the afternoon I went to the beach with Liz. We talked and walked, leaving our bags with some workmen who were taking a break. There is such a beauty emanates from trust – young people have it and Liz will keep it. When she looks at you, she opens her heart to the whole human race.

Our photographer, Ki, arranged me in a Welsh flag and took a picture for our publicity and then I went back for more interviews which I share with Joe. I enjoy these local interviews and appreciate spending so much time with my dear son. We had a supportive and passionate meeting and this time two local councillors attended but they were anti-fracking. The pro-frackers still don't come. We went to the Indian restaurant.

On Friday, we woke up in Hammersmith, I said goodbye (love you all) and walked over the road to the tube. Home by 7.30 a.m.

THURS 19 JUNE RENAISSANCE MASTERS AT THE PALACE

Dinner at Buckingham Palace in support of the Royal (formerly Prince's) Drawing School. Some of the drawings from the Queen's collection were on display. Holbein, Claude, Raphael and Michaelangelo. These last two Italians lived at the same time as the French writer Rabelais, who I am going to read next. All men of the Renaissance.

Michaelangelo is so different from Raphael. I describe Raphael's drawings as three-dimensional lines; he drew at the same time as he looked – from spirit to hand. Michaelangelo worked on his bodies, aware of flesh, skin and bones all together as one and built them up; he has the finest shading surrounded by a strong line that holds them in its perimeter so you see everything at once – you see them alive – he gives you the man. Raphael is just as dramatic but he doesn't give you everything, you have to join him, go into the drawing.

The Royal Drawing School students are allowed to handle the drawings. I don't know if they are then allowed to try to copy them. But the only way to become your own master is to copy the masterworks.

FRI 20 JUNE MAN SHOW IN MILAN

Farms not Factories at our MAN Show in Milan.

To Milan with Andreas to work on the MAN show. This season's new Red Label (ladies collection) was also ready in the showroom. I was scared of looking at it because even though it should be great you never know. I'd never seen the clothes made in the right fabrics and you don't know how they will turn out. (This is different from Gold Label where we make all the samples ourselves – the difference is because we sell Red a month before the August holiday – in order to sell more – and Gold a month after.) I did a deal with Andreas: he looked at the Red and I styled the MAN show. One day later we swapped. Andreas thinks the Red is great.

I did our press release for MAN promoting Tracy Worcester's Farms Not Factories campaign to stop factory-farming pigs.

JULY 2014

TUES 1 JULY VIRGIN COSTUMES AND BLONDIE

Invitations to go out four nights in a row, unusual for me – as you know, I like to stay at home except on special occasions when I go to the theatre or a classical music concert. Tonight, Virgin Air launch the uniforms we designed. We did enjoy doing this collection, not only uniforms for stewardesses but for all the different functions down to masseurs and waiters. The stewardesses really did look nice. Whoever did their hair, it was good, all caught up from the back and high on the head. I liked the steward's uniform, the texture and subtle colour mix of threads in the fabrics.

One shirt collar was too small – I hate small collars usually; we'll change it. The fabrics are the most eco-friendly, we worked on that. Blondie played at the event – she must be so bored having to do these private parties. Me, too.

WEDS 2 JULY BRYAN ADAMS'S PICNIC

Bryan Adams's picnic to raise money to support veterans' charities and War Child. Venue: the Chelsea Hospital with operatic concert in the church. This Wren building is immaculate – the golden mean – a harmony between aspiration and restraint. Bryan sang a little at the beginning. He has an incredible voice. No wonder he loves singing: he still does one gig a month worldwide and this gives him the time to do other things he's interested in – his photography and time spent with his family. He's a good cook: vegetarian. We talked to Eva Herzigova and her husband Gregorio.

THURS 3 JULY TRACEY EMIN'S BIRTHDAY

Tracey Emin's birthday at Mark's Club. Too many people for Tracey to be able to talk to us. Haven't seen her for ages. She says the answer is that she will come and visit us – just her – and stay 24 hours. Her agent is Jay Jopling of White Cube. His father is so proud of Jay. He was saying, 'Do you know my son?' The look I gave him caused Jay to rush in and tell him – Vivienne doesn't like modern art.

I was so pleased to find Eva and Gregorio there again and talk to them some more. They are such kind sincere people; he adores her and always wants to hear her opinion. She has three small boys; hard work. Eva remains a supermodel, so strong and powerful – a force to be reckoned with. She looks bigger than she is but size 8 or 10 fits her perfectly, still.

Happy Birthday, Tracey.

FRI 4 JULY OZZY OSBOURNE IN HYDE PARK

Sharon Osbourne invited us to come and see Ozzy perform in Hyde Park. I thought it was nice of her to think of us, though she and daughter Kelly do wear our clothes from time to time. I've never listened to Black Sabbath or any of the others but I do recognise heavy metal and if I ever hear a bit of it I like it. I know their daughter Kelly a little from the way she supports good causes and victims of injustice and I found the family friends interesting to talk to; they had a pretty good idea of what's going on in the world. Sharon's tough: she banished one regular gatecrasher, no messing.

Anyway, I still haven't heard Black Sabbath. We were at the back in the wings where you only hear noise and feel the beat. Ozzy just ran to one side then back to the other side waving his arms and the whole audience copied him, waving like a sea of corn. It's a shame my son Ben wasn't with us. He once split himself laughing describing how funny Ozzy can be. We left just as they were finishing so as not to get caught in the exodus. We could have rushed over to Jerry Hall's party in Richmond – we love her but we have too much to do to rave.

THURS 10 JULY VANESSA REDGRAVE

Shami Chakrabarti is a friend of Vanessa Redgrave and suggested that we should meet. Tizer and I biked over after work to a restaurant in Hammersmith where we were excited to meet Vanessa, but Shami warned us that she would have to leave early (ten-ish) to appear on TV to comment on the sneaky activity of the government (with Labour acceptance) in driving us further down the road to surveillance. Vanessa is dead clear against it. My opinion of governments is pragmatic. They don't care who their victims are so long as they look 'tough on crime' (Theresa May). They'll be making mistakes all over the place, getting the wrong people as victims of their paranoia, not supplying reasons for kidnapping people beyond the claim that they have secret information.

But this goes a lot further – right up to Orwell's world of *1984*. We're all potential victims and at the same time most of us think the secret information exists and accept that governments have a right to get it and act upon it. The system picks out arbitrary victims (especially today, if you happen to be Muslim – think of what happened to Shaker Aamer). People have been blacklisted and never got a job since they were involved in union activity, or other opposition to government policy.

It makes people self-centred. Shami said that an American friend of hers who had recently visited was a bag of nerves, thinking that because of who Shami is she would be under surveillance and that she, herself, would be marked as a dangerous threat. A week later, when Pamela came over and made an appointment to go to see Julian Assange, her son feared that she would not be allowed to return to California. Julian and Edward Snowden are America's most wanted men – because they defy the con.

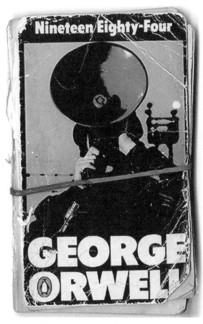

My copy of *1984*. In Orwell's story, people self-censor. Big Brother is watching you. But Big Brother doesn't exist.

WEDS 16 JULY EVERYTHING KEN CLARKE JUST SAID IS WRONG

After our tour against fracking – to which the pro-frackers had not come – Joe, myself and our team wondered what to do next. The pro-frackers had evaded our challenges; there didn't seem much point in continuing to invite them. Nevertheless, though we hadn't had our skirmish in the battle, we had alerted the media throughout the country to the fact of the battle.

Now the BBC had invited me to take part in the midday news programme. They showed the video we had pre-recorded (this bit is called 'Soapbox') and then I and the politicians on the panel – Ken Clarke and Liz Kendall (Labour) – were interviewed. I got one point across: it is not true that fracking in America was a success. Now that it has peaked, the frackers have lost money and are going bankrupt.

Ken Clarke waffled on, reassuringly. When I had a chance to reply, I didn't play the game of polite reply. I just said, 'Everything Ken Clarke just said is completely wrong!', then demolished his main claim. Liz Kendall was just as bad; speaking for Labour she said she was pro-fracking so long as safeguards were ensured. If she had ever applied one decibel of brainpower to the problem she would know that safeguards are impossible.

Listening to them, I put my head in my hands. Having done so, I kept them there a second so the camera could catch it. This, and that I took care to look good, were the most important weapons I had in such a short time to discuss the most important fight the Brits will ever face. It's most important because we have to win every battle in order to stop climate change.

There is a trick I must consider next time (if ever) I speak on TV: whatever the question, answer with one main thing you want to say. I would have chosen to say, 'These wells, which take up the space of Trafalgar Square, will be all over the country. Your house price will drop by 25 per cent and because of this the whole economy will collapse for ten to fifteen years. Because we'll be waiting this long before they can get enough gas.'

SAT 19 JULY LATITUDE FESTIVAL

Train to the Latitude Festival with film-maker Lorna Tucker, her cameraman and Tizer, who brings a picnic we eat on the train. Duffy's twin sister, Katy (not identical), meets us off the train as she works for Greenpeace. John Sauven will interview me and Frank Hewetson (Arctic 30) on stage for Greenpeace. Tent packed.

I admire the art of Keith Haring. He created a significant visual language. I met him in New York – a dear man – and he gave me some art work to use in my collection, *Witches* (1983). He was thrilled. This is my drawing, using his visual language, drawing like him. My margin dog in this book (signifying fracking) is also based on Keith's visuals.

John tries to find common factors in our lives. He talked about our childhoods – what made us rebels.

I said that my life was ideal. My parents loved their children, I lived in the country, that I became self-aware when experience pressed upon the rebellious nerve: why must things be this way and not that? And particularly regarding injustice and suffering: why should I be so lucky? When I look back, I think this is what shaped my life. Frank said how he looked up to his wonderful father. He mentioned that in World War II his father was told to shoot a prisoner. He took him round the back of the hut, he wouldn't do it, and told him to run. That must have been scary for the prisoner; it's a well-known way of killing somebody – to tell them to run and then shoot them in the back.

I seized the opportunity to talk about how we can stop climate change if only enough of us act now. Urgent! The only way out of this is:

"WHAT'S GOOD FOR THE PLANET IS GOOD FOR THE ECONOMY"
"WHAT'S BAD FOR THE PLANET IS BAD FOR THE ECONOMY"

This, of course, would change the world completely because a green economy is a world without war. Wars, since history began, have been waged to secure a monopoly on land for raw materials and exploitation of its people for cheap labour. We could say therefore it's inevitable and that by combating climate change – transferring from a world of finite resources to a sustainable world of peace – we will get the world we want – eventually. The only thing is that 'eventually' is too long.

Frank told of his time in jail in Russia. Cold ... bad, bad, bad. There for sixty-seven days. Didn't know if he would be there for months, years, or forever. Each day, he made string out of bits of whatever. At night, he tied a note on the end with the name of who he wished to receive it. At night, the prisoners hung these out of the window and, swinging them so that they caught in each other's strings, they passed them along. After about four hours you received a reply – there were many cells on different floors and it took time. The only person who ever opened the note was the recipient. Frank is a solid fighter for Greenpeace. He won't give up.

We got on the train home while it was still light. It stopped at every stop; we had to change and they held the train for us while we ran over the bridge. Then we stopped again at every stop and got into Liverpool Street at midnight. The best part of the day for me was the last couple of stops when groups of youngsters got on (ravers). They would have been between eighteen and twenty years old. A black boy sat down in the seat beside us; he had a medium-sized Afro with a rolled handkerchief tied round. I couldn't take my eyes off him, he was so good to look at; he was talking all the time to some friends behind us. His friend was good-looking too, he looked a mix between African and Indian, proud features, big. When we got off I saw that their friends were three white boys, not one more handsome than the other. They were so lovely together. In the streets lots of clubbers were around, girls in high heels with platforms (difficult to dance in?). They looked really glamorous, they were dressed like film-stars. I didn't know it was like that, really happening! But what the hell music do they dance to nowadays? Surely if there was anything good, we would get to know.

MON 21 JULY THE GENIUS OF WIKILEAKS

Went to see Julian Assange. We were happy to see each other. It's been a long time, we're both so busy. As in *1984*, governments misrepresent the truth and give out false history; but what makes our world different is that there is also a true record of facts called *WikiLeaks!* – a whole library which denies the official view, an archive accessible to all. So simple, so clever: anyone who wants to do so can publish the facts and the powers that be can do nothing. Any journalist can preface a fact with 'WikiLeaks says' and they can't be accused of libel.

THURS 24 JULY THE MARRIAGE OF FIGARO IN MUNICH

In summer each year we go to Andreas's family in the Tyrol. Munich is the nearest airport and we are staying there two nights, first. We arrive mid-afternoon and in the evening we go to the opera to see *The Marriage of Figaro*. Love Mozart. I was pleased that the costumes were eighteenth-century. It's safer to do it from the costumes of the time; you have to be clever to make modern dress work. The set was minimal – the stage was filled with a box of three white walls. They were super-white and lit with backlight. Token pieces of furniture were placed inside and changed in each scene; the best effect was in the scene where everyone was getting lost and mistaking each other in the garden at night – the floor was totally covered in a white sheet and when people wanted to hide behind a bush they got underneath it or picked up a separate square of white cloth and got underneath it. Nevertheless the effect was a bit thin. You were conscious of the figures looking precious against the white – kind of like porcelain figurines. You thought of them as figures rather than people.

FRI 25 JULY BECKMANN, DIX AND ORFEO

My friend Patricia who lives just outside Munich came to see me in the hotel, bringing her youngest child, Augustino, eight months; already standing, he should be an early walker. I taught her as a student in Berlin and she worked with us in London for a time as a design assistant. I enjoyed having her with me and her laugh is happiness itself. Then Andreas and I went to an art exhibition which was devastating yet uplifting. It was a double bill: Max Beckman and Otto Dix, who both served in World War I, and the exhibition was arranged according to the similarity of subject matter.

Both artists had drawn, etched and painted what they saw in the war and its results; Dix emphasised the message and arrested your attention. You had to bear witness to the horror, you had to look or immediately turn away. Beckman allowed you to look longer before the realisation hit you. I was shocked to know that Dix's shocking

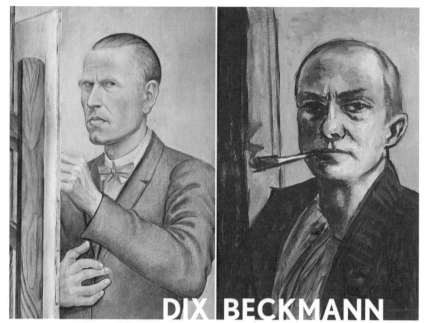

DIX BECKMANN
MYTHOS WELT

images were the truth; it was that bad. And we know this because Beckman painted the same thing, his war victims were the same. There were scenes of torture and scenes of horrific injuries and this cold end to soldiers' lives left my stomach heavy and drained of emotion. I had to turn myself away.

Before we went to the opera that night to see *L'Orfeo* by Monteverdi, I read the synopsis in English on Andreas's computer. Orpheus the shepherd played such beautiful music on his lyre that the birds and beasts came to listen. His beloved, Eurydice, dies from a snake bite. He went to Hell and Pluto gave him permission to take her back to life on condition that he did not look back at her as she followed him. As he got to the opening he turned to look and she faded back into the Shades. We were joined by Andreas's friend of many years, Bertram, and his sister, Silke. They met in their teens when Andreas worked evenings as an usher in the theatre and Bertram was a set designer. Bertram: well-cut features and a beautiful-shaped head, elegant, smoking.

The idea for the set and the costumes was very good. It was set in the 1970s and began with the hippy wedding of Orpheus and Eurydice. There were no scene changes. The costumes were hippy and intermixed with historical garments, which was true to the hippy period (remember Hendrix wearing a theatrical nineteenth-century soldier's jacket with gold braid) and went back to the time of Monteverdi. But everything was greyish or white; the floor of the stage was covered in a grey plastic sheet. Orpheus's suit was rubbish; it was in beige crumpled linen. Many theatre designers today think that without colour – and, therefore, neutral – you leave more room for the imagination. But I wish they would drop this boring convention.

The wigs were great and, in particular, the long dark wig of Charon – the ferryman who takes you over the River Styx and into Hell – suited so well the man who sang this role; his features were riveting, he had a sharp strong nose, eyes that flashed sapphire, and amazing white teeth. Pluto, the god of the underworld, was big and beautiful – really a god of a man – and he had a long silky, medium brown wig; he was wearing a vest and they had covered his arms and chest with matching hairs, long and floating and real-looking. I would love to have seen him riding his chariot – or a Harley. His queen, Proserpine, had a great dress, a long black gown filled with stars (little electric lights). She was the audience's favourite and they went crazy at the curtain. The performers rose to the highest aspiration of the sublime music.

Afterwards, we walked across the park with our friends to a restaurant bar where we ate traditional mash with fried egg.

SAT 26 JULY OFF TO THE MOUNTAIN

Before we left for the mountain we paid a visit to the Frauenkirche, the brick cathedral near to our hotel. It was incredibly beautiful inside, a high gothic nave with its two side aisles; tall pillars and arches all in white stone; a large simple crucifixion.

On the train to Jenbach we sat opposite a fat man whose belly spread into his lap. He was dressed casually and elegantly and his body language was delicate and refined as he talked to his daughter of around twenty. His son was reading. When we got off, Andreas told me that he had expressed himself at the highest level of the most beautiful German with a rich vocabulary.

I am going to start learning German during this holiday. I don't know why after all this time – I taught for thirteen years in Berlin (going seven or eight times a year for about four days each time), our pattern cutters are always German (they are the best), and I've been married to Andreas for more than twenty years. One reason is because I'm inspired by German painters and by Bach and Handel. And of course Mozart spoke German. Then there's Brecht … But I don't pick up a language by ear, I need a book. I speak French and Italian. I will then learn Chinese so I can read the characters. I think the characters each have their own story and that when you put the characters together they keep their story as well as contributing to the whole new story – and that this keeps the newly created story alive to deeper meanings.

Gregor, Andreas's nephew, collects us from the station and we drive to the mountain. We stop for a week's groceries then drive to the chalet, which is lower down the mountain to say hello to Martin, Andreas's brother and Gregor's dad, then drive on to the higher chalet. There are two chalets and Martin the farmer switches between them because the cows alternate between pastures. It is peaceful here; we will read and walk. We light the fire in the stove. The chalet has everything we need: cool cellar (no need for a fridge), solar electric light, pure water, milk, stars. The region we are in is the Inner Alpbachtal.

SUN 27 JULY THE BIRTH OF A CALF

We are invited to lunch with Martin and it is his birthday. Julia, Martin's wife, has a hairdressing salon in the village of Fugen at the bottom of the mountain. She has three children; she doesn't seem to get a day off and every Sunday she comes up to see Martin and to cook. There are other guests, too, including Andreas's father, Franz, and Auntie Herma.

I go with Martin to the barn where one of the cows is giving birth. The two front feet are out but we go back into the house because everything is okay; the cow is lying in a good position and Martin isn't needed yet. When we go back, the calf's nose is out. Martin puts his hand in and moves the calf's head forward a bit but it is still inside; you can see the shape of the calf's head covered by the distended fur-covered flesh of the mother. The feet and nose are white, a bluish white and I can't see any sign of life, except the calf's tongue, which is hanging out, moves. Martin ties a rope to its feet and does some serious pulling, sitting with his feet wedged against the mother's backside, and he moves his other hand round the head inside her, easing it forward. The calf's eyes are shut and all of a sudden the whole head is out. The mother stands up as the total calf sloshes out in the broken waters and lands on her hip. She is brown and white and her wide eyes are fringed with white lashes. I was shaking with emotion. I wanted to cry.

Martin kept the calf tied away from its mother – this was her first baby and he doesn't trust her; she's funny and once chased some hikers and he can't let her out anymore. I don't mind if the calf is separated from her mother because they get distressed if they are separated after they have bonded. I saw that the cow standing next to the mother was licking the mother clean. It's an intuitive response. It's the first time I have seen any animal born. I'm glad she's a girl because little bulls have a very short life. Within five minutes she was trying to stand. He's called her Vivienne.

I'm stupid. We would have had the best photo the diary's ever had but I never thought of getting someone to do it – I, myself, never take photos, I don't have a mobile phone. Gregor says the next time a cow calves he'll try to arrange one.

Unusually for the time of year the weather is terrible. We can't see anything; we are in cloud and the rain is constant, like strings sheeting down; sometimes we have storms with thunder and lightning around the chalet, sometimes hail. This lasts more or less

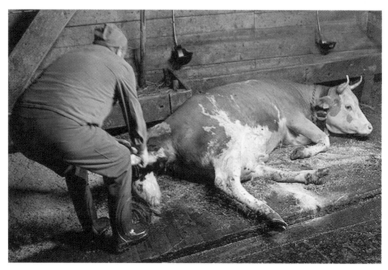

Gregor later sent this photo of another birth.

until the end of Thursday. Andreas managed one short walk during a break in the clouds. Miraculously, every night the clouds break and the sky is filled with stars.

WEDS 30 JULY INNSBRUCK

We are cosy in the chalet but the weather is impossible for walking, so we decide to go for the day to Innsbruck. Gregor collected us and on arrival we went to see Otmar, Franz's brother, who lives there. Christel, his wife, was not here and I missed her – I like them both. While the men were chatting, I looked at a supplement of German *Vogue*, which showed the last collections. There was a trouser suit from our Red Label collection. I noticed it because it was just about the only thing I liked. I thought most of the stuff was pretty bad and I don't think there was anything I would have accepted as a present. I mention this because normally I don't look at fashion magazines and the effect it had on me was to make me enthusiastic about doing our next collections. We all went into town for lunch. Some of the town is very old.

Then, following Andreas, I found myself inside a church looking at something I'd heard about when we were once in Vienna looking at art commissioned by Maximilian. It was his great tomb, built during his lifetime and wonderfully designed and worked. It contains only his heart. Twenty-eight bronze, larger-than-life figures surround it, watching over Maximilian in homage. The figures are heroes and ancestors chosen to give Maximilian a grand pedigree – of course the claims are not true, he is just manufacturing the importance of himself and his family for ongoing prestige. They were designed by the top artists of the day (Dürer was one) and they would first have been carved in wax, with precise detail, especially in the brocaded patterns of their rich garments. It is a momentous undertaking.

It is weird to us, this idea of burying different parts of the body of important people all over the place. In one of his travel journals, Aldous Huxley tells a story of how, in the time of Louis XIV, there was a funeral service for some of the remains of one of Louis's aunts. The remains were her guts which were inside a sealed urn but had fermented and caused the urn to explode, splattering everyone. Huxley called it an 'anatomic bomb'!

Maximilian's cenotaph is surrounded by twenty-eight large bronze statues (200–250cm) of ancestors, relatives and heroes.

AUGUST 2014

FRI 1 – SAT 2 AUG MOUNTAIN GLORY

Awoke to Mountain Glory – and the Sun in the Blue. Andreas went out walking to the top of the mountain. I missed the opportunity; I was reading and had a breakthrough – getting a glimmer of what I'm searching for and hoping to enrich my perspective on the world and who we are. (Rabelais – there's a lot still to read.) We went down the track to see a mudslide which had blocked it.

On Saturday, at last, I walked with Andreas to the top of the mountain and back through the woods. We didn't pick the porcini mushrooms which were everywhere because we'd been feasting on them for three days – people were sending us baskets of them. The porcini (French: cepes) are called *Steinpilze* (one was as big as a hat) and chanterelles are called *Pfifferlinge*. Andreas has been cooking.

SUN 3 – TUES 5 AUG LAKE CONSTANCE

The time has passed too quickly but we are going to Lake Constance to see Iris and her sons for two days (she was our pattern cutter/inventor, remember?). Gregor comes for us at 10 o'clock and we call in to say goodbye to Martin and to have traditional Sunday lunch (little crispy pancakes, bean and barley soup, buttermilk to drink, cake and coffee). Julia gives us another big bag of mushrooms to take to Iris.

On the way down the mountain we stop at a five-hundred-year-old grand chalet, perched on top of a steep slope; it is rented out but belongs to the family. Andreas talks of how one day he would like to give himself time and space to make it sound enough for another five hundred years. He would take it apart and strengthen every piece of it and put it all back as it is in immaculate condition.

There was never a house more elegant. It is true, built to last and at one with the environment. [*He is now doing it.*]

We caught the train from Innsbruck to Lindau. Iris and her boys Aamon and Hatto met us and took us to look around at Bad Schachen, a spa resort of the 1930s, the Riviera of the Germans. Everything is still original. An old man pushed a machine that looked like a lawn mower along the gravel paths stopping to let it burn off any grass under it, which had poked through the gravel. We saw such a lot on this holiday.

I stayed in Iris's house writing up my diary whilst the others went out. Also staying with the family were Florian and his daughter, Josephine, aged nine, whom they had met on holiday. Josephine did everything with the boys, hurtling down the hill on their scooters, jumping off the pier and canoeing in the lake. I saw them as they came home, barefoot, she naked except for a pair of long printed cotton shorts worn low and still wet (I guess it's a surfer's fashion). They are all so fit and skinny, at an age where they are completely unselfconscious and open to everything, sitting all close up on the settee. It's such a treat to be with children.

On our last evening at Iris's we had a party at some friends of hers, who have plans for an energy centre. On the hillside are a series of long buildings, now abandoned, which were once a holiday centre for orphan children. It would be ideal. Iris runs and does yoga (also teaches it) and for quite a time she has been practising energy work. She taught Andreas and had given me a bottle of pomander to try it. I put it on my hands, smell them and then pass them up over my head and down my body over the chakra points. I do this each morning to start the day. I don't know much more about it than this. But it must be a way to connect with cosmic forces and centre your own energy, empower you to help yourself and others. A Chinese friend once took my hands and moved my arms round my body, then let them go but so that I was able to collect my energy and draw it towards me. The weight felt like it would if you did this in water.

This part of the world is like a garden, lush and green with fruit trees everywhere laden. On our way to the party, our host told us that because the vines in the fields were cut by machine the grapes did not ripen well. He himself has a small vineyard and he says it is lovely work to trim the vines by hand; you need to leave the right amount of leaves with the fruit. A few years ago he began entering his wines in the most prestigious wine competition in the world – somewhere in Austria. They won gold or silver – to his complete surprise – and have done since. On a wall of his house the plaques are in rows, year on year – gold and silver.

THURS 7 AUG DREAMING OF PARIS

Home and back at work. We have a meeting with Simone, the architect who is working on our Paris building, shop, showrooms and flat – where Andreas and I would be able to stay a while, eventually. I would love to live in Paris and maybe we will be able to manage a week or two here and there. Oh, I would love to visit the French countryside, too; there is so much history there. I am a fan of French culture: life is too short to do everything we would like to do. We will open when we are ready.

FRI 8 AUG ADAM AND EVE

Andreas and I are acting as Adam and Eve in a film, *Trouble in Paradise*, for the movement to make ecocide a crime (End Ecocide on Earth). These people are brave and dedicated. I saw a short film that Marcus, their director, did for them and it really impressed me with its straightforward message. We were happy to take part in his next short film – and you'll love the costumes. Marcus was sweet and marvellous. He was asking a lot, the short scenes were many and it was a day's work for us. So he never asked us to repeat anything – just one take every time. He was able to do this because he had worked so hard so as to know exactly what he wanted – as well as leaving it open for us to be creative: total respect, great person, great team. Great day.

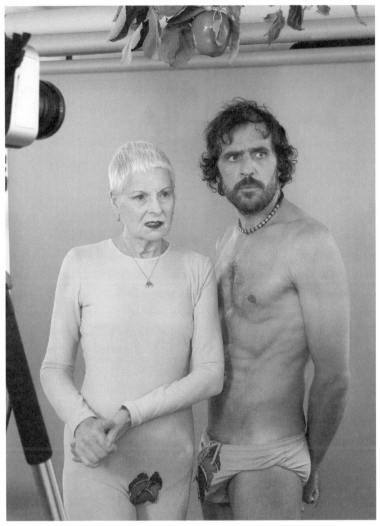

In costume as Adam and Eve for *Trouble in Paradise*.

WEDS 13 – THURS 14 AUG TO THE ARCTIC CIRCLE

We worked hard over the weekend and on Monday and Tuesday to bring things to a point with Red Label, our super-neglected but super-important collection. We got somewhere. It's good to go in on Sunday when we're not interrupted.

On Wednesday we set off for the Arctic Circle. John Sauven, who heads up UK Greenpeace, wanted me to go – they would be making a film. My objections: there is lots of film of the melting Arctic, why do we need another film right now? And why do you need me? Answer: people forget and they did need me. I said I'll go if I can take two young people, George Jibson, age sixteen, very impressive in his need to engage with the world, and Brandon, eighteen, our friend and Pamela's son who lives in California but is visiting England at the moment. Going gives me a chance to talk to them.

Our group included these two, John, Andreas and me, Lorna (filming) and her team James, Pietro and Ellie. We stopped overnight in Oslo. Andreas was great: when we arrived in mid-afternoon he got us all (except Brandon who crashed out) on the train to the art gallery. I'd never seen Munch except in reproduction. Here was a room of them. The power of communication is like a knife going in you; a superb and solid original, a genius.

We flew on to Spitzbergen: we give this name to the whole island but really it is just the name of the town (c. 2,000 people). The name of the island is Svalbard and it belongs to Norway. We are between latitude 75° and 85° north and the Greenpeace boat is anchored here in the bay. We are met by Jason, an Australian who will be our guide and has lived here for twenty years. He makes films at the moment and he worked with David Attenborough on his film about the Arctic. He knows everything.

He is typical of people who work with Greenpeace. Many are experts who have left their jobs because they were locked into the global economic system which they no longer wanted to serve. So they're now all activists and they come from every country. Jaspar (Denmark) was with us all the time because he's an expert on polar bears and was there to protect us (we didn't see any). I can't possibly tell you about the whole crew but we all agreed that the greatest experience was meeting them and spending some time with them. We crossed by dinghy to the boat, named the *Esperanza*; we climbed the rope ladder and strong hands pulled us in.

This was not the landscape of total snow and melting ice I was expecting. It was a world of great brown rocks and glaciers in the

On Svalbard with George Jibson and Brandon Lee.

valleys between. The weather was warm and sunny. Blue skies – unusual. The wind playing over the rocks seemed to change their colour – every colour passed over them, and this, against the colour of the glaciers with pink shadows and, in particular, shadows of electric blue. Oh, yeah, the sun never set; it's like that for six months – and dark for the other six. Andreas and Brandon wanted to go for a dip but somehow never got round to it. You have to be naked otherwise your clothes turn to ice and stick to you.

As we faced the glacier, Andreas talked of its power – enormous! – millions of tons of energy coming towards us. Brandon was fired by the idea of one day capturing that power. The glacier is forever moving and the sound of lumps crashing into the ocean is like gunshots. Previously the glaciers maintained their mass from the winter snowfall but now they are receding. Jason would say, 'You

see that rock in the sea, twenty years ago the glacier covered it.'
Brandon was choosing coloured bits of marble-type rock from the
glacier to take back to his mom. And what was George doing? He
was always the first to see where he could help and he was enjoying
himself. He interviewed the captain for Lorna's film. It really helped
having the crew explain to the boys what they're doing – it gives a
dimension and a clarity for us all.

The ship sailed around and we visited an abandoned mining
town, where we were met by two Russian guards. During the Cold
War Russia had rented a part of the island. It was their last outpost
and I expect they wanted the base just in case, so they used the
excuse of mining for coal – though it wasn't profitable. Within
twenty years of leaving the mining infrastructure is rusted over
and dilapidated. But the spirit of the Russian era is still standing
in its statues and weathered propaganda. It is photographically
attractive. It has only half a dozen blocks of flats, one of which

Svalbard – the abandoned Russian mining town.

serves as a cliff for the nesting kittiwakes. We had a drink in the cosy Russian bar of a hotel which operated for tourists – everywhere else was abandoned.

Back in Spitzbergen we had a really great last night where everybody except me and George got drunk. A Ukrainian man who fancied Lorna kept sending round shots of tequila. Everybody was laughing – a lot to do with Brandon's comments and jokes. We did all manage to catch the early flight back.

MON 18 AUG HELP!

People aren't all back at work yet but we managed a bit of fashion and the Climate Revolution team are here so I got stuff up. Really pleased with the finished piece on fracking entitled 'Help!' I used Keith Haring's visual language and I really enjoyed working within the website medium, reinforcing the focus always with the use of graphics, film and links. I don't know how long it will take but we have to think how to link an all young contingent to Climate Revolution. I hope George and Brandon will have some ideas.

FRI 22 AUG DEGAS

Met Joe and Cora at the National Gallery. Love Joe. So impressed by his anti-fracking strategy. Don't see enough of Cora. I talk to her and Joe about the paintings in the Impressionist rooms, then we wander off each on our own. Degas: I had seen a pastel in the Oslo gallery of a woman having her red hair drawn out and held for dressing; arms and hair stretching and compressing, holding the tension and the weight; colour and composition ruthless/ divine. Now I stood in front of *Young Spartans Exercising*, not many people around me. Unbelievable that Degas could do what he did. What catches you about this work is youth: he paints youth.

Degas – *Young Spartans Exercising*, in the National Gallery.

SEPTEMBER 2014

MON 1 SEPT YES FOR SCOTLAND

I accepted an award from the Scottish Fashion Council for lifetime's achievement. My love of tartan had a lot to do with it. I used my speech to talk on the importance of the Yes vote. I concentrated on the idea of democracy. In England there is nothing to choose between the main parties, therefore no democracy. I said: we English have to fight our government. You, Scotland can have the government you want. I was impressed by the young people – Scottish and English – who came up after to thank me for my speech. They all wanted Yes and they all knew why. Paul Weller's son and daughter seemed to know all about the purpose of the private banks.

SEPTEMBER 2014 | 339

Scotland could open the capitalist trap governments hold us in and build a true value economy based on people power. The UK is a small island but it has enormous credibility. Lucky – historically, geographically; financially at the centre of a world that speaks English. But it does everything America wants. A Yes vote would send shock waves through the world – the Angel of Democracy wearing tartan. Scotland could be the catalyst that saves our planet. We have no choice but to build a new economy starting with renewable energy.

DeMOcrACY IN THE U.K.

WEDS 10 SEPT CHRISSIE ILEY

I have to begin doing interviews for the about-to-happen launch of my biography. One today for the *Telegraph*, which I really enjoyed because it's with my old friend Chrissie Iley whom I hadn't seen for maybe twenty years. She was one of the first journalists to take an interest in my fashion. I remember her from when I worked in the little King's Road shop and she kept the clothes she bought as a regular customer. She still wears them all. She was wearing them now and they really suited her.

Afterwards I went downstairs to join Christina Hendricks, wearing our gowns for photos for *Hollywood Reporter*, to do with who wears what on the red carpet and who designs it. Andreas managed to join us. Christina's actor husband Geoffrey is enjoying his role in a TV political drama. They are a happy couple.

WEDS 17 SEPT SCOTTISH REFERENDUM

To Scotland on the eve of the referendum to take part in a Channel 4 debate with Jon Snow presenting. Yes and No are neck and neck. The possibility of Yes makes me think that this referendum is the most important event of my whole life. The potential ramifications could lead to change – and change has never before been needed so much as now in the whole history of the human race.

We won in the studio, okay. But?

Laura and I sit drinking in our hotel and a couple of guests join in an interesting conversation. Next morning we leave early and I've put so much care and thought into this possible event that I don't care now about the verdict. Drained. Later, after No wins, I do care, thinking wouldn't it have been great! I guess I had prepared myself before, that something so good might more likely not come about.

Alex Salmond is a real hero. The funniest reason given for voting No was: 'How do we know that if Scottish politicians win they won't turn out as bad as the ones in Westminster?' The Yes vote won on social media and with young people. It won't go away.

SUN 21 SEPT CLIMATE MARCH IN LONDON

Climate March from Temple Embankment to Parliament. I was at the front of the march (organised mostly by Avaaz) with Peter Gabriel, Emma Thompson and Peter Tatchell. Many colleagues from our company came. Thank you to Cindy and Peppe for organising this and the placards. By the time I gave my (same) speech the people

Models at our Red Label show wore Yes badges for Scottish independence.

still at Temple hadn't even set off. Estimated number: 40,000. Next time we should do it in Hyde Park – more camaraderie.

I was marching alongside Kye Gbangbola, whose legs were paralysed; he was being pushed in a wheelchair by his wife, Nicole.

Their son, Zane, died the night that water containing hydrogen cyanide gas flooded their home during the February floods in England. It also destroyed Kye's nerves and caused his paralysis. It is quite well known but I hadn't heard about it. The authorities had agreed the dumping of this cyanide in a nearby landfill. The government have avoided responsibility and offered no explanation or help. We should think about government behaviour towards Zane when we consider that they are trying to impose fracking upon us when all the evidence says that all fracking inevitably poisons water, ground and air.

WEDS 24 – SAT 27 SEPT GOLD LABEL SHOW: END ECOCIDE

To Paris on Wednesday for our Gold Label on Saturday. The theme is 'End Ecocide'. The show was well received and, of course, I liked it a lot. We stayed in Paris a couple of days, which was nice. Yasmine's little shop has officially opened. Apart from her job as a stylist, she designs her underwear – Yasmine Eslami. Such fragile/tough, pretty things. Andreas and I love her so much, always laughing.

We went to an exhibition at the Jaquemart-Andre museum: Perugino. Quite wonderful. And because Perugino inspired Raphael, there was also work by Raphael – and Raphael's painting is even deeper. I can't believe how anything can go that far, but he does. Andreas was suddenly adamant: 'Nobody, nobody can draw like Raphael.'

OCTOBER 2014

THURS 2 OCT TRUE WEST AT THE TRICYCLE

Invited by director Phillip Breen to the Tricycle Theatre, Kilburn, to see *True West*, a play from the 1970s by Sam Shepherd. Andreas and I enjoyed going on the tube, then walking up into Kilburn High Street. I don't think I've ever walked there before. Just different that's all. A lady who got off the train with us recognised me by my conker necklace which she had seen me wearing on TV the eve of the Scottish referendum. She said that she had wanted Scotland to stay in the UK but she changed her mind because 'All those people really want their own government. Don't think of us. Yes. Do it!'

The play was fab. It showed up the shit in the American dream. As relevant today as in the 1970s. What a great writer! Preposterous plot – madly unpredictable. Set – a kitchenette and a blue sky. Acting – Whew! Eugene O'Hare. Thanks Phillip. Tragic!

MON 6 – TUES 7 OCT LAUNCH OF THE BIOGRAPHY

On Monday, Ian Kelly invited us to the Doodle Bar for drinks and lovely cakes he'd made for us that morning. He wanted to thank all our staff for helping him with the biography. The launch was the next day at Mark's Club. Picador stuck our 'Map/Rot$' leaflet into the front of the books and it will be included in the reprints. I so much wish I'd thought of it in time for English and German editions. Cover portrait of me is by Juergen. The whole feel is of an important book.

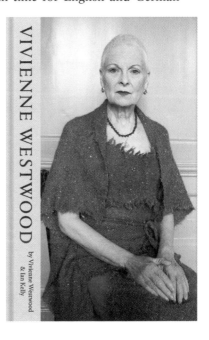

I'm so happy to see so many friends. Can't thank them all individually so I pick on Jerry (Hall) for my speech and talk about her in particular to let them know they're all as smashing as her. Jerry is the perfect hostess. She makes everybody feel special and we're already looking forward to her Thanksgiving dinner party. Told everyone how she pretended I was more important than her when she first modelled for Andreas and me, answering the excited press 'My husband got me the job' (Mick asked me at a party). She put perfume on first and went barefoot on the catwalk to show off a dress full of twirling chiffon frills and nearly dislocated her arm to get in and out of a dress when the zip jammed (if you'd have seen her!). We've all had a great fashion time.

WEDS 8 OCT NAOMI KLEIN IN OXFORD

To Oxford with Cynthia to meet Naomi Klein, who is giving a talk about her new book, *This Changes Everything*. Naomi has asked me to introduce her to the audience. We have been communicating because we share the same concern for urgent action to save the planet. I am very interested in the film that Naomi's husband, Avi Lewis, is finishing, which has a parallel message to that of the book: that tackling climate change will force us to create a better world, the world we want. The film highlights peoples who are already doing this. The only way to stop global warming is to rethink the way we relate to each other. Everybody needs to change. Right now there are the oppressed and the 1 per cent oppressors.

 ### FRI 10 OCT JOYCE DIDONATO IN ALCINA

Andreas and I go to see the opera diva Joyce DiDonato in Handel's *Alcina* at the Barbican. It is a concert performance, which means that the singers wear their own clothes and the orchestra is on stage. We have designed Joyce's evening gown.

Alcina is a witch who has charmed the hero, Ruggiero, to live with her on her island where she has turned people into animals. His beloved turns up to rescue him, disguised as a man. The other characters use this situation to further their own love interest. This silly scenario provides the opportunity for – limits everything to – the expression of human emotions.

Joyce's dress is perfect for the part. It's a dark sea green, almost anthracite, a brocade with a fish scale motif outlined in silver. The

Joyce Di Donato sings Alcina in our evening gown.

dress is asymmetrical and one side of the décolleté sticks up in a vicious point whilst the hem points up and down. The costume comes in three parts: in the first act Alcina's power is intact and she has enormous stiff puffed sleeves strapped on top, and below the jagged hem froths a tulle petticoat; as she begins to lose her power in the second act, she is more exposed and the sleeves are off; in the third act the petticoat is gone and she stamps around in boots. Joyce's hair is really something else, the back and sides are cut to half an inch and the top is a stand-up hedge five inches high.

TUES 14 – WEDS 15 OCT BIOGRAPHY INTERVIEWS

I have agreed to do several interviews in order to help promote my biography: *Rolling Stone*, *Woman's Hour*, *Guardian*, and a Radio 3 *Private Passions* interview with Michael Berkeley.

I enjoyed talking to all the interviewers. I liked them. Deborah Orr was particularly supportive. But then I was with her the longest. She is dry and funny and clever. What I hadn't realised – and this came out in all the interviews – was that my reason for doing everything throughout my life is just the same as it is now: I want to understand the world for its own sake and also to use this knowledge to make things better and then everyone can have the same chance as me. I'm glad I was born in the country and I love the seasons and the English climate. I'm glad that in those days children were not spoilt and distracted with consumer goods. So that later I had the discipline to cultivate my deep interest and become an art lover.

THURS 16 OCT JACK SHEPPARD

To Joe's shop opening – *Jack Sheppard* – in Charing Cross Road. It is named after the Clerkenwell criminal (see p.245), a hero of the poor, hanged aged twenty-two. Joe's done a marvellous job. Everything he touches is done with care and love and this is how he makes a business. What he loves most about the shop is that he's found a way to make all the clothes in England. He has his own little workshop, a factory up north, that would have closed but for of the Pakistani workmen taking it over, and a factory belonging to a Jewish friend's cousin in the East End. This man explained to me that he is fourth generation and though the skill base no longer exists amongst the English he is able to continue with workers whose countries were once behind the Iron Curtain. The clothes are really nicely made and Joe searches out deleted stocks of fabrics and invents uses for all the offcuts. The fabrics give real character.

At the opening I met Edward Tudor-Pole (Tenpole Tudor) who gigged with the Sex Pistols and was in *The Great Rock'n'Roll Swindle*. We wrote a song together, 'Who Killed Bambi?'. He still writes and performs. I gave him a Map/Rot$ leaflet as an idea for a song.

Re my own business: to live sustainably requires a symbiotic relation with Gaia and her eco-system. We can see this is possible in farming if we try to produce what is good for us to eat and waste nothing. Then Gaia's on our side. I am trying to do this with my fashion company. It's maxim is 'Quality versus Quantity' (*Q v. Q*) At the moment we have too much quantity and I am trying to control expansion. The

Joe's shop, detail.

idea is value for money, fair wages, full use of raw materials. The work is labour intensive providing development of skills and pride of achievement in the resulting quality. We offer real choice.

THURS 23 OCT PRINCE PHILIP AND RUSSELL BRAND

Duke of Edinburgh Awards, St James Palace. I've agreed to take part because I'm a fan of the Royal Family, especially Prince Charles.

Prince Philip, at the age of 93, still each day does three events (visits charities, functions, groups, workshops). This is his favourite. Young people have to do really important, empowering stuff to achieve the bronze, silver and gold awards. Nearly a quarter of a million have won gold this year and since the charity began there have been many millions throughout the world. I had no idea what an important role they wanted me to play until I got there. I was one of four presenters, each in different rooms and each with a hundred gold achievers and their families. I had to shake hands and give a hundred young people their certificate.

I had taken my leaflets and hoped to give some out. I spoke to a young woman, Laura, and she told me to speak to Paul, the master of ceremonies, whose full-time job is to look after these awards. I said, 'They're rather against the government.' He said that if I gave them to him then we could tell people to get them from him.

The speech I gave was 'End Capitalism': the same information as in the pamphlet, emphasising the need to transfer to a green economy and that young people could change everything by campaigning through social media, demonstrating on the streets and acting now. Urgent! Name capitalism as the problem. I might have even told them to vote Green. The young people loved it, and their schoolteachers and families. They all relaxed and felt that our world was inclusive, that you could say everything you wanted here in the palace. They thanked me and I was so pleased how deeply concerned they were. Paul told them my speech had been life-changing. That wasn't his exact phrase but that's what he said.

In the evening Cynthia and I went to listen to Russell Brand's Guardian Talk with Owen Jones. You know I don't follow the normal media much but I do know that Russell's got eight million followers on Twitter and that he tells them not to vote (I don't agree with tactical voting – voting for the lesser of two evils – but I would vote for the Greens if I had the opportunity). He was on the panel of the People's Assembly and said, 'We have to dismantle capitalism to save the environment.' What's great is that he attacks capitalism and our government head on. He's right and I think the government are the ones who are naive.

Cynthia and I are considering supporting the Green Party and so I'm interested to know if he's got any other ideas on how to get a government that helps the earth and its people. Though we believe it would make a big difference if young people did vote Green, there doesn't seem much chance in encouraging them if he's against it – because of his influence. He said, 'The reason I don't vote is the same reason I don't eat glitter: there's no point!' I agree with him completely and that's why people feel we don't have democracy.

Owen did his best to put the case for voting Green and Russell said, 'You can, I won't.' He said he tries to augment things: e.g. joining the women who refused to be evicted from their council houses so the government can profit. I decided to ask a question. I would have liked to argue with him about voting but that's not a question. So I asked what he's going to do to bring on the Climate Revolution. He said we should all do our bit, me my bit, him – his, and everybody theirs and join together – do things with others. He's so intense about doing this. But I say we have to do more. *The danger is too urgent.*

WEDS 29 OCT WHAT SHOULD I SAY TO BAN KI-MOON?

Every 24 hours I'm thinking how I can be the most effective in getting us all to fight climate change. Thank God everybody's talking about it. But governments all over the world are pushing us to the edge of the cliff and we have to stop them. Everything they say is rubbish. Everything they do is wrong.

Last night I talked on the phone with my friend Paul. I wanted to ask him about the UN. Reason: I have been offered the opportunity to talk to Ban Ki-moon, person to person for half an hour. But I have to fly to Vienna. I feel I should have a clear idea of what I would like to ask of him. Paul is an artist and a gardener and I consider him a political philosopher. He searches out information so as to form an opinion of what can be done for the better. He seems to remember everything.

I asked him about the American veto which makes the UN toothless. He gave me two examples: since the 1970s every country in the world opposes Israeli aggression in Palestine yet every call for action by the UN assembly is sabotaged by the American veto. In South Africa, finally America agreed with world opinion and lifted their veto and it was only then that apartheid ended. Yet I do know that the UN does good work and is respected. It runs the 'Work not Aid' project and our Africa bag project is linked to this. I think the UN was able to protect Edward Snowden at one point. How much power to influence has Ban Ki-moon?

I went to bed not knowing if I should go or not. I should go anyway for a sponsored event, because we designed a carpet against human trafficking, which Ban Ki-moon is attending. But I don't travel unless I have to and can't make up my mind if I ought to go.

As often as not I wake up in the middle of the night for two or three hours. Being awake is not a problem for me because I don't have to be at work so early. I have a lot on my mind and lying there one thought leads to another. I have been learning German and I was remembering new words: *schwierig* means 'difficult' and I put it into the sentence, 'These are difficult days'. This combined with my worries re the need for urgent action against climate change gave me the obvious solution as to what to ask Ban Ki-Moon. I will tell him my worries and see what he can do. Would he please keep telling everyone it's urgent!?

There is a swelling river against capitalism. In the words of Russell Brand, 'We must dismantle capitalism to save the environment.'

To save the environment we must convert to green energy. Now! Governments are hanging onto capitalism and that's why they impose austerity. [*At this point everyone is suddenly talking about capitalism; me, too. But there is some confusion. We are not talking about small business but about monopoly capitalism/neoliberalism/Rot$.*]

Well I didn't work out what to ask Ban Ki-moon straight away. I woke up with two words – *urgent* and *capitalism*. And so worried. There is so much protest and as people make the connections this protest will rise, but the urgency is still not strong enough. I was supposed to be getting ready to leave for work but I kept messing about – worrying. Finally I did half an hour of yoga and that fixed me. After that I took the words, 'These are difficult days' and made a kind of poem.

URGENT!

These are difficult days
We must save the world – now.
Or lose
The change from capitalism to a
green economy is easy
We know what to do
What's good for the planet
Is good for people
Vote Green.

Vivienne Westwood ♡

It was noon when I got to work. We had lunch: salad – lettuce, cooked beetroot, egg and walnuts; dressing – garlic, lemon, oil. I always take my raw food to work for lunch. The secret of a good diet (and staying slim) is to prepare your own food whenever possible.

I sent my leaflet to Ban Ki-moon so he can read it before I see him. The rest of the day I refused to be interrupted and managed to finish the plan for the allocation of fabrics for Red Label. I was pleased to add my 'poem' to a print and also use my culture heart scribble as placed embroidery. The need for true culture (not consumption) is half of my activism. At the end of the day I was happy.

 FRI 31 OCT THE SCOTTSBORO BOYS

Evening. Garrick Theatre: *The Scottsboro Boys*. My friend Bruno Wang invited me and my friend Giselle. He comes from a family of investors and he is not political, but I think everybody needs to be political right now. I give him my leaflet. He has something to do with investing in this musical. It is a famous true story of nine poor black boys, the youngest thirteen, who were hobos in the 1930s, looking for work and free-riding the railroad. Then they were charged with rape and given the death sentence (though that didn't happen due to public outcry). The story is presented as a minstrel show. They are wonderful people – victims yet heroes – and the macabre presentation helps you deal with your emotions.

NOVEMBER 2014

SAT 1 NOV LETTER TO CHELSEA MANNING

Wrote back to Chelsea Manning, whose letter from Fort Leavenworth prison just arrived.

To Chelsea Manning, Freedom Fighter

I was so delighted to receive your note from Fort Leavenworth which is proof we can communicate. You are a political prisoner. All activists throughout the world recognise the importance of the fight for your freedom. It is one step in reducing the power of our oppressor. Also, everything is connected – We must save the world! The matter is urgent but the solution is easy. We have identified the problem as Capitalism – and this economic system is run by a tiny percentage of people. It is easy to change from Capitalism to a Green Economy. For example, depending on our cooperation, Europe could convert to sustainable energy within three years. But the Green Economy is not only green energy, it's about the end of destruction. Capitalism is a war economy.

Love Vivienne

Chelsea E. Manning
89289
1300 North Warehouse Road
Fort Leavenworth, Kansas 66027-2304

2014.10.22

VIVIENNE WESTWOOD
9-15 ELCHO STREET
LONDON
SW11 4AU

Vivienne,

My sincerest apologies for not writing sooner. Thank you for your letters — I am recieving them! I get a lot of letters, but I dont have a lot of time to write back, which is very frustrating. I am working a lot, studying, working on the appeal and a lawsuit, on fundraising, writing articles, and trying to stay healthy. This doesn't leave me with a lot of time, but I will try harder!

I hope this letter finds you well.

With Warm Regards,
Chelsea Manning

CHELSEA E. MANNING

P.S. Thank you for all the work and assistance that you provided during my court-martial. I saw some of this work, and was glad that it helped (and looked fun too!)

SUN 2 NOV BAN KI-MOON IN VIENNA

Since Andreas was fourteen and at art school in Graz he's been best friends with Alex. Alex works with us. He designs scarves and ties and if we have a request for a charity project we hand it to Alex to sort out. He organised and designed our carpet for auction for the campaign against human trafficking and I have decided to go to the event – where I can meet Ban Ki-moon. So Alex picks me up and we fly to Vienna.

The evening event is held in the carpet emporium of Ali Rahimi. He and his wife do a lot of charity work; he helped sponsor the Life Ball – that's where we met. At the moment my speeches all begin from 'End Capitalism' so in this speech I linked it with human trafficking, leading out from the fact that capitalism is a war economy which exploits people (cannon fodder and cheap labour); they are dispensable cyphers in a mechanical system and our potential to develop all that makes us wonderful and human is suppressed and crushed.

I decide not to retire to an anti-room to talk to Ban Ki-moon, as he has read my leaflet 'End Capitalism'. He said he liked my speech and I said that the analyses and warnings from the UN never seemed urgent enough. 'Oh believe me it's urgent! We use all our power to stress the fact.' I asked him at every opportunity to mention two words: *Urgent* and *Capitalism*, capitalism being the cause and effect of climate change and the financial crisis.

MON 3 NOV VELÁZQUEZ IN VIENNA

Still in Vienna. The art gallery is closed but we have permission to visit the Velázquez exhibition because there are people working in the museum. (We know the director, Sabine, and Andreas is Austrian and they are proud of us.) This is one of the great world galleries and I look at the Brueghels. You have to. As spectacular and immaculate and alive as ever. Then on to Velázquez. I had seen every painting before but I was in heaven amongst them all. I always have the same sensation when I look at his work – and only with him: that the people are alive and that when you look again they won't be in the painting. I spoke to my friend Elke, who was working in her studio down below, and she came to join us. She is a picture restorer and works on world masterpieces. She knew just what I meant and explained some of the ways this effect happened – one of them being that some parts of the paintings are out of focus.

Which painting would I save if the fire bell went? I'll take the little Infanta Margarita Teresa aged three which belongs to the Vienna gallery. It's like Velázquez just dropped her into the painting and there she is, good as gold and patiently waiting to leave.

Diego Velázquez's *Infanta Margarita Teresa (aged three)*, in Vienna's Kunsthistorisches Museum.

TUES 4 NOV JULIAN HALL AND CRAIG MCDEAN

My neighbour in Clapham, Julian Hall, who risks getting kicked out of his house so the council can sell it – same thing Russell Brand is campaigning against – well, a film crew has come to talk to me about it. There is an anti-lethal imperative to build a green economy. The only way is to *actually do it*, starting with renewable energy. Meanwhile we must fight the present opposing system which is capitalism *in extremis*. Austerity, short-term cash to fill a gap or plug a hole! Storing up problems for the future. The worst problem about these council evictions, which sell the property to rich people and add to the housing list, is that it breaks up communities; something good is lost forever and the money the council gets is lost in the sand. The only party who wouldn't do that are the Green Party. The others are all alike – I call them 'the bloc'. Communities are essential when we build the green economy. Julian indeed stood for election as a Green councillor. Next time he should get in.

Another film crew in the afternoon. This time Craig McDean, who is doing a documentary on my old super-friend Gene Krell. A very, very interesting innovator of fashion. Without him a lot

Gene Krell when he worked in our shop Worlds End

wouldn't have happened. Of course he's in my biography, and of course we need a film about him. Thanks Craig.

WEDS 5 NOV MILLION MASK MARCH

Bonfire night is such an important night for an old girl like me. I've been to one every year of my life and the best ones were when I was a country child – a do-it yourself family festival, rituals and special foods. For whatever reasons I'm not going to a bonfire tonight but we're off to the Million Mask March in Trafalgar Square. I meet my friend Juergen Frisch from Berlin days when I was teaching fashion. He was my assistant. He teaches in Hamburg and he's here with ten students. Alice Dellal also comes.

The trouble with the march is that I don't know what it's about. It seems to be about: *we're against everything.* And it has no focus. I get bored and feel guilty about inviting people. What if it's their first march? They won't want to go on another. There were no speeches. We fucked off to the pub and enjoyed ourselves. But then we found out that Russell Brand spoke for a quarter of an hour while we were gone. Well, nobody told us that was going to happen.

THURS 6 NOV AT THE DOODLE BAR

Doodle Bar. To welcome the German students and talk about 'End Capitalism' we had also invited the students from the Royal College who are neighbours across from our studio. The idea is we will work with the Green Party. Main reason why: we need a focus for action and they have a national structure. Young people don't vote and if they voted Green it would send shock waves through the UK and through the world. Because Britain has more prestige re the capitalist set-up than any other country. Our young colleagues from work are enthusiastic about Climate Revolution and come to our meetings and they are up for fighting for the Greens. It was brilliant! Out of seventy college students, fifty want to do it and pooled their e-mails. So now I shall go to other colleges – one a week, starting soon.

FRI 7 NOV THE AGE OF ANXIETY BALLET

Royal Opera House, invited by Alex Beard the director. Three new ballets. Andreas said the middle one, *The Age of Anxiety*, was 'the best ballet I've ever seen'. Liam Scarlett, the choreographer, is a star: fresh and new. The four dancers were all equally superb: the girl, Laura Morera, was great and one of the men, Steven McRae, I've seen before – he has inexhaustible energy, fast and flickering like he's held on elastic. He played a sailor who comes into a bar – this is set in the 1940s – and makes friends all at once with the three other customers and gets them all relating. When they get chucked out of the bar they go to the girl's flat. Then two of them – the salesman in a worn light-brown suit and trilby and the young kid in a leather jacket – say goodbye. The kid is upset. He fancies the sailor and so the salesman, who isn't gay, kisses him on the lips as a token of affection and gives him his business card. When he's gone, the kid purposely drops the card.

I mention these details to give you an idea of the subtle relationships and endearing qualities of the characters – all expressed through dance. The end was super-happy when the enormous full stage opened up and the kid had the whole world before him and he ran and ran through the space as if he were flying.

MON 10 NOV PIG PLEDGE AT BELLAMY'S

Dinner party hosted by Tracy Worcester to raise money for her Pig Pledge campaign. Nice restaurant, Bellamy's, not vegetarian but you can usually find something. But I had fish. I do eat fish sometimes on social occasions. Some of my friends were there and Tracy did the auction herself. She's tall and skinny and she was wearing a T-shirt and a sarong – just nothing, a long bit of cloth. Chic!

TUES 11 NOV GM FOODS

I joined two dedicated American ladies – Pamm Larry and Diana Reeves – and we took their petition for the labelling of GM foods, signed by groups and organisations representing fifty-seven million Americans, (including Daryl Hannah, Susan Sarandon and Robert Kennedy Jnr) to No. 10. I'm afraid I said something that sounded stupid and annoyed people ('People should eat less' – but it sounded like 'Poor people should eat less'). But the press brought up public concerns over the farming methods of Big Ag, so we got the right publicity.

SUN 16 – MON 17 NOV NUREMBERG SHOOT

Worked with Andreas on Sunday, helping him finish the selection of clothes for the campaign shoot. These clothes will be sent tomorrow to Nuremberg where we are doing the shoot in the art school where Juergen teaches.

On Monday, we met Paz and her boyfriend Marcus at the airport. Paz is our model and Marcus will probably get involved, and if it works out the students can join in. We're shooting very strong women at the moment. Paz is Spanish and an actress living in California. Her name means peace but her real name is a long string of many names – so that means her family is rich. I ask her and it turns out they're a branch of Spanish royalty and she starts telling me her life story. I've never heard anything like it. And I've never met anyone like her, either. She uses her power all the time and what happens is that other people use their power too so we're all interacting on full power.

Throughout the shoot, Paz played a whole drama. Once I thought she'd lost her mind, then I realised she was play-acting. Between changes she was completely nude. She had ongoing jokes – e.g she loudly and beautifully called out 'Juergen, I'm ready!' – and because she persisted it got more funny. She continued dancing while a rock band played and people dressed and undressed her on the dance

Paz photographed by Juergen in Nuremberg.

floor. The students, everybody, was on full energy. The photos are something else.

Paz and Marcus are sincere and very serious people. They met while doing energy work with the native American shamans. Paz has her own charity helping poor Mexican kids get proper hospital treatment.

THURS 27 NOV JERRY HALL'S THANKSGIVING

We went to Jerry's for Thanksgiving dinner and I talked quite a bit with Gabriel's friends – he's Jerry's youngest son. I gave them leaflets for which they respectfully thanked me because they knew nothing about 'End Capitalism' and what it means. I give the leaflet out all the time (you might have noticed) and then I was talking to the grown-ups about (you might have guessed) Climate Revolution.

Marsha Hunt was telling me about the book she's written on her friend Jimi Hendrix. Jimi had to make it big in England, she said. It couldn't have happened in America. The Jimi Hendrix Experience was Jimi and two white British boys who together created the sound. But that story was airbrushed: Jimi was marketed by the US media as just Jimi – one black boy – not as part of a mixed-race group. It makes you realise that Obama probably could not have been president (no loss there) if Michelle was white.

Andreas was all the time talking to Jerry, whom he adores – as I do. Also to colleagues of Armand, Jerry's beau, as she calls him. He's a teacher at Imperial College so now Jerry has entered that intellectual milieu. (I want to talk to the students there. It's my plan to talk to young people to build Climate Revolution in time for the next election: Vote Green.)

I talked a little to Armand. He gave me his book, *The Lagoon*. Well, this book has been waiting for me. It's filling all my interest re the life and thought of Aristotle. But now I'm at a point where we get into detail – Aristotle's descriptions of each animal taken one by one from observation and dissection. I'll have to let you know how I get on. Armand is an evolutionary biologist.

SAT 29 NOV MACBETH AT OMNIBUS

After yoga I went to Omnibus, across the road from my house in Clapham. It is the old library, now a multi-arts centre, and we had tickets for *Macbeth*. I have wondered whether it is best to see Shakespeare when you have not read the play, or to read it first. I read *Macbeth* at school and saw it now for the first time. Though you may not catch all of it you 'get it'. Because it overwhelms you emotionally you get it aesthetically, through feeling. And now, later, I am reading the play with notes to examine it more carefully. Next time I see it I will be more informed: e.g. I'll know that Graymalkin is an affectionate name of a cat (Malkin is short for Matilda) and that Paddock is a provincial name for a toad. But I already guessed when watching that they were names of the witches' familiars.

The performance is 'promenade theatre' and Andreas and I met the other spectators at WC, a hundred-year-old water closet located at Clapham Common tube station, now turned into a wine bar. We were given those little lights you wear on a headband and set off onto the now dark common. At the empty paddling pool we meet the witches, who have a fire, all muffled up and chanting their plot as they await Macbeth and Banquo. One of them rode a scooter round the rim of the pool and had a sheet of plastic hanging down from under her bomber jacket by way of a wind break.

Then over the road to the library (Omnibus) and round the back to the fire escape, at the top of which – as if on the battlements of her castle – Lady Macbeth was leaning, reading Macbeth's letter. She was in her sleeping clothes – boxer shorts, vest and a white cotton short open wrap – smoking a roll-up. The costume design was ordinary modern clothes but really thought-through: e.g. when Macbeth put on his armour he just slipped on a bondage-type soldier's harness – the kind you fix a backpack on to – and when he became king he wore an old leather bandeau.

It was really romantic walking over the common, with Andreas and the others. I don't know if promenade theatre is more or less exciting than theatre on stage but it was so well done and my concentration was at full power.

What made this play was the acting, and of course Shakespeare's genius. It was one of the truly life-enhancing theatre experiences I've had. I'll always keep it. The casting, too, was well done – electric! Macbeth was skinny and beautiful; Lady Macbeth was little and tough. The convinced as a couple but I could imagine them as teenage kids – sexual attraction and wild ambition. (Macbeth in his letter calls her 'my dearest partner in greatness'.)

I need to stop here and mention again something that strikes me when I explore the past: the shortness of life. People died young and infant mortality was high, so childhood was not important – growing up was: girls married young. Shakespeare himself retired in his early fifties, perhaps to fulfil (in time) the life of a country gentleman. He died soon after.

This fact was in my mind when I 'got' Macbeth. Before, I had not been able to understand Macbeth – how he could do such a terrible murder. Now I realised – these two collaborators had to be quick and ruthless in their ambition to be great. And it was the sexual attraction and the fitting together in their acting that made

Jennifer Jackson and Gregory Finnegan as Lady Macbeth and Macbeth.

me believe in them. They were like James Dean and Natalie Wood in *Rebel Without a Cause*.

The idea of parted lovers – 'He's mine and I'm his. I would die for him and and he for me.' – is a theme throughout history and it is real in life and in literature. As a teenager in the 1950s I and my friends all wanted this: my guy, *La Vie en Rose*. I'm not so sure today's kids are into this, and as far as I know, lasting romantic relationships are not current in today's literary output.

MACBETH

A PROMENADE PRODUCTION
AT OMNIBUS AND CLAPHAM COMMON

CAST
In order of appearance

Lady Macduff / Witch 1 / Murderer / Gentlewoman	HANNAH JAMES-SCOTT
Malcolm / Witch 2 / Murderer	ALEX PHELPS
Witch 3 / Porter / Young Siward	LUKE ADAMSON
Macduff / Sergeant	JACK BENNETT
Duncan / Siward / Lord	STEPHEN SCOTT
Ross	FRANCESCA TOMLINSON
Macbeth	GREGORY FINNEGAN
Banquo / Seyton	SAMUEL COLLINGS
Lady Macbeth	JENNIFER JACKSON

CREATIVE TEAM

Director	GEMMA KERR
Producer	MICHELLE OWOO
Designer	LORNA RITCHIE
Lighting Designer	WILLIAM REYNOLDS
Sound Designer	EDWARD LEWIS

The Macbeths were committed to each other up to the hilt – don't forget their ambition and the shortness of life. They went too far, and this broke their bond. Macbeth lost his physical attraction for her. He was completely unnerved and when she cleaned up she could not believe King Duncan 'had so much blood in him'. Guilt finally overwhelmed her. Macbeth had to keep on going. In order to become a king he had become a murderer. He had to keep on murdering to cover up his crime and to legitimise it – to legitimise to himself his new identity: murderer and king.

Tomorrow, and tomorrow, and tomorrow,
Creeps in this petty pace from day to day

There is nothing more exciting than Shakespeare. The end is mega.

DECEMBER 2014

WEDS 3 DEC CARLO NERO'S FILMS

Some of us from work went to a film studio in Twickenham, invited by Vanessa Redgrave and her son Carlo Nero to see two half-hour films he has co-directed. *Bosnia Rising* concerns a detergent factory whose workers have not been paid by a crooked boss. This is against a background tide of poverty running through the country because there's not enough work. People there are on the last point of desperation: without the means to live, to help each other or feed themselves. They are protesting. *The Killing Fields* is about Wildwood, a forty-acre park in Herne Bay, set in ancient woodland, and where you can see wolves, bison, deer owls, foxes, red squirrels, wild boar, lynx, wild horses, badgers and beavers! (I want to go with Alice Dellal, who lives there.)

The two films have a message: we could conserve the world and eliminate poverty by reducing income taxes and replace them with Land Value Tax (on land and property). This is Green Party policy.

WEDS 10 – THURS 11 DEC DUBLIN WITH LORNA

To Dublin with my friend Lorna Tucker. She is following my activism, making a film and I'm here to be interviewed at the Facebook Women's Convention. It's in a luxury hotel, The Marker, decorated for Christmas – so many lights. Expensive menu: amongst the starters, pumpkin soup (exquisite) for £16.

I give my speech in exchange for some advertising on Facebook. We want to encourage the five million people who follow our main site to follow Climate Revolution. Remember – I want to concentrate our company under the banner of Quality not Quantity – and we don't sell on our main site, we just show people our best things.

I enjoyed talking to all these women and Nicole, who interviewed me, emanates love of life. The background to all my talks at the moment is 'End Vulture Capitalism'. Then I went on with 'Get a Life', the importance of engaging in the world through culture; the more you understand the people of the past, the more you understand the world you live in. 'You get out what you put in.' The women were delighted by what I said about Aristotle and the importance of fulfilling your own special potential. The basis of Aristotle's philosophy was the study of form: how it happened, how it worked and how it changed. He said, 'The acorn is happy to become an oak' (not in those exact words). This thought defines his idea of happiness: the acorn is programmed to become an oak and it is its destiny to become the greatest possible oak. We humans are born each with our individual character. Character is like a bag of tools and it's the only one you've got to live your life with. By following our deep interest we begin to use out talent. Happiness lies in fulfilling our potential.

Dublin is a wonderful city, architecture going right back but famous for its eighteenth century – everywhere. A world port, it was then richer than London. Cosmopolitan. Every side street seems an adventure. They haven't knocked everything down as London continues to do. We took the opportunity to have Seamus our driver show us around; he is a scholar and a thinker.

the acorn is happy to become an oak tree

TREES SAVE LIVES

THURS 18 DEC DOWNING STREET

Downing Street – fracking protest. Government advisors warned them that fracking could be the 'new asbestos'. So I went with Joe to present the Camerons with a box of (fake) asbestos.

THURS 25 – SAT 27 DEC CHRISTMAS AT JOE'S

Andreas and I met all my family and some of our friends down at Joe's place in Cornwall. Matthew Owen, who runs Cool Earth, came over on Boxing Day to meet Mike Hands from the Inga Foundation who is also doing amazing work on the rainforest. They both live in Cornwall so we all got together to discuss working together.

2015

JANUARY 2015

THURS 1 JAN HEROES

We had a small dinner party with Julian in the embassy for New Year's Eve. Julian is one of our thirteen heroes on the Climate Revolution website. I posted photos of them before Christmas and intend to write a text for each to celebrate what they are doing to fight for good. But so far I have only done Glenn Greenwald, Edward Snowden and Prince Charles. I will have to wait to do the others. Because Andreas and I are working every day on this season's fashion shows – and next season's collections.

Next time I visit Julian Assange I will ask him how he helped Edward Snowden escape capture.

THURS 15 – TUES 20 JAN MAN IN MILAN T-SHIRTS

Milan. The main event is the MAN show on Sunday but I am here to look at our other collections and the showrooms are filled with people come to buy. For the MAN collection I was very pleased with the unisex knitwear and jersey, including three T-shirts:

T-SHIRT 1 Andreas collected all these odd logos, symbols and fridge magnet type graphics and superimposed them on each other. We call it the 'Meaningless T-shirt'.

T-Shirt 2: Drillers in the Mist A film about Varunga, home of the mountain gorilla, shows how Soco International, an oil and gas company, planted seeds of corruption so they could drill in this protected park. They not only threaten the lives of the gorillas and the rangers who risk their own lives to protect them, but lead to the guerrilla armies/rebels coming into the reservation and killing people to get a cut of the corruption money.

T-Shirt 2: Prince Charles with Che-style beret When I was interviewed, I said that if he'd been world ruler for the last thirty years we would not have climate change. Some people don't like the idea of a royal family. I think the reason for that is that our left-wingers (can you call people 'left' when there is no political difference between right and left?) are what I call decadent Marxists – they don't like Marx but they still believe in his polarisation between 'bourgeois' and 'proletariat'.

FEBRUARY 2015

THURS 12 FEB RAVEL AND COLETTE

The first special event in February was a concert at the Festival Hall. Ben and his wife Tomoka invited us. Tomoka learned piano in Japan from age four – their flat was so small that her parents slept under the grand piano.

The programme was French. First Mitsuko Uchida, a tiger poised to attack a Ravel piano concerto. Then Ravel's *L'enfant et les sortileges* (magic spells). This was a concert performance, the singers taking various roles and adapting their costumes – sometimes just with an accessory – for each change of character. The story is of a naughty boy (a young female soprano) stuck in the house, refusing to do homework, thumbing his nose and pulling faces at 'Maman' and angry at the household objects who came to complain about him. It comes from Colette, who, as a young woman, was the pet of French intellectuals. The story of her adolescence in the country and her growing up, the *Claudine* novels, caused a sensation. If you want to embrace the Frenchness of France at the time of the belle époque – Picasso, Renoir, Chanel, Offenbach, Proust, Rimbaud, Josephine Baker, Cocteau – the list is endless – Bohemia, the salons – read Colette. This was the Western world at the peak of its intellectual output. It was said, 'When good Americans die, they go to Paris.'

Colette by Leopold Reutlingerin on stage in the the *Rêve d'Égypte*.

FEB 14 2015 SUPPORT THE GREEN PARTY

Valentine's Day. I am taking a day off. It is the middle of February and I am just writing up my diary. Andreas and I are under pressure to finish the Gold Label collection, which is in Paris on 7 March. In between we present the Red Label collection – which is finished – in London on 22 February.

As you know, we in Climate Revolution have been seriously campaigning with my son Joe against fracking in the UK. We have to win this battle, put a spoke in the wheel, halt the machine – run by the powerful 1 per cent – the antipeople. Their power controls the globe. But we have to start right here at home. For this reason we have decided to support the Green Party: myself working with Climate Revolution and Joe working with his anti-fracking team from Humanade. The Green Party are anti-fracking, anti-austerity, pro-community and pro-human rights. The rest of the parties – 'the bloc' – are the opposite. I just listened to a panel discussion with cross-party politicians – *Any Questions* on Radio 4. On fracking they all told the same bare-faced lies and on the health service their answers amounted to a complete muddle because it's difficult to rescue it from the mess our current system of vulture capitalism has caused – and they all believe in this system. No chance!

So now Climate Revolution supports the Green Party. We've had a couple of meetings. After the fashion collections I want to give weekly talks to young people in universities on how we can 'Get a Life' – our own lives – and save human life in the future, as well as how we can enrich our lives by an easy transfer to a green economy. The Green Party will help in this part of the discussion.

SUN 22 FEB RED LABEL GIRL

Our Red Label collection was delivered in good time, which gave us plenty of time to put the show together and enjoy it. Murray had worked with our jewellers to make the most super punk jewellery and suggested punk as a theme for the hair and make-up. I always like it to look like the girl did it herself. The models loved it.

I wrote about the Red Label girl on the press release:

VOTE GREEN

The girl who wears Red Label – I want to tell you about her, she's a bit like me. She was lucky enough to be born in the country and she moved with her family to London when she was seventeen. She knows the names of all the trees and she's always been a reader. Since she's been in London she's gone to the museums all the time. She's an art lover and she really thinks culture is very, very important. If we had true culture we would not be in the situation we're in. Culture has been replaced by consumption – which is quite a different thing.

At the moment we are controlled by 1 per cent of the world population who are in power. They preach consumption, and they preach war, and they're taking us into disaster. We are in incredible danger.

There is no point in voting for the others. She is going to vote Green.

MARCH 2015

SUN 1 MARCH AT THE ICE-CREAM PARLOUR

At work Sunday, designing the Gold Label with Andreas. Late home, walking over the Common, we went to the ice-cream parlour, where I was recognised and asked for a photo. This is usually a pleasure – to say hello to someone – and only takes a minute. But twice I've said no and regretted it, and I did it again today. There were six or seven girls of age ten or eleven – they were the sweetest and loveliest little things on earth – but I was feeling a bit stressed (worrying about the Gold Label) and I suddenly felt I couldn't cope with engaging with so many children and being the focus of everybody else in the parlour. I just got up and walked out – 'I have to go!' When we got home I felt so upset with myself that Andreas said, 'Let's go back.' I thought, it's too late, they won't be there. I should have done, anyway. I was miserable for two days.

TUES 3 MARCH VISITING JULIAN AND TIME TO ACT

I have arranged to visit Julian the first Tuesday of every month. I would like to see him more often but I know he's busy. Ben takes him lovely Japanese food made by Tomoka – vegetarian, organic – a couple of times a week. I know it's good because he drops a little of the same to me for my lunch at work.

Julian thinks it's good that I and Climate Revolution are supporting the Green Party. He says the public debate is far more important than the election. It immediately clicked, yes, what about the social media? Opposition to being governed by these main parties is growing like a tidal wave, so it's good, Julian says, if the Green Party, being part of that opposition, can take the debate into Parliament. Julian is excited about all those SNP MPs. I say, if only they can tip the balance away from disaster.

So what can people in England do? Vote Green and also add your power to the power of the social media, which has access to true facts. Form true opinions and smother the lies. Go on demonstrations. Start by stopping fracking. We, especially Cynthia, have been working with NGO partners to organise our demonstration, 'Time to Act'. We designed it as a poster for the London march and a T-shirt for the Gold Label in Paris. At the same time as the march our models are walking the catwalk and I will be sending a video message from Paris. Of course, you've noticed – I lay the title of my current activism on top of the collections, then talk about that, not the collections.

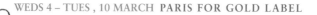

Off to Paris on Wednesday on Eurostar (the Tories have just sold it off in one of their corrupt bargain sales to the monopolies) to Paris to prepare our Gold Label show. In the Paris showroom we meet Sabina, who is working on the casting. She is a terrific stylist (never satisfied until she's tried everything). We'll be able to leave a lot to her. The clothes are nearly all here, which will make a total difference. When they arrive late we're working all night before the show.

The show is Saturday. Catwalk music is Die Hartjungs live. This collection is something else! Unisex. The same size suit (Savile Row tailoring – from Huddersfield) fits a woman – bolero with shoulder pads buttoned inside – and a man (model size) – sleeves and pants too short. Cool! They look like queens/kings. I liked the make-up idea: frowns. Paz and Marcus were Bride and Groom.

Gwendoline Christie did our show and after it finished we went straight on and did our shoot with her and Leebo Freeman, with Juergen Teller, for our advertising campaign. Done! Everybody satisfied. At dinner I wanted to talk to my friends, especially Paz and Marcus, but they were so polite and considerate – they left me in passionate conversation with Gwendoline. We were talking about Shakespeare.

Our Unisex suit at the Paris show.

Gwendolene modelling our campaign with Leebo – photo by Juergen Teller.

TUES 10 – THURS 12 MARCH CATHAR COUNTRY

In Paris we began an important discussion regarding Q v. Q with our people working in Asia. We need to continue before one director goes back to Japan. This will be on Friday in England. Therefore we will have to cut short the little break we had planned whilst in France. But we have a few days.

Gare de Lyon. It's so romantic for me travelling down through France. My English education is so connected with its history and culture. We are going to Perpignan, close to the border with Spain, at the foothills of the Pyrenees. As we near our destination the train stops more often. The names. From Nîmes we come to Montpellier. We are by the sea with *etangs* and flamingoes.

At Narbonne Tizer meets us in a hire car. We are staying in her mother's little house in Padern. Out of the way. No shops. When a van of produce arrives each week a loudspeaker from the *mairie* announces the opportunity to stock up. We just loved it. The house so rudimentary, collecting kindling and wood from the side of the little road, which wound up the steep hillside to the Château of Padern. Tizer cooked and put us a hot-water-bottle in bed.

The weather was glorious blue. We only had one full day – Wednesday – and went to Peyreperteuse. This is the most dramatic of the Cathar castles built on and embedded within the outcrops of limestone which rise up crowning the hills. The castles run along the French-Spanish border. From the approach road it is difficult to see where the rock stops and the castle starts. I have never seen this kind of limestone terrain before. Rivers crashing and winding, deep pools where you can dive and swim. Tizer has been coming here with her family every summer. Hippies live here and there are organic markets with fantastic wine. The crops you see are vines and almond trees are in blossom amid the landscape.

Anne, Tizer's neighbour, tells us the Romans were here – ancient tribes always stay near water. They mined tin. How did hunter-gatherers before that survive? I've never thought of this before. They must have known so much that we don't know. It was the novelty to me of this old landscape that made me think of it. How did they survive anywhere? Here there are wild boars and in a section of a stream we saw dozens of big frogs.

On Thursday, on our way to the airport, we passed a sign leading to a Neanderthal cave. We couldn't go. No time. The Neanderthals were here for 200,000 years before Homo sapiens came to Europe 45,000 years ago and within 5,000 years of that event they were gone. The theory is that we were cleverer at getting our food. Recently dogs' bones dating from 30,000 years ago were found. They were like wolves but with shorter snouts suggesting that our ancestors tamed and bred dogs from wolves.

WEDS 18 MARCH REMEMBERING RACHEL CORRIE

Amnesty International came to interview me for a film about activists. I remembered Rachel Corrie, a young woman of twenty-three who travelled to Palestine to join a group trying to stop Israeli seizure of Arab land. She wrote a diary there, and this was turned into a play, which I saw. She was in Palestine only two or three weeks when she stood in front of an Israeli bulldozer, which kept coming and killed her.

FRI 20 MARCH EVGENY KISSIN AT THE BARBICAN

Pianist Evgeny Kissin at the Barbican. Andreas is in Italy so I gave his ticket to my son Joe. Kissin first played a Beethoven sonata. Dramatic and so fast you could only just keep up with him. Beethoven is self-consciously clever and seems to hammer the point by repeating himself. It conjured up a picture of charming Victorian ladies in crinolines self-consciously appreciating the countryside. Next Prokofiev. This is great. I wished I could hear it again. Either I didn't concentrate enough or I did not let myself go enough. I don't know. Except I did know that it had the integrity of great art. After the interval came Chopin and this carried me away. It was like Kissin owned the music and gave it to you, communicated it to you. I was now completely opened up. Next Liszt and, ravished with pleasure, we travelled on with Kissin into eternity.

WEDS 25 MARCH SMILE

Mark, the artist cab-driver, called for me and interviewed me in his cab on video. He's really engaged with what is happening in the world and is desperate, like me, to expose the criminal political-financial structure that kills us. When we said goodbye – Gosh! – he gave me the sweetest smile.

THURS 26 MARCH THE BEST BOOK ON FOOTWEAR

An evening event in St Margaret Pattens church in Eastcheap. Our host is Jenny Tiramani. She and my friend Santina Levey are dedicated to their work. They are costume historians, researchers and curators and they publish the work of Janet Arnold, to whom I am grateful, as I discovered historical cuts from the diagrams in her books. Santina is a leading expert on lace and Jenny was costume designer at The Globe. They founded their own school, The School of Historical Dress. This occasion was a launch for a book on footwear by Alan and Vanessa Hopkins. Its lay-out is different to any books published today. Alan said, 'When you employ a designer you pay for white spaces.' There are none. But the real difference is the love he put into it. The school hopes to find a house in order to open to the public their archive of historical clothes.

The back of one of the shoes showing the seam where the covering ribbon has been worn away.

Fashion plate from *The Lady's Monthly Museum*, August 1799.

The top of the heel and part of the sole of one of the

A pair of buckles of the style that might have been worn with the shoes. They are silver with paste stones.

Fashion plate from a lady's pocketbook, 1756.

Drinking wine, listening to speeches from people with such knowledge and passion in this treasure of Wren's church architecture is typical of Jenny. Everything she touches is exquisite.

APRIL 2015

FRI 3 – SUN 5 APRIL WILD GARLIC

Afternoon concert at the Barbican with Andreas, Ben and Tomoka: Bach's St Matthew's Passion. Didn't quite gel. From there we all drove down to Joe and Faye in Cornwall for Easter. Faye with the horses. Blue sky and lovely to walk the beaches and woods and to do nothing. Picked big bags of wild garlic.

WEDS 8 APRIL BIRTHDAY PARTY – THANK YOU, SARA

My birthday. How many flowers I had and thoughtful presents! Sara (Stockbridge) gave me a party at her home and invited my friends. I gave a little talk to tell everyone where I'm up to, what been happening. It is useful to have a formal talk – it helps make a party more of an event. The big problem for all activists is how do we get through to people? I enjoyed myself and realised how important my friends are to me. Thank you, Sara, for everything.

FRI 17 APRIL SIMON AND BARBARA

I see friends that I work with and we talk about work and a bit about background events – personal and universal. But I am so busy that it is a treat to see other friends. Simon, a son of my cousin Christine who died young, called into our studio in Battersea, down from Scotland with his partner Barbara. They were staying with his friend who is working on the restoration of Westminster Abbey and have been experiencing it as the friend shows them his work. They are both carers but Simon has a new job – for the past two weeks he's been a bus driver. His caring job had deteriorated. It is now run for profit, not for the best interests of people. Barbara is Polish and very dedicated, studying with a view to having more responsibility in her job. They just stayed in my room, talking with me and my son Ben, then had a little tour of our building and the different operations. They are going on the Eye tomorrow and maybe to the British Museum. I asked Simon what were his hobbies. He said, 'You won't like me when I tell you.' He goes shooting in the woods. I told him I thought some of the wood pigeons are endangered.

SAT 18 APRIL TTIP – POLITICIANS ARE CRIMINALS

Yoga. Then to Shepherd's Bush Green to speak at an anti-TTIP rally. TTIP (Transatlantic Trade and Investment Partnership) is a trade deal which is being negotiated in secret between the US and the EU. (Are chlorine-washed chickens coming here to roost?)

An example of what can happen is in El Salvador, where the water has been poisoned by mining, the public demonstrated and the government stopped permission for further mines. Now a giant Canadian mining monopoly is suing the government for (I don't remember) millions or billions for loss of earnings. TTIP uses the ISDS (Investor-State Dispute Settlement) legislation which gives the same rights to giant monopolies as to governments, which means that these giants can sue anything or anybody by claiming loss of earnings. They can wreck the planet and smash every law which protects us. It is a catch-all law. TTIP can stop all workers' rights, stop protest, impose fracking, privatise the NHS – anything. We would be ruled by giant monopolies, criminal governments and the faceless evil of the private banks.

By the wish to impose TTIP, governments have exposed themselves. They now have the confidence to show their hand. They have drawn the line. They are pro-profit and anti-people. They are *criminals* and every one of their policies is a crime against humanity. They are movers in a giant game and they thrive on power: people are pawns – collateral damage, cheap labour.

I now know what to do. I was with Cynthia. I said we have to make a point of calling politicians *criminals*. She said people do that already. I have sometimes heard them called 'crooks' but I

have not heard 'criminal'. Cynthia works with computers and the social media. I don't. I rely on her as my medium, she tells me what's happening out there. I said we are activists and we have to tell everyone to say *criminal*. We never say 'politician' unless the politician is a good politician. Then, by constantly referring to criminals, it might sink in: change public opinion.

SUN 19 APRIL NOBODY NICER THAN AMERICANS

On Sunday evening Andreas and I went to see my old friend Dennita Sewell. We last saw her in the archive of the Metropolitan Museum, New York, at the time of our 'Vive la Cocotte' collection. We copied a Dior suit; Andreas took measurements and called it the 'Metropolitan suit'. Dennita has been head of fashion at the Phoenix Art Museum for fifteen years and she was on a fashion tour with a group of twenty women supporters and trustees of the museum. They invited us for dinner at the Lansdowne Club and Andreas remarked that he was the only man.

Dennita's ladies are Jeffersonians. I talked about +5 *degrees* and *End Monopoly Capitalism* and they were very encouraging, indeed they did their best to cheer me up. They too want a better world. Andreas enjoyed being with such people. We love art historians and when Americans are nice there is nobody nicer.

TUES 21 – SUN 26 APRIL PRATO

Andreas and I went to Rosita and Paola's in Prato, near Florence. These are our friends who produce for us in Italy and we stay with them in their home. Andreas and I worked together – he mostly on the Red Carpet dresses (fabrics now chosen) and me on unisex knitwear. On Saturday morning we drive half an hour through Tuscan hills, past miles of nurseries, to Viareggio, with its long beach and restaurants on the sand. In its heyday it was very rich and popular but some of the great hotels are now boarded up.

I came back on my own because Andreas caught the train to go and see his father in the Tyrol.

MON 27 APRIL HIGH-RISE LONDON: A MODEST PROPOSAL

Wrote article for *Huffington Post* about the scandal of London being torn down for the building of high-rise flats for speculators. I pointed out that as the flats are empty no one need build them. The government could just issue bonds – IOU the right to build a high-rise, then the speculators could just keep selling them on until it all goes bust.

THURS 30 APRIL RAMSGATE ELECTION

To Ramsgate with Joe. Our friend Nigel Askew lives there. He's popular here in his home town and is standing for the Reality Party against Nigel Farage. He has a bus, a double-decker, which he's had

At the opening of Evolution cafe with Nigel and Joe.

for twenty years, and he uses it to raise awareness for good causes at festivals and for anything else useful; e.g. ten years ago they fed homeless people from the bus and campaigned for their shelter and support in London. I first met him when we travelled in the bus in Malcolm's funeral procession, up through Camden to Highgate Cemetery. And since then we travel in it and use it as a base in anti-fracking demonstrations.

We are in Ramsgate and Margate to support his campaign in the general election and the local council election. And I am also here to open Joe's Evolution Café. This has good vegetarian food and snacks like beetburgers (beetroot – scrumptious). The innovative chefs Tom Batterby and Giuseppe are young lads and the waitresses are local girl activists. One of them, Laura Hackett, wrote Nigel Askew's campaign speeches. A great idea is that if people enjoy their meal they can buy a meal ticket which is pinned on a board and anyone who is poor can ask for one.

Ramsgate, Joe says, is 'artist-led'. People who find London expensive move down here and the resort, once dilapidated, has been very much renovated. But there are still a lot of poor.

MAY 2015

SARURDAY, 2 MAY TAX AND THE GREEN PARTY

Myself and Climate Revolution and Joe have been working with the Green Party since Christmas. I gave a donation which enabled them to field more candidates for the coming election. We had meetings. What inspired me to get involved was of course that they are the only English party who care about the environment and that this and everything else is connected. I was impressed by the small leaflet I was handed at an anti-fracking demo which listed their main aspirations. I urged them to stick to it. Keep it simple. Stick to your four big aspirations: against fracking, against austerity, pro-community, pro-human rights. You are the polar opposite of the other parties. We were delighted. A day or two later their message was an image of Luke Skywalker with a green-lit baton and the text: *We are the Revolt.*

Just before Easter we got an email of a poster for their billboards. I was feeling stressed (tell you why in a bit) and I

freaked out. I thought the poster was terrible. Negative. Where was the aspiration? It seemed only detail and off-putting. My enthusiasm drained away. But then next day I started to see that, though I would have done it differently, it was their poster and it suited them. But I really shocked myself and doubted myself. How could I have been so extreme in my passionate dislike? There was nothing wrong with the poster. It was rather clever. And by the tone and feeling I saw that we did have the same vision and our discussions had helped.

At the time of our Gold Label Paris show (7 March), the *Telegraph* did an article citing an item extracted from my company's tax accounts, which they claimed had deprived the British government of tax. It did not worry me at all because I am quite comfortable that not only legally but morally I pay the right amount of tax. Of course the paper linked this claim to the donation I had made to the Green Party. A good week later when I got back to England I decided to make a statement against the smear, especially because the Green Party needed this cleared up. First, I went through everything with my accountants, asking questions. I wished to make a simple statement but I kept thinking I needed to supply some detail, but every time I tried, the detail led to more detail and I found myself at every spare moment and in the middle of the night holding imaginary conversations with the world at large explaining why I had not morally avoided paying tax. At the time of the poster I still hadn't done this statement. I was frustrated.

So right now in the diary, even though this stupid story has evaporated, I would like to use the opportunity to make a general statement – and there's an end:

An offshore company is a convenience. It means you build a company as you go along. When the company makes a profit, I receive it in the form of a dividend on which I pay full income tax in England (45 per cent). In this way I end up paying more tax here because the profit is greater than it would otherwise be. I am not a non-dom. I live here.

Nevertheless the Young Greens, bless them, weren't happy; I wasn't pure enough for them. Shame they believed the *Telegraph*. They went on our planned tour without me. We had proposed a series of public lectures and debate with economics expert Andrew Simms: 'How to get from Here to a Green Economy'. We were to visit eight towns throughout the country, focusing where strong Green candidates were. I thought, 'Why should I create a fuss for me and the whole of the Green Party? Give yourself a break.' And they went off without us, I think. A wasted opportunity.

It is important to have this debate:

* Make clear that the Greens expect political power and they are seen to be preparing for this.
* Show that a green economy could build a fair, comfortable, kind and safe society. Not just green jobs but education, social life, art and culture.
* Show the Greens to have the only responsible financial vision.
* What's good for the planet is good for the economy. What's bad for the planet is bad for the economy.

I have met very good people in the Green Party, friends, dedicated and inspiring. I am so glad there is a party you can believe and vote for. By the time you read this the election will be over and then we've really got to get it together. We will have to fight the next government on every issue – prevent their crimes. Hopefully, the SNP will also take the fight into parliament.

TUES 5 MAY MAN AND SUPERMAN AT THE NT

Visit Julian, then to the National Theatre with Andreas – *Man and Superman* by Bernard Shaw, starring Ralph Fiennes as John Tanner/ Don Juan, and Indira Varma as Anne. It was first played in 1905 at a time of socialism, the campaign for worker's rights (build-up of trade unions) and women's rights. The core of the drama is of a man and a woman completely attracted to each other. He wishes to preserve his bachelor state of noble isolation as a sceptic and thinker (Superman) and will not be sucked into marriage and the daily social round of the idle middle class (Man) by the young woman, who at every twist and turn defies all logic by her idiosyncratic and unexpected wiles as she baffles and twists him round her finger. Everything is unexpected except the inevitable ending. The drama turns on the outrageous opinions of all the cast and exposes English morals by reversing them all.

The play has three times as many lines as a play written today, lines which compound the irony. Fiennes was on stage almost the whole time and he sped through the lines in their hundreds. Shaw didn't give us time to stop thinking; we were kept on our toes throughout and didn't miss a turn. This was a virtuoso collaboration between writer and actor. Consummate skill. Sheer concentration of mind. Bravo! Bravo!

Tanner/Don Juan goes to Hell in the middle acts. I am thinking of reworking Faust into a new play: Mephistopheles would be the press, taking us to Hell on Earth.

THURS 7 MAY ELECTION RESULTS

Tories won. Old people duped by their obvious lies. Nothing changes – we will have to fight on every issue. Our campaign, 'Politicians are Criminals', aims to polarise the opposition – on the one side a few criminals and on the other public opinion.

SAT 9 MAY EVERYMAN AT THE NT

My friend Susan came to stay. Remember, we met at teacher training college aged eighteen. She is two days older than me. In the evening we went, with Cynthia and Peter Olive, to the National Theatre to see *Everyman*. Another Faustian theme. It starred Chiwetel Ejiofor – terrific actor – and the text was a new adaptation by Carol Ann Duffy. Her poetry is really good; this is in a rap style.

Everyman is a morality play from medieval England and its story is bang up to date because Everyman ('Ev' in this version) has wasted his life on self-indulgence, consumption and irresponsibility to family and to the higher things in life (God/good deeds). God tells his servant, Death, to kill him even though he's in the prime of his life because God demands a reckoning. Ev has an accident and in the few moments before he dies he makes a journey, a review of his life, so he can tell God what good his life had been. He can't find any and desperately tries to do something. A good scene is where 'Fellowship' has left and he, Ev, has left 'Worldly Goods' and thrown away his credit cards. He is sitting in a rubbish dump with a wino. She shares her drink. 'Knowledge' (Penny Laden) is the wino and she wakes in him the realisation of his ignorance. Knowledge is the only one who will accompany him into death.

For myself, I see God as a concept of our perfection. Ev had not followed his deep curiosity to understand the world; not engaged with the human genius through culture; not honoured God. Knowledge says: 'Everyman, I will go with thee and be the guide in thy most need to be by thy side'. This is my story. Knowledge is my friend in my need and throughout my life till the end. Knowledge is when you personally really know something. You have to find it – by following your deep curiosity and comparing things. My motto is 'you get out what you put in'.

The end of the play was beautiful. Ev told the truth. He remembered the beautiful things he had seen and the moments of

Culture being a pursuit of our total perfection by means of getting to know the best which has been thought and said in the world; and through this knowledge, turning a stream of fresh and free thought upon our stock notions and habits

Culture

love. Again, National Theatre: best acting. And the programmes are always full of knowledge and so well designed. This one refers to *Everyman* as a 'Play for the Anthropocene Age'. Carol Ann Duffy is our Poet Laureate. We should be proud.

THURS 14 – SUN 17 MAY SAVANNAH, GEORGIA

Andreas and I flew to New York with Christopher (our marketing director) and Laura (head of our press). There we met André Leon Talley and flew to Savannah in Georgia – to Savannah College of Art and Design, where André is a mentor and trustee. André is part of fashion, very well known in our circle; as a teenager he became protégé and assistant of Diana Vreeland, the legendary editor of American *Vogue*, and he has worked with Anna Wintour.

The college, SCAD, is to give me the André Leon Talley Award for lifetime achievement. We have installed an exhibition, *Dress Up Story – 1990 Until Now*, which covers the last twenty-five years of Andreas and I working together. SCAD has a museum of paintings and furniture and applied art – a small random collection. Andreas selected some artefacts from photos SCAD sent us, in particular a collection of English portraits to create an environment for our exhibition. He worked on it in England with the director of our archive, Rafael, who had gone ahead to install it. It was well done.

We saw the students' work in their diploma fashion show. It went fast and slick, which was a shame. It's not like you're in Paris and everybody has to rush to fit into the timing of a grand schedule with all the top designers. I would have liked to look longer.

Paula Wallace is the founder, owner and director of the school. She sold the family house and moved to Savannah where she bought a building and set up the school. Savannah had many untouched old buildings – it is *Gone with the Wind* and it had been in decline for a century. The buildings were cheap and she bought more. The school has now 11,000 students – including branches in Atlanta, Hong Kong and Lacoste. The town is now regenerated.

I feel I should tell you of the hotel we all shared in Savannah. Paula's husband had decorated it and it was full of curiosities – every painting, every object had been chosen because it was peculiar or gross. Over our bed hung a giant-branched candelabra that had come from some baronial-sized hall; running out of our fireplace was a herd of twenty plastic horses; large old books with cloth or leather bindings were used as decor everywhere, colour co-ordinated blue. We didn't take any pictures because we didn't like anything – invasive decor! But then we got used to it and it seemed friendly and like home. Wonderful vegetarian food. We tried grits at breakfast!

We enjoyed spending time with our colleagues and so very much with André, and Danny, our organiser, driver and guide. And we enjoyed Savannah. Each morning at sunrise Andreas had a run through 'fairyland' as he described it. It is set out in squares designed by a philanthropist, John Forsyth, with grand trees to shade the heat and absorb the humidity. The trees are oaks with wide branches and are hung with Spanish moss, which is a parasite but an air plant. The best experience was on Sunday morning when Andre took us to the First African Baptist Church: singing – ravishing – 'soul'.

There was lots of press, also from New York and countrywide. I launched our 'Politicians are Criminals' campaign.

MON 18 MAY – THURS 21 MAY NEW YORK

Flew back to New York and said goodbye to dear André for the moment. Treated ourselves to staying in the Carlyle Hotel. Met my dear friend Terry Doctor who is, among other things, an outstanding follower of fashion; he knows everything – also about politics.

Andreas is here to check a few things about the shop we will open and Laura and Christopher are working to choose an American PR. I told Terry I might not come for the shop opening. I might never come to New York again – I only travel if I have to.

We went to the Met to see the current exhibition – *China: Through the Looking Glass* (of fashion). Yves St. Laurent's, Poiret's and Dior's designs from his Chinese collection were the stars of the show. Then we met Stella Schnabel and her sweet friend Theodora, Keith Richard's daughter; she and Stella had been to the same school as our friend Paz. We got take-away pizza. I don't like pizza but that's what we did because the restaurants were too noisy and we met at our friend Sabina's flat. I had spent the day with Sabina and Andreas because they wanted to look at second-hand clothes in Brooklyn. Sabina is a super stylist and queen of the flea markets. She will be helping again at our forthcoming shows.

I wish we had taken a photo of Stella – she was wearing an old dress and it suited her. She is riveting, her posture and her voice give her the authority of an oracle. She is an actress. Her latest project is original. *My Hindu Friend.* So original that I can't remember what it is. We were enjoying each other so much and probably getting drunk. I must have told them about my politicians/criminals campaign.

FRI 22 MAY – SUN 24 MAY WOODSTOCK

Let's look at a bit more of America, I had said, because I might not go again. So we went to stay in a house Sabina had bought in upstate New York. I enjoyed driving up through Harlem and over George Washington Bridge and into the green forests and rolling hills, like England on a much bigger scale, on an almost empty road. Three hours' drive.

Sabina's house is in Andes, not far from Woodstock, and like Ramsgate it is becoming more populated by people from the city, this time New York, living there or buying a second home. There are many more organic and vegetarian restaurants than in England. Here, but also in the city – and it's the same in LA. This area was rich when New York was rising, supplying milk and other foods, but it lost importance with refrigeration and distribution from other parts and particularly from California. There are still farms but they are often abandoned. We went looking inside one: tools and machinery were all left rusting and on one floor were dummies for home dressmaking and effects of female life. On a shelf was a shoebox of letters. I took one, just pulled it out at random for this diary. It was dated January 1914:

Dear "Taffie"

I know I should have written sooner, but the drug store has kept me on the go, as usual.

First I want to tell you that I am writing on the stationery which my niece, Audrey, gave me. There are larger sheets, too.

I got 2 more Xmas presents which I didn't tell you about. One is a tailored red cloth jacket with an open pleat in the back – it's darling. I got a green sailor dress, too. I'm not so crazy about that, though.

I'd like to see your blue dress. I bet it's cute. Do you think you can come up either for Lincoln's or Washington's birthday?

I got a card from my paratrooper last week saying his furlough is delayed. He'll be home around the 15th, and that's almost here. Oh boy!

We got our report cards the other day, and I got all 90s, excpet for an 85 in ancient history. How are you making out?

You know, the stationery I gave you looked swell in the box when I bought it, but now it doesn't look good or like what it was worth. I'll do better next time hence. I'm mad at myself, now, for buying it.

My sister Bea is going to give me a 'Charm-curl Permanent' in two more weeks. I can't wait until I try it.

I have to write to a soldier now, and I don't know how I'm ever going to get his letter done as I'm tired as a dead dog. Bye now.

Love Ida

WEDS 27 – THURS 28 MAY TWINKLE, TWINKLE, LITTLE BAT

We flew back to London on Monday and went back to work the next day. We are discussing with the architect the rebuilding of our studio. It has been hotch-potched. But it's best not to keep doing that and we should rebuild for a better working environment.

Thursday afternoon to our Conduit Street shop to an event organised and decorated by our clever visual merchandising manager, Lorraine. I am reading a passage from *Alice in Wonderland*. Of course I chose the famous scene, the Mad Hatter's Tea Party. He murdered Time when he sang the song, 'Twinkle, twinkle, little bat' – so said the Queen of Hearts – therefore their lives are stuck at six o'clock, which is tea time.

JUNE 2015

MON 8 – WEDS 10 JUNE DUSSELDORF

Andreas accompanied me to Dusseldorf where I'm to give a talk. I could choose any subject I liked and there is a fee. This is a regular event for speakers with ideas, sponsored and attended by German businessmen and also by the ticket-buying public. It was sold out. An audience of 2,000. Peter, whose marketing company arranged the event, looked after us so well and our schedule was comfortable. My talk was about the 'Politicians R CRIMINALS' campaign and at the word 'CRIMINALS' spontaneous clapping broke out. Very encouraging – helps me feel I'm on the right track – getting through.

I gave my fee to Cool Earth and at Peter's suggestion we had hung their banners in the reception area. Matthew Owen (Cool Earth director) came, so afterwards I sat signing my biography and Matthew sat by my side giving out leaflets to those queuing and we raised another €12,000.

Dusseldorf is famous for its textiles, which now include industrial textiles like car-seat covers, and on the third day we were shown round a soon-to-be-opened textile museum. The machines are all operational and we watched them demonstrated. My mother was a weaver and she had twenty-four looms; she replaced the bobbins and tied the threads as they were about to run out, and whilst the machines were running, so that none stopped. During the demonstration the machines got faster and faster. Something scared me; it was that the smallest most simple innovation could unleash such power – at first just a bar of wood in the right place, then in a few more innovations; blinding thunder. I was scared by the machines because I am scared of the power of people.

The museum has an archive in the form of a basement room filled with thousands of bottles of vegetable dyes, each one a different colour; each needs its personal mordant to fix it and it will be thrilling to see one day the new colours applied. I expect most have never found a mordant. I once read a book called *Mauve* (by Simon Garfield). The colour mauve was the first synthetic dye, made from coal tar. It became a rage; it was the only fashionable colour for a time during the nineteenth century and women wore no other colour. It was one of the most important discoveries ever made because from this the synthetic industry grew synthetic fabrics and plastic and the whole perfume and pharmaceutical industry.

THURS 11 JUNE A TISCHBEIN PAINTING

Andreas is thinking of buying a little painting we both loved when we saw it. It's late eighteenth-century by the painter Tischbein the Younger (1742–1808). It reminds me of Watteau because of its attitude. Watteau, born in 1684, died of TB aged thirty-six. He tells the truth in his paintings. You can find his work in the Wallace Collection. Two artists who copy him, Pater and Lancret, are there in the same room. Their paintings are decorative pieces but they don't tell the truth – the gestures are self-conscious.

Andreas was telling me what he wanted to say about the painting and not listening to me.

'Watteau was telling the truth!' I said.

Andreas: 'Yes, he probably invented the truth. You know when people die, they say the soul flies off, that little trembling of life.' He fluttered his fingers near his mouth and whisped out slightly his breath, referring to the little Tischbein. 'You know, the dog licking his crotch and the other climbing up on her skirt, she with her

Johann Heinrich Tischbein the Younger's 'An Elegant Couple Out Hawking'.

hawk and the man behind the horses – he could be her servant –
her lover?'

What Andreas is describing is it's so arbitrary – that's what's real.

FRI 12 JUNE TEDDY JOINS CR

Teddy has come to work for Climate Revolution. He, together with
Cynthia and Cindy, makes up our team of three. Teddy is Andreas's
cousin. His name is Otmar Kronthaler. When his mother brought
the new baby home and put him on the floor in his basket his fifteen-
month-old brother toddled over, put his arms out and said 'Teddy'.

SUN 14 JUNE BERNARD HAITINK

Andreas and I to the Barbican: Mozart Violin Concerto No. 3,
Mahler Symphony No. 1 ('Titan'); Bernard Haitink, conductor, and
Alina Ibragimova, violin. Mahler really titanic. Haitink – I've had
some of my most exciting times with the famous conductor and
this was one of them. It is probably twenty years ago I remember
stamping and whistling from the highest balcony at the end of
Daphnis and Chloe. An orchestra is the high point of human
achievement.

TUES 23 JUNE PRESTON VOTES AGAINST FRACKING

Got back from Milan (for our MAN show) last night. Now off to
Preston to support the fantastic local campaign against fracking. It's
local but they also protest nationally and internationally. They are
up to the hilt informed re the dangers of fracking. Tina Louise is one
of the major spokespeople; she comes from Blackpool, near where
Cuadrilla fracked then had to stop after they caused an earthquake.

I'm up here with Cynthia and Joe, who concentrates his activism
on fracking. His team, Talk Fracking, have worked with Tina Louise

before. Our CRIMINALS have no clue of the dangers of fracking or the immediate damage it would do to the economy. They are totally irresponsible, except to the GIANTS. They are pledged to the reflex action: 'If it's good for business, it's good for everybody!' (knee-jerk response from Vince Cable to John Hilary from War on Want).

I speak around the idea 'Politicians R CRIMINALS' and because of that my speech gets reported on mainstream media. If we keep calling them CRIMINALS we'll get through.

Major WIN! The Preston council voted against fracking.

MON 29 JUNE VAL GARLAND

Val Garland, the make-up artist we love to work with, comes to our Battersea studio. She wants us to contribute to a film she is making about her art for students. She looks lovely wearing one of our dresses like a coat.

JULY 2015

WEDS 1 – THURS 2 JULY MEPHISTOPHELES

Wednesday: Andreas is off to Cataldi in Italy to work on Gold Label and to go to the beach on the weekend. I do an interview for Lorna for a film she is making re my activism. She wants me to talk about my childhood. I do another interview in a couple of weeks' time and then she can keep putting everything together.

On Thursday I do a talk to camera for the internet on CRIMINAL. We will put up the film each Thursday and build the campaign one point at a time. For the 'first' talk I will ask people one thing: say CRIMINAL. Though people know politicians are criminals they focus on petty things – stuff like the expenses scandal, even though they feel it's bigger than that. They know austerity's a fiddle and many of us hate Tony Blair as a war criminal, a man who is responsible for deaths by the thousand and is free to deny it. I need to get it across that every one of their policies is a crime against humanity. TTIP gives absolute proof. Any politician who wishes to implement TTIP is a criminal because he is anti-people. I never thought politicians would have the gall to show their hand so obviously. But they did with TTIP. It's like they are proud to be CRIMINALS. So now we know and we have to deal with them. They feel so safe playing their game of destruction, together with the Giants (monopolies) and backed by the Faceless Evil (Central Banks) and the American War Machine, and served by their PR – the mainstream media.

I have begun to see our global politics as a war game run by criminals who are going to wipe the board clean. The press is Mephistopheles (Joker) and we are Faust who put up no opposition. We sold our soul for consumption and we're led along to Hell. I think it would be possible to rework Marlowe's play.

Together with the Joker I did this graphic for CRIMINALS. We use them on T shirts, badges + publicity.

Checkerboard

The game is: Rot $$ = designed to create poverty + syphon off profits for the rich. → the poor get poorer + the rich get fewer. Taken to its logical conclusion = Total Poverty: there will be no market left — people will be either poor or dead. Game over. Nothing on the board but the word DESTROY + the faceless evil.

Politicians must be able to tick four boxes to qualify. The rest (most of them) are CRIMINALS. They must be against fracking, against TTIP, pro community, pro human rights. We have already found two politicans: Caroline Lucas and Jeremy Corbyn. We need real politicians if we are going to save life on earth.

FRI 3 JULY LOVE TO JULIAN, MOST WANTED MAN IN THE WORLD

Julian's birthday party. I wrote him a card which said 'Love to Julian, the most wanted man in the world'. Andreas and I enjoyed talking to WikiLeaks workers from different parts of the world and to South American diplomats. We like the new Ecuadorian ambassador and his wife.

MON 13 JULY ANDY GOTTS FOR GREENPEACE

It's taken a long time – six months – for photographer Andy Gotts to photograph sixty celebs all wearing the same T-shirt designed by Andreas for Greenpeace's campaign (see p.276). The first to be photographed was George Clooney, the last Julian Assange.

I had thought: great to have all this on social media! What else can we do? A book? An exhibition? All wearing the same T-shirt? Even though a lot of them pull a powerful face. John Sauven, who heads Greenpeace UK, had the answer. What a brilliant idea! Take advantage of everybody wearing the same graphics – the London Underground escalator at Waterloo! That's where Shell staff go up to work at the giant Shell building on the South Bank.

We all met for coffee before we went down to the escalator. John couldn't be there – a hornet had bitten him and he was in hospital with antibiotics. The press were waiting and I went down with activists Sadie Frost and Leebo Freeman.

I was knocked out – the effect was tremendous. I had never looked at or even noticed adverts on the escalators before. Now, all wearing the same white shirt in the same framed format the

Our Greenpeace Arctic campaign with celebrity photos by Andy Gotts.

portraits plunged down to Hell either side of the moving escalator, then streamed up to Heaven when you got to the bottom. It became a new space for art – an art exhibition experience. It's there for two weeks. It's an experience. One journalist who had interviewed Shell told me they said, 'Oh, it's just a one-off event with celebrities.' I replied, 'Wouldn't they just like that support?' Many more stars want to join in and have a photo. We just donated seventy more T-shirts because people want to do it in other countries.

TUES 14 JULY DINNER AT THE WALLACE COLLECTION

My friend, Bruno Wang, invited us to dinner at the Wallace Collection. We talked to Grayson Perry, all dolled up, a happy man. Andreas sat next to him and he confirmed to me Grayson's reputation as a keen observer and thinker. We also talked to Zaha Hadid who looked stunning in frills of different browns because they toned with her brown skin; they fell from her like feathers and set off her eagle nose. She looked so beautiful, like a carving. I sat next to her architect partner, Patrick.

There was a lady on our table I felt friendly towards as she and her husband came from a family of English diplomats in China and I'm a big fan of her relation Maggie Keswick, whose book *The Chinese Garden* is one of my treasures. I think China up till the late nineteenth century was the greatest civilisation of all. Patrick thought the English lord of the nineteenth century was perhaps the upstanding specimen of civilisation. I said that after what Lord Elgin did to the Summer Palace in China I was not too sure. I claimed rather that France in the last quarter of the nineteenth century, up until World War I, arrived at the peak of Western civilisation and that the salon – hosted typically by society women, e.g. Mme Strauss, the wife of a rich banker and friend of Proust – was the catalyst which made it happen. I am aware of all this because it was a special subject of my friend Gary.

I told the joke of Oscar Wilde who said that an English lady opened a salon only to find she had opened a saloon. The lady I had been friendly to came back at me, 'At least the English understand justice. Their law is superior to the French.' I was flabbergasted. Where has she been the last hundred years? Her view might have been the jingoism of the past – but now! English law has been mined away, especially recently. Human rights! We're back to before the Magna Carta because politicians are now making blanket laws which overule all previous law. I said, 'Napoleon called us a nation of shopkeepers and I take that to mean the businessmen and the government which supports them would sell their grandmothers.' That is true of Cameron, selling not only our financial assets but also disposing of our laws in exchange for favours from America. She came back at me again, 'In a world of great and rising population it is wonderful that London is rapidly building so many high-rise flats.' I buried my head in my hands – how can anybody think like that? I said the flats were for speculators and that they were pulling down the social housing. 'Pah!' – she pulled a face and waved me away. I said, 'Exactly. Pah!' and gave her the same face and gesture.

I am sure Lewis Carrol was thinking of Victorian society, especially the socialite dons, deans and their wives of Oxford (Alice's family?), when he devised the Mad Hatter's Tea Party – talking nonsense, riddles which left a hole in the air and time stopped forever at six o'clock tea time.

WEDS 15 JULY TALKING PUNK

Back to Lorna to finish my interview. She films in a room in the Groucho Club, which has nice light coming from the skylight. I balk at the need to discuss punk – but I managed. I hope that's the end of it! Punk wasn't important, just a marketing opportunity. I do love the look, though, and that's really all it was – except that I learnt a lot from it. But to most people it was a marketing opportunity.

SAT 25 JULY GAELLE

Gaelle arrives from Paris. She was once our fitting model and we had great fun. Andreas adores her. She is now an actress and she's staying with us for three weeks while she attends summer school at LAMDA. I have an idea for her and her friend Marie to create their own show called 'Culture for Beginners'. Choose a venue where you can have an intimate rapport with your audience. Put together a programme of poetry and readings but also talk about these and put them in the context of the world they came from, telling the audience things that are normally written in the programme and connecting things, ending with the *Map/Rot$* leaflet.

[*She did it. First performance in June 2016 – central action 'Introspection' by Peter Handke. She'll do more.*]

I want to add – just so you know – that I spend an increasing amount of time, more than I spend on either design or CR, in improving the structure of my company, but I shan't speak of it any more even though it's a very human story because it's about people and their skills. I also think it's very good for the environment to have a company efficient in human happiness, resources and team work: quality in human values.

AUGUST 2015

TUES 4 AUG JULIAN AND ORPHEUS

I went to see Julian, this time taking Teddy: I want him to take a few notes and put them up on the site. Julian's view is so sharp, it gives me ammunition. We're both in this fight for human rights and to halt the destruction. The people in the embassy are so kind and I do appreciate my best cup of coffee.

 Then with Andreas to the Albert Hall. We are friends of John Eliot Gardiner and are really privileged to be invited to a concert performance (remember we saw the opera in Munich) by his Monteverdi Choir. The music is different, brighter and clearer – due in part, I imagine, to the use of old instruments. The opera is Monteverdi's *L'Orfeo*. Though Orpheus (sung by Krystian Adam) goes to hell, a metaphor for the exhilaration caused in me would rather be a climb up to the gods of Mount Olympus.

THURS 6 – SAT 15 AUG TINOS AND STONER

Yesterday Andreas couldn't make his mind up if he should visit Yasmine who had rented a house on the island of Tinos. You know who she is – my French friend, stylist – works on our shows and has her own lingerie collection – Yasmine Eslami. My luxury is to stay at home and I wanted to write. But at the last moment I said, okay, I'll come. So we are off, for a week. The plane left at eleven at night and when we got to Athens it was still dark. We had two hours to wait for the boat, and this was my favourite part of the holiday. I was dressed in a sack-cloth short cape, long black skirt, brown socks and white medium high heels and I felt glamorous, as if I was travelling in an earlier decade, when to travel was glamorous – sitting at dawn in one of the rough cafés on the quay, watching people as they turned up.

Tinos is barren hills and rocks with tiny one-cell churches here and there (I think they are visited just on their saint's day) and bird houses, cubes of stones and holes, perhaps from previous years when people farmed here – perhaps for pigeons or doves. There were walls all over the hills, mostly embedded into the hills. We think they are to hold the ground; much of the land was for goats, though not now. Small trees looked like giant heather. Yasmine said they were called tamarisks.

Yasmine's house overlooked the sea and we could walk down to the shore. It was wonderful – lying under the tamarisks – the warm calm sea of the ancient Mediterranean. There was a wind which kept the climate comfortable.

Yasmine was with her boyfriend, Dominic. I had not spoken to him much before, because he thinks his English is so bad. I never realised. Yasmine's friends are always speaking English and I thought

Here I am on the terrace in Tinos giving a talk to camera on 'Politicians R Criminals'.

he was the quiet one. I could have practiced my French. Anyway we got talking and he's great. My holiday was about reading John Williams's *Stoner*, and afterwards I stole Andreas's copy of another Williams novel, *Augustus*, when I could. *Stoner* was written in 1965 and has just been rediscovered, and now everybody hails it. Andreas says: 'The words have such a wonderful flow; he's found the essence of what he wanted to say – nothing to add, nothing to take away. It seems the most incredible English. With a few words you're drawn in: an extraordinary labour of simplification.'

The day Stoner falls in love with literature is the most memorable event in the novel. His teacher is called Archer Sloane and sets him to read Shakespeare's Sonnet 73. The novel has the power of a Greek tragedy. The characters are lit like monuments, revealed according to the events of the daily drama. At the end I marvelled at the integrity of Stoner – of a life fully realised. Only truth is left.

I also did my last 'talk to camera' video but we did not have the technology to send it. I need two days to do a talk – think about it and work out how to say it – how to get the message across, then memorise it, then do it. I find myself able to concentrate on nothing else until it's done. So I did not go with the others when they went shopping for food down at the port town.

The rest of the time was about dinner at the taverna with Yasmine's friends. I discovered that Tinos is popular with French fashion people, they rent houses and know each other. Andreas bumped into John Galliano on the beach one day and he was surprised to hear I was here, too, as I don't go on seaside holidays.

TUES 18 AUG CANTERBURY TALES

Evening get-together for staff and friends at the Doodle Bar. We showed Pasolini's *Canterbury Tales*. Pasolini was a genius film-maker who was murdered in mid-life, aged fifty-three.

The costumes and the casting were really good. The cast were not film stars but real people and therefore a very unusual bunch from what you usually see in film – they were just as good as actors but their real pimples and crooked teeth made you constantly aware that the images in front of you are actually real people pretending. This got you personally involved and taking part in the fun.

The Doodle Bar will be demolished along with anything else interesting – that or empty high-rise flats, unaffordable and for speculators, and the amount of concrete, the amount of stuff to build them. We are being overruled by the **antipeople**.

We take advantage of the Doodle Bar whilst we have it. I am pleased the Vauxhall Tavern won't be wrecked.

TUES 25 AUG HAMLET AND SONNET 73

Hamlet. Barbican. A big production, great use of the Barbican stage, lots of running up and down. Viridian green with an electric-blue glow (sometimes strobe lighting); in the second half, black slag had blown in and buried everything. Costume reference: Edwardian mixed in with today. In the beginning (e.g. at the banquet) the court was staid, whereas the play gives out that it is decadent, corrupt and drunken. Hamlet contradicts the staid impression by telling it like it is. And the invading slang in the second half confirms it. I agree with the press criticism. Benedict Cumberbatch was wonderfully intelligent in understanding his role yet he did not move you. But Ophelia moved me more than any I've seen.

At the end of August the lamps were out in Battersea Park. Cycling home, Andreas got a different impression of the twilight, the trees were somehow ever more present but yet they loomed and filtered into the universal shade. I had memorised the Shakespeare sonnet that is discussed in *Stoner*, and I quoted it ('In me thou see'st the twilight of such day/As after sunset fadeth in the West'). Andreas: 'That's it. I must have kept the poem and that's what I noticed.'

The sonnet (no. 73) is about ageing. If you read it, let the poem find its way to tell you of the beauty that fuses you with the world.

WEDS AUG 26 YOUNG WERTHER

Andreas bought me Goethe's *The Sorrows of Young Werther*. It was the first tragic novel and it caused a sensation – and was one of the factors that led to the Romantic movement. It was translated into languages across the world. Napoleon took *Werther* on his Egyptian campaign in 1798 and when he met Goethe in 1808 he told him that he had read the book seven times – he decorated him. *Werther* became a model for the Romantics. On the cover of my copy of the book is a self-portrait by Philipp Otto Runge – still wearing Werther's blue frock coat and buff leather waistcoat and breeches in 1805 (thirty years after the book).

The book is based on a true story combining Goethe's own experience and that of a man he knew called Karl Wilhelm Jerusalem, who shot himself after declaring his love to another man's wife. It is the first confessional novel and takes the form of letters from Werther to Wilhelm, a one-sided communication. Goethe wrote it in six weeks at the age of twenty-four.

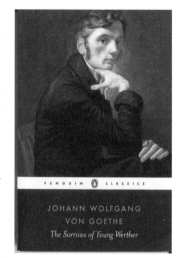

His hero follows his heart and loses himself. Young Werther was the happiest of men. Under the sun he lay in the warm grass and knew the teeming life of the microbes. His heart was his proudest possession and he marvelled at the power of his love which fitted in the whole creation; his soul rose in ecstasy to meet its heaven, the wind and the stars and the divine mystery of the cosmos. I write this in criticism: he believed that it was noble to indulge his finer feelings beyond the bounds of sanity. Because of this practice, his love for another man's wife – convinced that she was his one soul mate – turned from joy and collapsed into the unbearable pain of depression until at last he found the calm to shoot himself under the self-delusion that his life was a sacrifice to her.

Why was Werther so passionate/desperate? Why did the Romantics abandon themselves to the task of living on the edge? The first reason given is always that the Romantics reacted against the cold dry reason of the eighteenth-century Enlightenment. The *Encyclopedia* was the engine which clarified opinion during this time. Diderot was in charge of it and it was a monumental task; it attempted to amass all knowledge and great thinkers contributed essays. It had a moral purpose: to combat (1) the supernatural and fabulous in history, (2) religion on irrational grounds, e.g. the doctrine of eternal damnation, (3) intolerance and persecution.

The Romantics didn't agree that reason gave truth, they found it limiting: knowledge isn't just stuff you can measure and argue about. And it was all too materialistic. The heart gives knowledge through direct experience and one's soul experience eternal truth. So the Romantic poets and their muses went round showing off their noble emotions; posing as beautiful women without mercy, dying saints, vampires, over-sensitives, wild gypsies, necromancers; they flew to anything morbid or exotic, deviant, virginal or mystic; they looked like medieval dandies or like they'd come through a storm – consumers of an idea.

Today we are still Romantics, millions of posers who just consume. Any old rubbish will do; status lies in catching the latest thing. That's why we have no original ideas. So I didn't feel so sympathetic to Werther. But it's an important book and wonderfully written. And it's about someone young and sincere – and, yes, noble, letting himself get carried away.

SEPTEMBER 2015

THURS 3 SEPT CONTRIBUTORIA

Contributoria, the newspaper I edited for an issue on the environment and our 'Politicians are Criminals' campaign – came out, and I was pleased. The graphics were exciting. *Contributoria* was affiliated to the *Guardian* but now they want to cut loose so as to have complete editorial freedom. Good luck!

Lush campaigned against TTIP. We did the packaging and the shops gave away copies of *Contributoria*.

SUN 20 SEP RED LABEL SHOW

I'll just pick out one more special detail here. It's about Lizzie Jagger and her walk. Though she's been educated mostly in England she

Mirror the World

The most important philosophical question ever asked is 'What is a good life?' A good life is one that mirrors the world.

That means that you understand the world through art and culture. You understand the genius of the human race and you understand yourself in relation to it. You're like a little tiny shard of mirror glass that's exactly a copy of the whole world. You're very beautiful because you understand the beauty of the world and you understand the human race and you want to do your best.

So what are we doing? There is a demonstration outside the fashion show today. These people are model and activist friends of mine, they have asked me 'What can we do?' and I said to them 'You've got to demonstrate! Let's build demonstrations. Public opinon will stop them.'

They look great and the idea is that you can have a good time at a demonstration but more importantly, it's a matter of life and death. I'm saying something you don't hear, and we should be hearing it. And we've got to keep saying that Politicians R Criminals and that way people will get the idea that we're being completely misled and lied to.

sounds just like her mum – from Texas. She is charismatic, with such a giggle filled with happiness. You can't get enough of it. This is her walk as Andreas described it:

'The walk of Lizzie Jagger! She exudes presence. As if the Roman legions had been sent out in advance to prepare for her – the path of her triumph. She proceeds without molestation, one step at a time. She thinks about every step, when she turns a corner she thinks,

Lizzie Jagger, Red Label show.

now I turn the corner, takes a little step back to adjust her position, hands on kidneys at the back, pushing herself forward. And the emperor went forth and the multitude acknowledged her. I never thought I'd see the day!'

FRI 25 SEPT DON'T LET ME DIE IN JAIL

Leonard Peltier has been in jail for forty years; we know he did not commit that crime. Many years ago I was collecting VIP signatures for the Leonard Peltier is Innocent petition – that's how I met Pamela. Geri from Ireland, a committed supporter of Leonard Peltier, came to see me. She told me that now is the time to build the campaign for Obama to free Leonard. Leonard is in a high-security jail and has been quite sick. The prison officers requested that he be transferred to a more lenient prison, but unfortunately just one person said no. So Leonard is really suffering: 'Don't let me die in jail.'

WEDS 30 SEPT EVENTS

September was busy. I am always working to improve the structure of our company and I had a visit from the lovely people who weave our blankets and cloaks in the Scottish Borders. And I took part in dear Tracy Worcester's film to campaign against the terrible suffering of animals in pig factories. Ninety per cent of your bacon comes from them – three major animal monopolies. Her campaign is 'Farms not Factories' and you can stop this by how you shop (Take the Pig Pledge). Or be vegetarian like me.

I went to six evening events this month to support other NGO friends – fundraising. One was a film about Malala and her work. Another was our own event with Cool Earth which raised £400,000. In between I worked on our next fashion collections whilst Andreas was finishing the one for Sunday.

OCTOBER 2015

THURS 1 – SUN 4 OCT GOLD LABEL IN PARIS

We went to Paris on Wednesday for the show called *Salva Venezia* on Sunday. On the night before we left I was exhausted but I had one thing left to do. I had promised Andreas to make a dress out of a long elastic net of two-inch-hole mesh and embroidered with sequins. The idea was to stretch it out onto the stand/dummy/mannequin then pull it round into a tube and 'sew' the sides together by pushing a strip of gossamer fabric through the holes.

I pulled the elastic net out of the bag. It came out all together like a bouncing solid pipe, a snake of sequins. I threw it on the stand; I didn't know where to begin. I couldn't. Andreas wound it round his neck, hanging like a boa and played around with that idea. He was on form. He then pulled it around him and held it and walked with it and posed. This is the dress he made in five minutes. You could do anything with this net. It was like chewing gum, it fitted anything and it stayed where you put it. The hardest thing in fashion is the right use of fabric.

Andreas did this Gold Label collection solo but of course with our team. I hardly touched it. When we arrived in Paris on Wednesday afternoon Andreas was relaxed and in a good mood, though tired. And now I'm going to tell you something about love, which is an unusual thing for me to do.

Yasmine's shop, selling her underwear, is next to one of the best flower shops in Paris. We met her with the idea of getting something to eat and for Andreas to get flowers for our hotel which is in the same street, Rue de Richelieu. Andreas always does this. He loves flowers, it's a routine. I told Andreas to buy these white freesias. I love flowers in season and they were just beginning to come out and they smelled with a very concentrated spicy freesia smell; the stems were especially green and strong.

The florist wanted to do her thing and add more flowers and I kept saying no. Andreas thought I had a cheek telling the woman that we just liked the single bunch of freesia. He looked upon her

Gold Label – the dress Andreas made in five minutes.

as a priestess of flowers whose authority was sacred. So we ended up with the freesias with just their heads showing and embedded amongst a bouquet of white blossoms with woody stems.

While we waited for our light meal in a little café, I said two or three times, I couldn't help it – I don't like the flowers. Andreas got up, said I was terrible – 'I worked my arse off' – stuck his hand in the flowers, broke off their heads and walked out, leaving his lunch untouched. We found him later and I apologised.

The next day I stayed in our room writing the press release and he left. Half an hour later the maid came to the door with a vase of flowers – just a bunch of the same white freesias. I had not realised before that Andreas liked me, loved me, so much.

MON 5 OCT PAUL WATSON AND SEA SHEPHERD

Pamela invited Paul Watson of Sea Shepherd to the show and next day Andreas and I met with him and his wife, Yana, in his local café. One of the most important meetings in my life. The first thing I asked Paul was, 'Is there a chance to save the world?' He said, 'No, we are not too late. We must regenerate the seas. The seas give us 80 per cent of everything we need; oxygen, waste disposal, it sequesters 80 per cent of CO_2.'

I always thought that big fish eat little fish, so we start with bacteria and plankton and krill. Paul says, 'No, it's a cycle. It's the whales' shit and not only that, these huge creatures bring up the iron and nitrogen from the bottom of the sea. The more predators in the sea, the more fish you get. Every creature on this earth gives and takes – this is biodiversity – except us. We only take. At the moment the world's biodiversity can only deal with 50 per cent of our poison and waste.'

He gave me his short manual on how to save the world. Each page was a set of bullet points to identify a particular problem and suggestions of how to solve it: nothing vague, just a practical

RESTORE. CONSERVE. PROTECT.

We must replenish biodiversity in the ocean.
Humanity has been diminishing biodiversity to the state of collapse.
Biodiversity in the ocean has been reduced by 90% by a species that holds absolutely no ecological niche within the marine ecosystem.
We take. We do not give back.
Whales, fish, sea birds, seals and all marine species contribute to the life support system that is the ocean.
We do not. That is the problem.
We need to shut down all industrialized fishing operations.
To replenish the ocean we need to stop taking from it.
Seven billion people cannot continue to devour the ocean. *Here*
There are no sustainable industrial fisheries.
All government subsidies to fishing industries must be ended.
The fish cannot survive the continued onslaught of super trawlers, draggers, long-liners, drift netters, gill-netters, seiners and aquarium collectors.

Solution — start here — if you did that the whole over-fishing would stop — Those guys wouldn't make a profit (our money)

26

A page from Paul Watson's booklet, *Ocean: Solutions to Climate Change.*

programme. It is the best tool every activist has been waiting for. An example from one page: it gave me the idea for BE SPECIFIC!

He is expecting a life-size replica of the blue whale down on the quay of the Seine for the COP21 (climate change conference) in Paris, at the beginning of December.

I will join Paul there and hopefully take part in the COP21 mobilisation campaign.

SAT 17 OCT ONE HUNDRED MILLION POUNDS

I agreed to give a talk to open the Frieze Art Fair. Why, when I deny any status other than 'rubbish' to so-called modern art? Benedikt, PA to Andreas and me, came to me three days in a row asking please give me an answer. Yet he had only just told me that my friend Gregor was asking me to do it. Gregor doesn't mind my opinion because he thinks what I say is interesting and he needed an answer now because he needed to go to press. I agreed because Benedikt told me that Gregor had first asked a month ago and he had 'lost' the email – so I couldn't let Gregor down.

Also I had a painting (which is really a collage) I wanted to sell to raise money for the rainforest. Cool Earth, the charity which has a simple plan to save the rainforest by working with indigenous tribes, have already saved 541,035 acres. They are on target and need another £100 million in order to save all three great equatorial forests.

At the last election the polling station was in the local school and I saw the collage on the wall. It was done by a class of six-year-olds – about the environment. I thought I'd rather have that on my wall than something by Andy Warhol or Jeff Koons. I'll try to sell it, it will be a challenge – a challenge to 'What is art?' So I did my talk: Great art is timeless; it is always original, as alive today as when it was first done; there is no progress in art (because it is perfect), though there can be decadence. Art gives culture. Today we have consumption instead of culture – for the mass of people. If we had culture we would have different values, the values of our human genius, and we would not have climate change.

Who will own the Rainforest.
What does it mean?
£100,000,000 ?

Though people were deeply interested I started to feel mad: here I was trying to save the rainforest with a kids' collage. I said: 'I feel crazy. There is no relation between the littleness of my means and the enormity of the task. I am just going to get down and lie on the floor until somebody comes to take me away.' Then when they were clapping I suddenly sat up with an inspiration, 'I know the value of the collage! One hundred million pounds. Buy the painting and you save the rainforest. I demand one hundred million pounds!'

MON 26 OCT **FASHION CHARACTER**

I met a party of Chinese people in our showroom in Conduit Street, visiting England on a shopping tour. They are rich and because of that I imagine influential and they are interested in the environment. I gave them my leaflet with the map 'Rotten Financial System' and they invited me to come to Shanghai to receive an award at a grand event – an auction and dinner with the rest of their group, 'Fashion

Character'. I did not do this, but of course the hope is that they might help with fundraising for Cool Earth and use their influence towards building the Green Economy, which is a matter of life and death. I will keep in touch with them. However, I've had this money kind of thing before. Also: 'Talk to this blogger who has millions of fans.' They usually want something from you but they don't come across to help you.

TUES 27 OCT BJÖRK

Björk is in London and she came to see us. She brought a gift – two boxes containing LPs with all her music. She is doing everything she can to fight the present government of Iceland to stop wrecking the country. Love her.

NOVEMBER 2015

FRI 6 NOV ENGLISH CHAMPAGNE

Vineyard visit. English champagne (we have to call it English sparkling wine). Nyetimber is the name of the champagne and also the residence. I didn't know we were going. I was told yesterday that we had accepted. If I had been told about the invitation earlier I would have said no – I don't have time. But Lorna Tucker, the film-maker, came with us and I had been too busy whenever she had wanted to show me her new baby. So now on the train I had the chance to meet baby Lola Vivienne and to talk to her about Leonard Peltier. I also relaxed and talked with colleagues – about work.

Nyetimber is on the South Downs, such a gorgeous part of the world, and the house is unbelievably beautiful with a large pond landscaped with plants, gardens on the surrounding bank, woods and barns. The undulating fields of vines, a mile or two away from the sea, were separated from the woods by a curving path. The warm wind carried a little rain and you walked into it with the sound of the autumn leaves whipped in the branches above you. This is good soil for vines, something to do also with natural drainage.

We were here for wine tasting and lunch. Nyetimber sponsor the wine at some of our events. Now was the chance to really appreciate it. Delicate and subtle sensations. I will never drink again without stopping to savour the pleasure. This day I had lived in the present.

THURS 12 NOV ZEITZ FOUNDATION

Went with Teddy to Shad Thames, for an evening gathering with the Zeitz Foundation. When I went to Kenya I stayed at the Segera ranch and wildlife park, one of Jochen Zeitz's enterprises for his Long Run charity. The idea is that each of their projects regenerate the wild territory until it is sustainable – funded by luxury tourism. Andreas and I are patrons and in particular of Uaso Nyiro Primary School. Tribal people there now live more sustainably (solar not firewood) and healthily (gardens from rainwater collection). I met retired businessman Alan and his wife who have built the new school for Uaso Nyiro, which won a prize as 'Earth's Greenest School'. Jochen asked me to open his contemporary art museum in South Africa but I can't, it's too near to the collection in February.

MON 16 NOV TAKING A TANK TO THE CAMERONS

Tank to Cameron's house near Witney, organised by Joe and his 'Talk Fracking' team. Cameron has exempted his house from fracking permits but allowed them in the surrounding land. Aim: to poison the garden of the poisoner. The Nanas were waiting for us and had brought their grandchildren. They are so important – a focus group against fracking. Their support must have been so useful to the Preston council in refusing planning permission for

We got front-page coverage on the papers for this anti-fracking protest.

fracking. And I think they have been crucial in focusing public opinion against fracking – which is now at 87 per cent. The photos of the tank went everywhere. It was even featured in China.

I went back home in the car with Ben and Tomoka and dog Jackie. We stopped in Witney – so attractive. Being vegetarian, you can't find decent food when you travel, only rock-bottom prepared food produced to make the most profit. There was only cheese and gooey white bread, so we had fish and chips. I eat fish sometimes and I do like sushi, when there is nothing else.

THURS 19 – SAT 21 NOV PHOTO SHOOT IN VENICE

To Venice shooting our campaign, *Salva Venezia*. We will meet Juergen there. We were early in the airport at Gatwick having a coffee when the three models turned up one by one. They were all adorable, slim and young. I asked one of them, Naleye, about his name. His father is African-Asian and his mother Dutch. He told me that when he left New York the news on CNN was full of the grief from the Paris suicide bombings but never mentioned, obviously, that the men who became ISIS were trained by the US, UK and France. He is so friendly. Later, when we were airborne, he tore this page out of his book and gave it to me.

What's your name? I asked the girl with waist-length thick hair. Ee-A! (Ia) she boomed. Up for anything. Very sweet with this strong voice – made direct observations and questions. Amelia, caring and committed, comes from Dominican Republic. She liked coming to Europe. In her country it is dangerous to go out at night, and it is racist – people with dark skin are ostracised, with no means of

Andreas and I also model in the campaigns. Juergen took this shot of me on the Grand Canal. The jacket is covered in buttons.

income, and Haitians who were born there are now stateless and have nowhere to go.

Nadia joined us with her big suitcase of products for hair and make-up. The models are so young and lovely that make-up doesn't enhance. We did almost nothing. Naleye had a sty but it didn't matter. When we do a show we paint a theme on the face – or a device. My favourite is still the one when Andreas said, 'Make them look like horses.'

None of the models had been to Venice before. They were excited in the taxi boat. We had lunch. Juergen took us out to a little shop with fish tanks. The tiny fish tickle you by eating the dead skin and you come out with your legs smooth.

That evening our team, including, importantly, Sabina (super stylist), put together the outfits for the shoot and tried them on the models, and Colby, our fourth model, arrived. He is a porn star. When Andreas had shown me his photo and asked my opinion I said, immediately, I know why he's a porn star: because he looks

After the shoot, someone threw away our big cardboard box containing all the hats packed in tissue paper. They thought it was rubbish. The models are Amelle and Ia.

like the sweetest nicest person. And that's how it turned out. He is observant and knows more about Venice than me. He knows what we're up against regarding the environment.

Next day the plan was to hire a taxi boat and a barge and sail around. Juergen wasn't liking these tourist photos so luckily we took advantage of the invitation of Jane da Mosto to film in her palazzo. Contessa Jane da Mosto is very important. She's a scientist and has been campaigning to save Venice. In 1966 there was a terrible flood and since then people have been analysing the problem and proposing solutions. The lagoon is one of the most wonderful wetlands in the world: exquisite symbiosis between the animals and plants that stabilise the sediment from the freshwater rivers, and Venice itself which has grown with the lagoon. If Venice were not there the wetlands would have become either land or a bay – the sea having swept away the sediment. The lagoon protects Venice from storms and inundations by the sea. The biggest problem now seems to be the cruise ships which tear up the lagoon. Total false economy to allow them. Jane says that

Venice is the canary in the mine. If we can't save Venice, how do we save the world?

Here is the press release I wrote:

SALVA VENEZIA

Today we present our Gold Label show called 'Salva Venezia' and it's about saving Venice. The problem there is one of repair but also of climate change. In 12th Century Venice great houses on stilts lined the canals. They were trading posts and they each belonged to rich families and on the ground floor of these houses were shops. All the luxury goods from the East came there and merchants and rich people travelled there to shop. The prosperity of these families was out of this world and they built grand palaces painted and gilded on the outside as well as in.

Bellini, Giorgione, Titian – it was the period of the greatest flourishing of art that the West has ever known. Venice was an emporium of culture. Carnival – everyone in disguise in St. Mark's Square or disappearing round corners into those narrow streets. The mask hides a time of altered states where the poor become rich and vice versa or the ugly become attractive. It dates from a primitive time when people indulged in excess so that their sins could be forgiven before the new spring.

Come on our march on November 29th in London. The People's March for Climate, Justice and Jobs. Bring your children, it will be massive. The more people the better the chance to change the world. Come! To mirror the world: be beautiful as the world – you must engage with the world.

TUES 22 NOV MORE IMPORTANT THINGS

Party at the Shard. We did a Christmas Tree, decorated to promote awareness of Cool Earth. Why does a party have boom-boom music in an area where there is no dance floor. Can't talk. I like to talk. I prefer it to constant photos. Irvine Sellar was presented to me, who produced the Shard and put up the money. He's doing another building, a bit taller now. We had a photo taken. He was so full of his own importance. I said, 'Are you coming to the march against climate change on Sunday?' He sneered, 'I've got more important things to do.' I said, 'Like what? – Die?'

SUN 29 NOV CLIMATE MARCH

The march. Blustery day. 70,000 people. Hyde Park Corner to Houses of Parliament. Speeches before – Caroline Lucas, me, Jeremy Corbyn. (I got Caroline's speech later: superb.) So much organisation goes into a march. Avaaz and Friends of the Earth were the main NGOs. Cynthia worked with them for months and thinks they are splendid.

Then off we went. A lot of our young gang wore crowns which stand for 'We are the People, we rule the world'. It's great talking to people as you go along, especially the young ones and meeting your friends. At the end were more speeches. Everything was on such a high level. Listening to rap poet Mic Righteous and later Kate Tempest – Andreas said she was 'Shakespeare – The Best!' I remember something my friend Gary once said: 'The world

On the march with Jeremy Corbyn and Labour's Shadow Secretary of State for Energy and Climate Change, Lisa Nandy.

suffers from the isolation of intellectuals.' I suddenly understood; everybody who came on this march is an intellectual.

DECEMBER 2015

END OF DEC PARIS CLIMATE CHANGE CONFERENCE

I have not done diary entries for December. Apart from work and Christmas, the overwhelming fact was the Climate Change Conference in Paris – COP21. I attended the Alternative COP21 and there was a lot happening – thousands of NGOs. Half the people of Europe understand what is going on. The plan of the official COP21 is a mirror of death. The scientists and NGOs will now fight for our lives against the governments of the rich countries.

I shall be selective of the other things. I need more time – for my fashion design – and to clear the way for an eventual block of time to see if I can manage to put together the idea I have for a play. I mentioned already that I think you could update Faust. Mephistopheles would be the Press and the aim would be to show how easy it is in the 'democratic' system we have today for the mainstream media to lie to the public by giving out bits of information so as to hide the complete picture.

END OF DEC LIPPI MURALS IN PRATO

Just before Christmas we were in Prato working with our producers in Studio Cataldi. We went with Rosita to the old town (a little Sunday morning holiday) and into an antique shop where every single thing was desirable – something you would really want to have. Climbed the steps up into the castle and overlooked a large grassed courtyard where horses and riders were practising for an event in the afternoon – the boy sitting upright, the arched neck of the horse as he stepped to the rhythm.

Lippi's fresco in Prato cathedral of Herod's Banquet.

Then to the cathedral to look at the Lippi frescoes. I had been allowed to see the murals before, but only partially, standing on scaffolding whilst they were being restored. These amazing works – you wouldn't find them unless you knew they were there. We climbed a few steps then along behind the balustrade into the chancel and a lady happened to be there and switched on a light. On one side is the life of St. Stephen. We see him in three stages of his life – he was stoned to death – amongst crowds. On the other side is Salome, dancing at the banquet where she asks for the head of John the Baptist, and she is in the same picture again, down on one knee, looking out at us whilst presenting John's head to her mother on a big plate. We are present at the whole thing and it is held together by every person's relation to each other and what is happening.

Coming home, Andreas wrote on the back of his air ticket: '*Art can touch you to such an extent that you want to change your life.*' He is alluding to Rainer Maria Rilke from his poem regarding the remains of a broken statue – the Torso of Apollo – 'du mußt dein Leben ändern.'

END OF DEC CHRISTMAS

Andreas went back to Tyrol for Christmas. He had to help his father move from the family house to a smaller home. On Christmas Eve I drove to Cornwall with Ben and Tomoka and our friend Krishna to stay with Joe and his girl, Faye. Three things:

First, *Game of Thrones*. I watched some episodes and thought it was really good – it's about right and wrong and that's what interests us all – it rings true.

Second, Joe, Tomoka and I were standing on the shingled slope of a narrow bay watching the waves of the incoming tide which was now reaching the extent of its flow. It was cold and wild at the end of a grey afternoon. The bay enclosed our vision of the waves as they smashed upon the rocks at the cliff side – our horizon was this wall of waves at eye level, because we were on a slope. Body and soul controlled by the forever-coming waves; fulfilled as our breath comes in with the sea. We were at one with the world, gladdened and renewed. But it is not quite the same experience as the experience in front of Filippo Lippi because we do stay, we don't leave the world. That is my experience.

Third: Ben has campaigned for Shaker Aamer. He has just been released from Guantanamo after all those years – just picked up with no evidence because he happened to be in Afghanistan doing charity work. Ben collected signatures from all our work people – on a very big Christmas card (even though Shaker is Muslim) saying, 'Welcome Home'.

Vital: Our task is to form *Intellectuals Unite*.

INTELLECTUALS UNITE

We are student intellectuals spreading IoU (I owe you the world) through the colleges of the UK.

Intellectuals Unite. The world suffers from the isolation of intellectuals. During the Renaissance, intellectuals were the most influential members of society. I am an intellectual; I am a reader and an art lover. I need to understand the past to understand the present. As an activist, today I spend more and more time on the problem of climate change and how to save ourselves. I must therefore give a very broad view of what is an intellectual: even a kid on a demonstration who has had little education is already an intellectual – the reason he's on the demo is because he wants the world to be a better place. An intellectual is someone, like me, who wishes to understand the world as it is, and his place in it.

We have already begun to form a movement; in six colleges and schools young people are forming active cells to oppose governments and fight climate change. They will ask their professors and visiting speakers to join, they will expand the movement to other colleges and link with intellectuals from all walks of life. The beauty of such a movement is that it is inclusive, open to everyone.

If intellectuals reunite they will lead public opinion; this would enable democracy to protect the public interest. Otherwise we have Donald Trump. Britain will lead by example.

It is time to swap the old myth of fossil fuel for the green revolution.

JANUARY 2016

MON 4 – MON 11 JAN HEAVEN AND HELL

To Los Angeles. We agreed to do the concept for a charity event, Art of Elysium, for critically ill children. Our theme was 'Heaven and Hell'. The floral decorations were really something – the florist had spent three days foraging for wild plants and branches to make a Paradise. And our friend Stewart's band, Wild Daughter, really rocks – and is to dance to – not just boringly bob about, like most stuff. We met some nice people and I talked about Leonard. I hope some of them will support his request for presidential clemency. Won't know until Christmas. Be brave/stay strong, Leonard!

We also went to dinner with James Costa and guests at his vegan restaurant, Crossroads, in support of Sea Shepherd. Paul (Watson) spoke to everyone live by video link, and Pamela, his close friend for many years, was there to welcome us all.

THURS 14 JAN BE SPECIFIC

To Milan for the MAN show on Sunday. Fantastic casting. Lots of models letting their hair grow. Our unisex look is Punkature (punk couture/puncture). 'Be Specific' is the title of our show. I got the idea from Paul Watson of Sea Shepherd.

New punk look at the Milan MAN show.

- ✳ Be Specific: Save Venice – Stop the Cruise Ships
  weareherevenice.org
- ✳ Be Specific: Save our Rainforest – Cool Earth *coolearth.org*
- ✳ Be Specific: Save our Ocean – Stop $ubsidies to Industrial
  Fishing *seashepherd.org*
- ✳ Be Specific: You – Switch to Green Energy *ecotricity.co.uk*

Jane da Mosto came – Save Venice being part of 'Be Specific' – and
we put Italian PR Emanuela Barbieri in touch with her organisation.

I also went through the Red Label (women's) collection, which
had just been delivered to the Milan showroom. It is the first time
we have seen everything made up in the right fabric.

I like Save OUR Rainforest
Save OUR Ocean.
Who do our! politicians think they are?
Who gives them the right to WRECK the Earth?
Vivienne Westwood

TUES 19 JAN BABY BAMBOO

Back home in the morning Ben phoned to tell me Bamboo had
arrived. We went to see Tomoka and her baby, just down the road
in Chelsea and Westminster Hospital. I love him. We ate sushi in a
nearby restaurant, then cycled home.

SUN 24 JAN THE NEW PARIS SHOP

To Paris. Andreas had just caught a cold and he had quite a fever. So
we waited and in the afternoon he felt better and we just turned up

at the Eurostar, though our tickets were now no good. What a lovely woman the supervisor was. She knew we were telling the truth and she checked with someone and took us through. She seemed to have a cold, too. Bless her!

Next day, we met the architect for the interior of the French shop, Simona, and her assistant Caterina. We worked all day and for me one particular decision happened. The walls were painted grey and Andreas pointed out that whereas some of the walls were walls others were plasterboard just so as to box in the wiring and infrastructure. These he hated. I am not sensitive enough to my surroundings to have noticed this, but then I understood and completely agreed.

Andreas said it would help if the cold grey could be a warmer tone and he indicated the colour of a piece of plasterboard: 'What do you think?'

'I would like it if they could actually be plasterboard,' I said.

The next day Simona told Andreas that that's what they would do – real plasterboard with ordinary builders' screws showing. I am excited.

LATE JAN T-SHIRTS AND MATHS

Still spending lots of time streamlining the structure of our company and edit our products. For this reason Andreas and I have decided to clarify the collections. Gold Label will become *Andreas Kronthaler for Vivienne Westwood*. He designs it, I assist him when I have time. Red Label will be *Vivienne Westwood*. Andreas said that when he was last in Italy he went with Rosita to this special doctor she has. The doctor told Andreas, you have a completely mathematical mind, were you good at maths at school? 'Absolutely not! But I know what he meant!'

I collect everything. I have to have everything there – I set it all out. You see how I behaved to get these T-shirts. Six graphics pulled out from all this rubbish. I like them. Plus colours and fabrics. First I have to decide the forms. I decided on three shapes (one normal classic, one long-sleeved with gussets, one oversized with long sleeves puffed up at the sleeve-head). Then when I have decided which graphics match the shapes, I edit, reduce, change it around. There are endless possibilities and when the possibilities really are endless I go mad. (I know about endlessness; if you want to know endlessness listen to Mahler – we did the night before.) Then at the end I took the paper bag which had the print of ladybirds on it. I love ladybirds. I needed it for the sleeves of one T-shirt. Then I added another T-shirt – the classic one all made in this same jersey with the ladybirds print and that gave me the chance to use my OM graphic on top. I don't care how it's printed – it can be a mess. And then I will stick on the bee patch. I love the yellow bee with its blue wings against the red ladybirds. I am happy.

FEBRUARY 2016

MON 1 FEB A MODEL COMPANY

Catherina, the daughter of my American friend Frank, came for work experience. I gave her a special task. We are fusing our Climate Revolution website with the main Vivienne Westwood site. This will happen in July. Meanwhile, we double up on what we post. I believe our website is the motor for everything I want to promote. We promote quality.

I asked Catherina to analyse the structure of the marketing and digital marketing team right up through to the people who sell.

Obviously my main reason for asking this is because I want to know. (Though I direct the sites, I don't use a computer. I write by hand and tell people what I want.) But also because otherwise I will never get round to doing this. These people work for me and most of them I haven't met until now. And that's what I want to do – link personally. I read some of her report: short, concise and really so well done. With Catherina, we have begun to talk to the people concerned. I really want to be sure that the message is my message.

My aim is to have a perfect company, a model for the new Green Economy. Efficient in every respect, efficient in happiness and job satisfaction. Our people are skilled and their work is labour intensive. To our customers we say, 'Buy less, choose well, make it last'. I believe this is a company of the future.

BUYLESS CHOOSEWELL MAKEITLAST

THURS 4 FEB MONTHLY VISIT TO JULIAN

My monthly visit to Julian. There were lots of photographers outside the embassy because he was waiting for the decision of the UN who next day ruled that he was illegally detained. I was really glad to be photographed on this important day because I support Julian and I feel privileged that people know that.

I don't want to say anything until I have been back to talk to Julian, other than that the government and press response thrives on libellous lies. They don't care because at the moment they are getting away with it. And though one refutes the lies, once the lies are out, for the moment they stick.

SAT 6 FEB SUPPORT THE JUNIOR DOCTORS

To speak at the rally for the junior doctors. Vanessa Redgrave spoke and also my son Ben spoke as a member of the public who is grateful for the National Health and for the stand the junior doctors are taking to protect the NHS from government sabotage and sell off.

Lauren, one of the organisers, started to tell me some of the stuff that's going on. How can somebody have so much information and remember all that detail? I said, does she work? Yes. She works as a specialist registrar in adult psychiatry in London. I'm astonished by how clever she is. Cindy has asked her to talk to some of the groups of intellectuals she is helping to form.

WEDS 10 FEB GOLDFINCHES

For some months I have seen only one or two loyal birds in my little back garden. There used to be so many. Either they weren't there or I missed them. Today the mimosa tree is full of goldfinches and the tomtit and the lady blackbird have got partners. The best time to catch them is 8.30 in the morning.

WEDS 17 – SUN 21 FEB INTELLECTUALS UNITE

Our fashion show – which will soon change name to *Vivienne Westwood* (from Red Label) – is on Sunday. Its title is 'Intellectuals Unite' and I have written a rap about this – which I did to camera. I also used it for the press release and Mic Righteous wants me to do the rap as a guest on his next album.

All this week I will be working on the show, choosing outfits, fitting models, fixing the running order. Andreas will help. Yasmine is here, staying in my home, already casting. Tomorrow we try out the hair and make-up. I knew the tailoring worked well. It is classic – it would have been as fashionable ten years ago as it will be ten years from now. But to put a fashion show together is such a big

climate revolution. co. uk

LEONARD PELTIER IS INNOCENT

Vivienne Westwood

#VWAW1617

We are Climate Revolution. We are intellectuals. We are building the intellectual movement starting within the colleges and universities. You must come and join us. We will win/Stop climate change/Build a green economy.

Everybody is talking / But only our map gives the complete picture.

The ice is melting / Fracking releases tons of methane / Water is more precious than oil / Plastic kills the albatross / There is no end to migrants / Perpetual War / Floods + hurricanes.

Sow the whirlwind,
Reap the " !
If the bees die, we die / Au$terity is stupid / Violence is....

Intellectuals Unite!
Murdering mainstream media / Killing us with Confusion / Scatterbrains.
Bits of information / Lies / Non-stop Distraction
Intellectuals tell the Truth!
Give us the picture.—
You know the past, present + future
Speak with one Voice!
— Culture not consumption.
(Go to Frank Auerbach at Tate Britain)
Give us the map—
Red is uninhabitable / Green is all that's left.

Vivienne Westwood

job; it took me and Andreas three days (afternoon and evening). It is not until we start cross-styling that we get the looks. Exciting.

MARCH 2016

THURS 3 MARCH FRANK AUERBACH AT TATE BRITAIN

I have been to see Frank Auerbach at Tate Britain twice and I shall go again. It is a life-changing experience. Its power is so profound.

William Feaver, one of the people who sat for him, writes in the exhibition notes about how he did sessions every Monday evening for twelve years, 'changing position every nine months or so'. The reuslt, he says, is 'something marvellous: an image hatched, a sense of animation perpetuated and let out into the world. These paintings give such a sense of being alive that I for one am pleased that here, whew, I'm still breathing.'

Perhaps Frank Auerbach painted layer on layer because he saw fresh every time. The paint is thick! Auerbach himself says that in dealing with 'the problem' (we don't know what the problem is) he sometimes stopped finally out of frustration.

It is so well exhibited. Auerbach himself hung all but the last room. I could not leave the first room – heads; they just held me there. Then I continued. I was so pleased to meet the landscapes because I felt I knew them. You just know, that's real, that's true.

I went again and this time I 'got' one of the landscapes which had puzzled me on the first visit, titled *The Origin of the Great Bear*. You see the constellation thrown up over the hill into the sky, the stars are bluish. The whole surface is acid yellow – sky and earth, except for a patch of night sky torn through the clouds which looks like a dark-blue giant bird. I suddenly felt I was seeing the whole of creation, back beyond civilisation, back beyond the Greeks yet including that, and forward to the end of our time on earth: the world seen through human eyes.

I said this to Cynthia. She said that was exactly what happened to her. This does not mean anything. We don't believe our experience is mysteriously embedded in the painting. We don't know what Auerbach saw, but we believe it is something primary.

SAT 5 MARCH PARIS SHOW: ANDREAS KRONTHALER FOR VW

Andreas presented our top fashion, which he designs in the main, under his own name: *Andreas Kronthaler for Vivienne Westwood*. We are trying to make ours into a model company and this is a way of clarifying what we do. It was great.

The photo opposite is of my favourite outfit, which I call 'Medea'. She was the barbaric princess who helped Jason steal the Golden Fleece and later killed their two sons when he married another woman. See the amazing film with Maria Callas by Pasolini.

WEDS 16 MARCH OPEN LETTER TO DAVID CAMERON

I sent an open letter about fracking to David Cameron, also signed by Mark Ruffalo, Colin Firth, Livia Firth, Bianca Jagger, Taron Egerton, Rupert Friend, Aimee Mullins and Felicity Blunt. We noted that 'fracking in the US has caused thousands of cases of groundwater and surface water contamination, made many people sick, has been linked to infant health issues, serious air pollution problems, and more.' But the main point is that Cameron had said that communities would have a voice in whether fracking would happen near them – but now these local decisions are at risk of being overturned by central government.

The government actually intend to force-frack – the whole country – with the help of the big energy companies (not Ecotricity). But eighty per cent of people don't want fracking.

The government = **antipeople**.

'Medea' from the new 'Andreas Kronthaler for Vivienne Westwood' collection.

Easter. We were invited to the Barbican by Isabella Gardiner to see the St Matthew Passion, with the Monteverdi Choir conducted by John Eliot Gardiner.

I am glad I was brought up to believe in God. Our village life centred round the church (and school); the sense of community, the rituals and the singing, the feeling of being at one with oneself and with the world (spiritual cleansing). I was religious until age twenty-three, after that, not; though I agree that one's spirit or soul is a fact of experience. I like the Christian concept of God: made in our image (or vice versa), a symbol of our perfection; the idea that by becoming more human we can evolve into better creatures.

65 Aria (Bass)

Mache dich, mein Herze, rein,	Purify thyself, my heart,
Ich will Jesum selbst begraben.	I myself will bury Jesus.
Denn er soll nunmehr in mir	For he shall henceforth
Für und für	evermore
Seine süsse Ruhe haben.	sweetly take his rest in me.
Welt, geh' aus, lass Jesum ein!	World, go hence, let Jesus in!

When I went to the St John Passion – I've said it before – I flew. The music carried me away. The St Matthew Passion is longer, with a large choir. The arias are soul-wrenching and full of guilt. It was a triumphant and perfect performance. Yet afterwards whilst we were having a drink, John Eliot came up to me and I said, 'The Matthew Passion is more sick than the St John.' That was rude of me and he came right back, 'No it's not!'

I'd like to explain. Leading up to my rejection of the Christian religion, we Protestants had found the Catholic religion morbid and kitsch – flaming medical hearts, blood, agony, bones, God on a cloud – it made me think of the Spanish Inquisition. But then I began to think that all Christian religion was sick. That's what turned me off, and it came crashing down like a house of cards. The Bible says: 'For God so loved the world, that he gave his only begotten Son, that whosoever believeth in him should not perish, but have everlasting life.' Rubbish! If God wanted to save the world, why didn't he just do it if he could? No need to torture and kill his son. I expect the implication is that we must suffer too if we want everlasting life.

Yes, I do think the Christian religion is rooted in morbid superstition and causes a confusion of unhealthy emotion: a mixture of love and guilt. By killing Jesus we become cleansed of sin. He is the chosen sacrificial victim, the redeemer king, who dies for the love of us, so that we might be forgiven. We perform the necessary magic by having killed him; we now eat his body and drink his blood so that we may have eternal life. He led the way.

Religion comes from magic ritual. Lord Raglan, in his small book *Jocasta's Crime*, tells us that myths are the stories that accompany the ritual – the myth tells them how to perform the rite properly – and which are still passed down the generations when the ritual is forgotten. He refers to the diffusion of culture: an invention (e.g. stone axes) occurred in one place only and passed slowly over the years from one tribe to another. In the same way this happened with magic ritual. The same rituals passed all over the world and some of them must have done so as far back as when the continents were connected. That is why the myths of the world tell the same stories.

In the days after the Passion I was still thinking of a play I had seen earlier that month, because they each left me with some of the same feelings. My friend Susan came to stay the weekend and we saw *Cleansed* by Sarah Kane at the National Theatre. The play was full of violence. I was worried about that, especially that somebody was going to have his tongue cut out with a pair of scissors. It happened early on. Was that it? Thank God for that! I can cope. It was all done matter-of-fact. The victim didn't scream.

Patients/victims, sometimes hands tied, or gagged, were bundled around or pushed down into chairs. Black-clad orderlies, their heads covered by thick black stockings, passed back and forth. Two men were pushed into chairs seated at a small table and supervised whilst

Bernini's *The Ecstasy of Santa Teresa*. The angel holds an arrow, he is piercing her heart with love for Jesus. She is in ecstasy. Nuns wear a wedding ring, they are married to Jesus. Jesus the sacrificial victim is sometimes called the 'bridegroom'.

they argued over their commitment to each other. They promised, like the lovers in Orwell's *1984*, never to betray, whatever happened. One man said 'I love you'. He was the one who had his tongue cut out. This was the longest piece of dialogue; there was hardly any other. A thrum-thrum of music and beat was continuous except a few times when a pop song was broadcast, when someone would dance madly and fling his or her arms like a windmill. Everything was stage direction. Now and again a striptease dancer was wheeled on in a portable shower for the benefit of the man who seemed to run things, to wank. She came out of the shower box and said she loved him and he hated her.

They all accepted the continuous acts of violence. It reminded me of what an ex-prisoner of Guantanamo once said: he felt so guilty for being free when his friends were still in there being tortured that he wanted to go back and share in the pain.

Why did these two events, the play and the Passion, leave me thinking they were linked? The St Matthew does leave you feeling cleansed: a hypnotic rhythm underlies the soaring music and when it's over you feel complete and elated and conscious of your breathing. With the Sarah Kane play, the ethos was sadomasochistic to the point of death.

It is worth taking into account that people have said that Christian religious ceremony has a parallel in sexual feeling – 'dying' – to transcend as in orgasm. Ascetics persecuted their body so as to transcend into religious ecstasy – fleas and hair shirts to combat the pricking of desire and lust; children felt the sexual feeling – Jean-Paul Sartre as a little child fantasised about doing a pee-pee in the font. What we are discussing here is morbid though it gives a thrill – sin locked into guilt. S+M is linked to sex. Guilt is paid for by self-denial.

In the aria the singer will love only Jesus, there is no room for anybody else, certainly not himself. He wants to be pure. Sexual repression is relieved by pain. The objective is to achieve ecstasy but avoid orgasm (this can be sexually thrilling). If orgasm occurs, then S+M becomes a vicious circle.

APRIL 2016

SAT 23 APRIL GIORGIONE AT THE ROYAL ACADEMY

The current Royal Academy exhibition is *In the Age of Giorgione*. In the sixteenth-century, Venetian painting was at its height. It signalled the Renaissance with its Humanism and discovery of the Greek mind. It had probably the first use of the word 'modern' when Vasari, the first art historian, used the phrase *maniera moderna* to describe what was happening.

I want to talk about four works in the show. The first is a *Virgin and Child* by Bellini. When you say Bellini, you have to say first, colour: unsurpassed! Though engaged with each other, the people in this painting keep their distance from the viewer; the painting is an icon to be worshipped. His portraits also keep their distance.

Giorgione includes the viewer. This is the difference between the old formula and the new. Now we get involved in the emotions; each painting is a vision, a story, a world, a life. In his *Portrait of a Man*, Giorgione was able to capture his direct relationship with the sitter. Giorgione, who died from the plague in 1510, aged around thirty-three, is a legend. We know little about him and over the years critics have debated which paintings can be firmly attributed to him – very few. He intrigues because his work has an internal mystery; he paints what he sees, what only he can call forth.

Portraits by Albrecht Dürer are also included in the exhibition. He too attracts the viewer to the living emotional character of the subjects of this paintings. He was working in Venice at the time as Giorgione, who admired him. He had walked to Venice from Nuremberg – people did in those days – stopping at inns along the way. I find it awesome that Dürer's mother had fourteen children and that he (genius) was the only one who survived.

Giorgione was a master by the age of twenty and famous in Venice. Titian – who trained with Bellini at twenty, was five years younger when he worked with Giorgione on the frescoes of the façade of the

Anticlockwise, from top: Bellini's *Virgin and Child*, Giorgione's *Portrait of a Man*, Titian's *Christ and the Adulteress*, Dürer's *Portrait of the Artist's Mother*.

city's Fondaco dei Tedeschi. Titian copied his method, lived to be old and (Andreas tells me) went on to invent three quarters of all the original ideas of painting.

His painting *Christ and the Adulteress* (1508) tells the whole of a story from the Bible in one go. A woman 'taken in adultery' is dragged off to be stoned. Jesus says, 'Let him who is without sin cast the first stone.' Nobody does. A Hollywood film could not tell the story so well.

JUNE–AUGUST 2016

These are my last entries before this diary goes to press. I have been working continuously: on fashion (a third of my life is dedicated to Quality v. Quantity – reducing, clarifying, controlling – so that we become a model company for the future – Buy less, choose well, make it last!); Climate Revolution; and, on top of that, after our publisher had edited the diaries, reducing them to a half from the online entries, I have been doing the final edit.

The reason for the diary is to clarify opinion. Reading it, you will access my point of view, which is completely heretical to that of the status quo regarding culture and political economy. You will get all this – and it is easier to assimilate in a book than on the internet.

I did not want a long book. The reason the fashion shows are not given equal weight is because when I referred to them in the online diary, sometimes just mentioning them, they were covered equally on our main VW website (now fused with the Climate Revolution site). I have added a few texts and graphics which were not in the diary but are on the websites. Square brackets and italic text indicate comments I made whilst editing.

Writing a diary is a great thing to do for yourself. It marks your life, you know where you're up to, and where you're going. You pin down your ideas, adjust and develop: a constant resumé and improvement. I already told you that my job as an activist is to pin down, clarify, analyse. You can't fight until you know your enemy.

Our enemy is that globally a few thousand control seven billion. We in England have to fight the present government – they belong to these few [antipeople].

THURS 9 JUNE DANIIL TRIFONOV

I am picking out only the really important events for these months. This was major. Daniil Trifonov, the latest thing; Rachmaninov, Wigmore Hall. He covered the keys and the piano and he covered me and the rest of the world. A big musican, cut fine – a beauty, straight hair all the time hitting his face. Focus! Shit! Half the time his eyes were shut.

SUN 19 JUNE *FIRST THEY CAME FOR ASSANGE* SHOW

MAN show Milan. We fused the VW collections MAN and women – unisex. We won't do a separate women's catwalk show. But next season we will present them both together in London.

First they came for Assange. This was the title and our show was one of a number of simultaneous events, including Patti Smith, Brian Eno and Noam Chomsky, taking place in ten countries across the world to protest the illegal detention (this in accord with UN ruling) of Julian, beginning his fifth year in the embassy.

The man next to me is so cool in his simple knitted toga dress. I too am wearing a toga – just a tube of sequins which I have pulled down to show my 'I am Julian Assange T-shirt' (my face). I think the British press do not support human rights for Julian because they are jealous. *He tells the truth and they are not allowed.*

FRI 24 JUNE BREXIT

Brexit. The night before, I went to the Ecuadorian Embassy where Julian was interviewing people for live transmission on social media. I gave a speech asking people to vote Remain – on the basic principle that Peace and Co-operation is better than War and Competition.

The result next day – 'Britain is out of Europe' – immediately translated itself in my mind as 'No hope to save the Planet'. Because our economic system (Rot$) is based on war and competition. The only way to get out of this destruction is the Green Economy. How do you get enough people to see that? I think if I don't manage to move something within two years then … I really am desperate. I have purposely written 'I' not 'we' here because I have to find a way to link that will work.

I read accounts of why people voted Brexit. They were lovely people, sincere and motivated. One strong sentiment was, 'We Brits can roll our sleeves up, we don't need them taking our money and telling us what to do.' Whatever the reason, they all made the same mistake, the same mistake as I did. We all think of ourselves as 'we'. Who are 'we'? We are in solidarity with the Brits; in my case we are in solidarity with Europe. Mistake: let's remember – globally a few thousand control seven billion.

'We' does not exist politically. Britain is sixty-four million people completely confused by the mainstream media and controlled by 500 politicians who ignore public opinion except at elections, when they make fantastic promises. So even though the Brexit result was unexpected, political control stayed with the antipeople. Theresa May, David Cameron, Tony Blair, Barack Obama, Angela Merkel – some worse than others, you might think: they're all the same. They belong to a global club. All profit goes to the club. A few thousand antipeople control seven billion people.

One thing Brexit will expose more clearly to people is that government policy is making them ever poorer.

Economy after Brexit
UK cut off from the world

✳ Bank of England loses its position as the world's most important bank. Greater focus shifts to national central banks in Paris and Frankfurt.

✳ Headquarters of multinational companies – the big players of Canary Wharf – leave and relocate.

✳ UK politicians increase tax breaks for corporations and rich investors to encourage the Chinese and others to come. EU residents in the UK lose their status.

✳ London: Land-grabbing for hundreds of glass tower blocks/ skyscrapers stops. They remain empty.

✳ House prices fall.

✳ Because of London's cultural institutions, tourism continues. It is possibly our only relationship to the US.

✳ Our present shambolic antipeople government accepts TTIP trade deal – Britain is fed to corporate lions to carve up and wreck.

✳ London is poorer/whole country faces poverty.

✳ Tax cuts for the rich = more austerity.

Which is what caused Brexit in the first place

FRI 15 JULY LAND TAX

Fred Harrison, Director of the Land Research Trust, and member of IoU from its first general meeting, came to talk to Climate Revolution about Land Tax. At the moment CR is the motor of IoU, and when we develop our strategies Land Tax could be part of that. He explained that Denmark is always top of the happiest country polls and has no big housing problem because its tax system rests on a Land Tax, which gives fair distribution of wealth. Important for building the Green Economy.

TUES 19 JULY GREEN GRASS GAS

My son Joe, who campaigns against fracking, came to see us, along with Dale Vince from Ecotricity – a not for profit company that delivers 19 per cent of our electricity supply. Dale is now challenging government imposition of fracking policy (80 per cent of our population is against it) by applying for planning permission for Green Grass Gas, offering farmers money for the grass in their field instead of them agreeing to the danger of fracking.

If NGOs would announce their support for Ecotricity by asking all of us to switch our energy supply to green energy that would stop antipeople subsidy (it's our money) for fossil fuels (for the benefit of investors: first battle won).

THURS 21 JULY MONSANTO – END ECOCIDE

I'm a big supporter of End Ecocide, and they asked me to make a two-minute video to camera. Here is what I performed:

Monsanto

The crime of ecocide is the greatest crime of all
Everything is connected
If the grass dies we die
If the worms die we die
If the insects die we die
Without birds we die
Without fish we die
Without plankton we die
Everything is connected, we all die together

SAT 23 JULY THE SEAGULL AT THE NATIONAL

The Seagull at the National Theatre with friends Dominic Hourd and Peter Olive. Stunning – set, acting. I'm having trouble with theatre – going a bit deaf – missed details of the relationships but got all the agony the actors projected. My God, by the end I was literally holding myself together. I couldn't clap.

TUES 26 JULY MONTEVERDI CHOIR

We designed the ladies' new jacket for the Monteverdi Choir. It will go well with the men's black and white and the shining wood of the musical instruments.

Our new ladies' jackets for the Monteverdi Choir.

THURS 28 JULY TAKE FLYING MORE SERIOUSLY

Dominic sent me a copy of *The Seagull* and I read it on the way to the Tyrol. The plane was delayed and we were four hours waiting in the airport. I didn't mind as I hate airports and I think it's good we suffer, just so we take flying more seriously and don't think we can come and go as easy as we please.

FRI 29 JULY – WEDS 3 AUG IN THE TYROL AGAIN

In the Tyrol with Andreas's family: walking, writing some of the tracts for this last diary entry, reading. Andreas has recommended *Things Fall Apart* by Chinua Achebe. Nelson Mandela had called him 'the writer in whose company the prison walls came down'. Achebe's novel is about the tribes of the lower Niger: how the British had set up a trading post with their courts and missionaries and ruled all the black people who were held together in clusters or separate tribes – different ethics. It is one book of a trilogy. I am now halfway through the second book. The insight, the wisdom of the author! This really is who we are – a mirror of Homo sapiens.

Mattias, a boy of nine, was helping Andreas's brother Martin with the cows. He did the work of a man, rising at six and going to bed at ten. He liked milking best – you have to begin milking by hand and only then can you attach the mechanical system, when the milk will run. He played the accordion with panache: you wanted to dance. Martin is so proud of him and Andreas loved him, called him (to me) a Buddha, because he has big ear lobes and is sweet and wise. Here he was asked to get into the cart and flatten the hay and he can't get out again yet. Oh yes, when he's back at school he loves in his free time to go riding in the forest on his motorbike.

Mattias – the little Buddha.

Talking and eating on occasion with the family, I miss Franz, Andreas's father. *Ruhe in Frieden.* Franz died at the beginning of May, aged 86. I went with Andreas to the funeral in Fügen – there must have been near to 300 people there plus the local firemen, because he had for twenty years, at some period of his life, been a chief of the fire brigade. He was the life and soul of the village, always laughing. Andreas's family are farmers; on the father's side, they are smiths. It's a tradition in Austria that all the gravestones are made out of wrought iron, so if you go to the graveyard there, they're made by Franz or his father. Each one is different in design.

He was famous throughout the area and in northern Italy for wrought-iron chandeliers, balustrades, gates. Andreas was very emotional – his father didn't realise how talented he (Franz) was. What a superior craftsman and designer.

THURS 4 – SAT 6 AUG SALZBURG FESTIVAL

On the train to Salzburg. Still writing.

Salzburg: flat land surrounds a giant rock, on top of which are castle walls enclosing an entire village with court, prison, workshops. The first builder was a cardinal who in c.1150, for his own protection, sided with the pope in his wars with the Holy Roman Emperor. Impregnable of course. Rich.

Here for the festival (down below), staying with our friend, Thaddeus. He is really important, working exhaustively for the festival. Many guests, including Bianca Jagger, who is a big music lover. Thaddeus is an art dealer and many guests respect modern art as having its place, although they don't understand it. Count me in with them except that I consider most of it a mistake: i.e. it has no reason to exist and just adds to the confusion. But I really like Thaddeus and I enjoyed particularly talking to Fritz, a cardiac doctor who told me his view of the world – and he did know. There was not much I could add; he understood it like I do. The Queen of Sweden supports the festival and came to dinner but as she is above politics she had not heard of Julian. I will write to her.

Thaddeus knows my views on art and thinks I should give again the talk I gave at Frieze with a view to selling the collage.

I won't tell about the two operas we saw (I love the opportunity to dress up) because I don't think you will learn much from the descriptions. But on the third night we went to a concert with a wonderful programme and performance: Arvo Pärt, *Swansong*; Gustav Mahler, *Kindertotenlieder*; Anton Bruckner, *Symphony No.4 in E flat major* and *WAB 104* – Romantic. Bianca was in raptures and afterwards stayed talking to Zubin Mehta, the conductor. 'Did you notice he did the Bruchner without a score?' Andreas has been designing the new uniform of the Vienna Philharmonic.

SAT 6 AUG SALZBURG RESIDENZ

Great! Our visit to the Salzburg Archbishop's Residence. Michael Rottmayr. Big painter in the eighteenth century – ceilings, walls, fresco and oil, intimate works; reduction of means, raw fact and bravura. A special exhibition, going through 1.5 kilometres of rooms, showed a selection of the Princely Collections of Lichtenstein. Mostly about nudity. During the Renaissance, artists' subject matter focused on pagan gods: nudity was allowed to gods but not to men and women. We stayed four hours and saw paintings and sculpture but missed the musical instruments and curiosities.

My favourite painting was Rembrandt's *Cupid with the Soap Bubble*. This little boy blowing bubbles has just looked up at you. I was weak with emotion. It was like you were looking at your own child, it rang so true. You have to see the real thing, not a photo. Discussing it later, Andreas compared this Cupid to the *Red Boy*,

John the Baptist bronze.

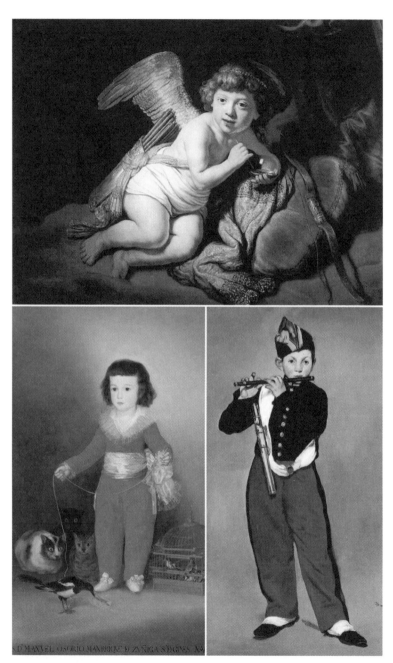

Rembrandt's *Cupid with the Soap Bubble* (1634); Goya's *Red Boy* (1784–92); and Manet's *Fifer* (1866). .

with a bird on a string and his toys on the floor around. Goya in the Metropolitan Gallery in New York. Andreas loves that child even more. I mentioned Manet's young flute player. Yes, they are as good.

Twelve bronze sculptures of height were displayed in a circle in one room. Each one had achieved the perfection of Shakespeare's aspiration in the first lines of *Henry V*: 'Oh, for a muse of fire, that would ascend the brightest heaven of invention!'

If I wanted to be an artist I would try to copy those and if I succeeded in that process I would try my own. Andreas said, I would give all the paintings if I could have one of these. He took a photo of John the Baptist.

SUN 7 – MON 8 AUG LAKE ATTERSEE

Our friend Georg, who lives in Salzburg and had attended the festival with us, drove us to Attersee, a lake half an hour away. We met our friends Yasmine and Sabina and their friends and family. The lake is outside my window but on the second day I still haven't been down there. I am finishing up the diary because the book has to go to press when we get back to London. We go back tomorrow. If Andreas comes for me I will go down; it's about five o'clock.

WHAT DO WE NEED TO DO FOR CR IN THE NEAR FUTURE?

*   I have applied to visit Leonard Peltier. I want to give him courage as he awaits the decision of Obama to set him free or not when he leaves office. My friend Lorna has made a film about the whole situation which led to Leonard's wrongful conviction for the murder of the two young agents. It is an impartial film and shows that on that day people did not know that it would end in tragedy. She has talked to some of the FBI men who were there and she feels that they trust her. The hope is that freedom for Leonard means that people can feel more at peace and get on with their lives. Leonard's lawyer is really good and the plea for release is most professional. Leonard has served his people

by sticking to the truth and his principles. He has planned and paid for his funeral. On the rez.

✱ I plan an art exhibition including the children's collage to raise money for rainforest and other charities.

✱ I did not finish the Politicians R Criminals campaign. There is still one more video to do. Having left it so long I don't know when would be a good time to do it. Perhaps when I find the time to write the play about Faust. You see, this set of videos is a basic research for Faust.

This is the fourth Politicans R Criminals video – me dressed as the Joker/ Mephistopheles/the Press.

The game played by – politicians = CRIMINALS, monopolies = GIANTS, banks = FACELESS EVIL! I now refer to them all for convenience as the antipeople. The press support them and they are taking us to Hell on Earth.

MORE ABOUT THE ANTIPEOPLE

• They belong to a club owned by the rich and powerful antipeople who control Rot$.

• They need the right reflexes to enter: Don't think, simply reflex, 'If it's good for Rot $, it's good for us.'

• Once they're in, they stay – unless they start to think / empathise with Homo sapiens. They, too, will become rich.

• The same antipeople are always in power. Even after a revolution! Revolutions have never yet worked. The rich and powerful antipeople make sure that the same antipeople get back in.

• Today the antipeople control the media and enough people believe in Rot$ to win an election.

• Antipeople are not us. We try to think. We care about Homo sapiens.

• Like aliens they come from another planet. They ignore the real world and live on the planet they create: Planet Rot$.

✳ **IoU.** Climate Revolution is the motor of IoU. At this point student IoUs in six universities are working out how and what to discuss and act upon, so that the movement sustains: culture as well as activism; culture is activism. When ready, they spread to other colleges. There will be events in September at The Box and LSE for Resist Festival.

I o U a Life
Save whirl'd // Win or Lose
Hope Time // Too Late
M A S S I V E
O P P O S I T I O N
Brit. Gov't → v. ← Brit. People
< O P E N T O A L L >
Will the NGO's join tog. + IoU
?
Separate stunts + demos not enough
Oxfam - Green Peace - Friends - ALL

Butterflies
Sick with nerves - if only 1
- our dear friends Junior Doctors,
it would be a start / T I A W T'NAƆ
Mirror the World

NGOs UNITE

NGOs Unite! We have our websites. We can broadcast direct to social media and through news sites. A quarter of the mainstream media are intellectuals anyway. Come! We are open to all to join; so strong will we be. Everyone can engage with us, starting with celebrities, professionals, scientists and everyone who is desperate to stop the destruction and Get a Life. Here is a proposal draft of our first challenge. We have to work through government, put pressure on them to change policy. We will be strong enough to do it. There are many ways.

A LETTER TO THE NEW PRIME MINISTER

Aug 2016

Dear Theresa May,

We are trying to focus, then build opposition – open to all – to the financial policies of your government. Globally a few thousand antipeople control seven billion people.

We want to expose this, starting with Britain. In Britain at the last election let's say 37 per cent of the electorate voted for the antipeople present government. Therefore, the majority do not agree with your political programme.

We are the opposition.

We are IoU together with Greenpeace, etc., etc.

We condemn Trident – cost estimates between £40 billion and £100 billion. The money could be spent on doctors and nurses – on the NHS. We ask the public to connect this colossal waste of money with the fact that austerity is not necessary, it's a con.

Our economic system is designed to cause poverty and syphon off profit for the rich.

It is also the cause of climate change. Yet you have just shut down the Ministry for Climate Change.

Everything is connected, yet the press make sure we never get the complete picture; which causes confusion.

We challenge government dishonesty. We tell you: Address the facts. Demolish the problem you have created. The easy way out of this is the Green Economy.

GIVE THE COMPLETE PICTURE
* **Many ways to clarify and build public opinion in accordance with the facts – give the *complete* picture:**
* e.g. make the connections: 'growth' is the means by which the antipeople syphon off profit; according to the Rot$ the world is technically bankrupt, the state of the economy is measured according to what is good for investors. These are mostly bubbles, sold on like 'passing the parcel' – the one holding the parcel when the music stops goes bust.
* e.g. the terrific escalation of rise in temperature comes not only from fossil fuels and their extraction but from desertification of land by Big Ag. and factory farming – release of methane (eighty times more potent than CO2) and all the other shit the GIANTS are doing.

ONE LAST THING
One last thing. Our friend Bertram just died, aged forty-nine. It took since the time of Queen Elizabeth I until now to make the connection between cancer and smoking. We have not made the connection between climate change and mass extinction but the antipeople accept it and continue the Rot$ which causes it.

Generally, we also accept it, it's just part of coffee-bar chat. Perhaps the reason for this is our belief in the myth we live by.

The Myth that the End Purpose of Evolution is Hom. Sap.

One day the world was ready
One celled creatures grouped together.
Experiments. Attractive:
One by one they lived & died
Evolution.
One thing after another
Leading to us.
Stuff teamed all over the place.
Ready for our use.
Finally we appeared: Homo Sapiens.

We were the best hunter-gatherers,
More clever than the Neanderthals
Who disappeared — Left us the field
We made special tools & hunted with dogs
Life was easy. Women gathered seeds & fruit
Men killed all the large prehistoric animals
Except the elephant who had evolved with us
And knew our power— avoiding us.
We sat by the fire, we had time
To carve & sew & paint. Wow!
Those cave paintings.

Farming was harder but it gave us
Organization / Civilization / + finally,
Democracy.
Such a big responsibility. We had to delegate.
Such a task — to manage the world's wealth
So that even the poor can grow equally rich.
If we don't like our politicians / we can
                    kick them out! (joke)
Life is easy. Follow the Times! Hom. Sap
is marching into the future.

One thing after another / So now we have
Austerity / Our way of life is not
Sustainable / It won't last for ever.
That's the price we pay for our
Comfort. It can't be otherwise.
Maybe they'll do s'thing. I'll be
Dead along with the animals.

End
     Sorry, mass extinction is not inevitable.
Get lost! Get off yr. arse! Get a life!
— for you + yr. children.

MON 15 AUG BUILDING THE IOU MOVEMENT!

Here is the speech I gave to the NGOs at the IoU meeting:
This is about global political financialisation which gives governments
power to do what they like and how the only credible opposition are
NGOs. They can save the world from disaster and climate change. It
is set out like a theorem; QED-Unite!

Think of the position we're in – globally! Everything has become
dramatically polarised.

* The rotten financial system called neoliberalism is now
  imposed the world over. Its global term is financialisation.
* A tiny percent control seven billion people.
* Thousands of NGOs – unprecedented! Every problem is
  being tackled.
* Direct and immediate communication through social media
  – an aid to truth telling.
* Mass extinction has begun.

Only the last has ever happened before on a global scale (end of the
dinosaurs).

If we connect the dots of these five bullet points the problem we
have created and its solution is staring us in the face:

* If a few control seven billion that is not democracy. (We
  know how they do it – by means of the political-economic
  system. Politicians are its public face.)
* The work of NGOs is not effective in opposing the financial
  policy of neoliberalism. Proceeding by the polarisation of
  wealth the policy creates poverty and causes climate change.

The answer to the problem is that NGOs and charities make real
the power they have, speak with one voice. Unite! Only we can do it.
Everything depends on us. Others don't have time to build a global
solution. We have already built it through our work. We are the
solution. We just have to continue doing what we do, but do it together.

A solution is what people want. We will attract potentially everyone – intellectuals, businessmen, celebrities, people from all walks of life. We will tell truth through the social media. We have immense credibility. Britain is a good place to start. As things get worse our government is aggressively imposing policy which caused our problem in the first place.

We can achieve a Green Economy. That is the solution.

It's the Olympics, which means the four-year anniversary of the launch of Climate Revolution. Time flies but we are trying to get somewhere. We are holding an IoU meeting. I have some hope that the NGOs and charities will unite. John Sauven, who is head of Greenpeace UK, is nothing if not practical. He tells us that we already have an affiliation of NGOs (including the trade unions!) in the Climate Coalition. We are members, too; I had forgotten. Its potential has not been tapped. He's going to try something. I know Cynthia will also work on this. Once IoU becomes more solid then it is united with the most powerful UNIT in the world – the NGOs. John is so full of knowledge, he must have made a lasting impression on the student IoUs. (A fact he noted: when recently the government pulled the small subsidy on renewable energy, yet subsidised the fossil fuel industries by £30 billion, 12,000 solar jobs were lost yet the press never mentioned it. It was the same number of jobs we just lost in the steel industry, where the press made a fuss.)

We want the IoU movement to become as big as the hippies. (Make love not war.) But it has to sustain and the way it will do that is if it is anchored to the pursuit of art and culture. It takes commitment to read a book (you get out what you put in). The movement has to come together in each university as a club with regular meetings and I suggest as a practical linchpin that they begin meetings by reading the current diary entry.

Sow the whirlwind / Reap the whirlwind.

Everything is connected. War is connected with climate change. War is part of the fact that a few thousand control seven billion.

Perpetual death and destruction is caused by the war industry and the neocons (conservatives) who support Hillary Clinton.

This looms over our solution to save our world. Nevertheless the solution is in the practise.

"WHAT'S GOOD FOR THE PLANET IS GOOD FOR THE ECONOMY"
"WHAT'S BAD FOR THE PLANET IS BAD FOR THE ECONOMY"

What's good for People is good for the planet.

Follow it like a rule of thumb.

Vivienne
Westwood

PHOTO CREDITS

Serpents Tail and Vivienne Westwood are grateful to all the photographers who gave permission for use of their images in this book. All these images are copyright as credited below. While every effort has been made to contact copyright-holders of illustrations, the author and publishers would be grateful for information about any illustrations where they have been unable to trace them, and would be glad to make amendments in further editions.

Mark Allan: p.345.

Catherine Ashmole: p.222.

Paolo Colaiocco: pp.56, 424.

Stephen Cummiskey/Royal Court Theatre: p.116.

Mark Ellingham: p.164.

David Ellis: p.161.

Environmental Justice Foundation: p.64.

Alicia Fox/Cool Earth: pp.59, 62, 69, 163.

Farms Not Factories: p.104.

Getty Images: p.73 (Jon Kopaloff); p.75 (Hiroyuki Ito/Hulton Archive); p.83 (Samir Hussein/WireImage); p.136 (Olga Bermejo/Film Magic); p.141 (Michel Dufour/French Select); p.176 (Ian Gavan); p.193 (Joerg Koch); p.195 (Split Second/Corbis); p.200 (Randy Brooke/WireImage); p.229 (Kristian Buus); p.295 (Juergen Vollmer/Redferns); p.426 (David M. Benett); p.441 (Victor Virgile).

Andy Gotts: p.276.

Roger Grace/Greenpeace: p.194.

Alistair Guy/Cool Earth: p.88.

Milan Ilnycky/Syndark: p.206.

Innsbruck Tourismus/Roger Rovira: p.329.

Evgeniy Kazannik/Trouble in Paradise: p.333.

Kamil Kustosz: p.449.

François Lamy: p.253.

Neil Mackenzie Matthews: p.356.

Marcio Madeira: p.43.

Craig McDean: p.78.

Cindy Palmano: p.90.

Tom Parker/Omnibus: p.363.

Johan Persson/ArenaPAL: p.281.

Press Association: pp.149, 454 (both Jonathan Brady/ PA Archive).

Ki Price: pp.288, 311, 312, 367, 383, 410, 421.

Rankin: p.50 (courtesy *Harper's Bazaar*); p.303 (courtesy *The Times* magazine).

REX/Shutterstock: p.316 (Richard Young).

Jiri Rezac/Greenpeace: p.260.

Lina Scheynius: p.45.

Jeffry Scott: p.153.

Dmitri Sharomov/Greenpeace: p.243.

Clare Skeats: p.343 (cover design; photo by Juergen Teller).

Juergen Teller: pp.36, 61, 265, 304, 343, 360, 375, 423.

Lorna Tucker/Finished Films: pp.335, 336.

Ugo Camera: pp.25, 26, 28, 97, 133, 134, 151, 184, 213, 234, 239, 273, 283, 314, 341, 374, 411, 414, 432.

Virgin Airlines: p.315.

Ben Westwood: pp.270, 347.

Vivienne Westwood artwork: pp.1, 5, 6, 8, 31, 46, 94, 123, 125, 128, 157, 158, 169, 182, 204, 217, 237, 240, 254, 255, 256, 265, 293, 300, 309, 320, 339, 351, 366, 371, 381, 388, 398, 399, 430, 432, 435, 436, 438, 452, 462, 464, 468–9.

Vivienne Westwood personal and company archive: pp.1, 5, 6, 8, 48, 52, 58, 82, 108, 112, 114, 119, 121, 138, 143, 144, 147, 167, 181, 197, 208, 215, 220, 230, 248, 251, 252, 296, 298, 328, 405, 455, 460.

THANKS

Thanks to all those at Vivienne Westwood Ltd (Beata de Campos, Joe de Campos, Cynthia King, Laura McCuaig, Colette Thurlow, Anthony Santolla) and Serpents Tail (Peter Dyer, Susanne Hillen, Steve Panton, Simon Shelmerdine, Hannah Westland), and to all the photographers (especially Ugo Camera, Juergen Teller and Ki Price), for their help with this project.

Mark Ellingham, Editor, Serpents Tail.